PARTICIPATION WORKS:

BUSINESS CASES FROM
AROUND THE WORLD

PARTICIPATION WORKS:

BUSINESS CASES FROM AROUND THE WORLD

James P. Troxel, General Editor

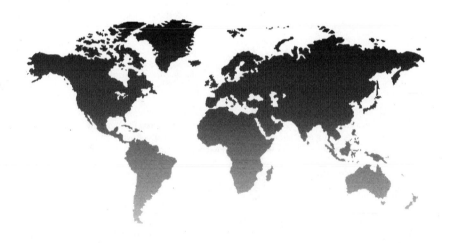

◆

AN ANTHOLOGY OF READINGS
ON PARTICIPATION IN PRIVATE COMPANIES

◆

Miles River Press

1009 Duke Street, Alexandria, Virginia 22314

Published by:
Miles River Press
1009 Duke Street
Alexandria, VA 22314
(703) 683-1500, Fax: (703) 683-0827
(800) 767-1501

Miles River Press Team
Peg Paul, Publisher
Elizabeth Katz, Project Editor
Libby Schroeder, Marketing Coordinator
Nancy Speights, Word Processing
Deadlines, Inc., Publication Technology, Corp., Production

Editorial Note:

- *Selections reflect the cultural patterns and diversity of the contributors' experiences; editors have made an effort to retain the original meaning while making language consistent with American English spelling and usage.*
- *Level of familiarity of address is case specific.*
- *Graphics appear in the form as used by each company.*
- *The editors express appreciation to the company leaders who gave permission to share their stories for use in this book.*

Library of Congress Cataloging-in-Publication Data:
Participation works : business cases from around the world : an anthology of readings on participation in private companies / James P. Troxel, general editor.
    p.   cm.
    Includes bibliographical references.
    ISBN 0-917917-03-0
    1. Management—Employee participation—Case studies. I. Troxel,
James P., 1946-
HD5650.P3325   1993
658.3' 152—dc20   93-31681
                                                CIP

Printed in the United States of America

Printed on acid-free and recycled paper that meets the strictest state and U.S. guidelines for recycled paper (50% recycled waste, including 10% postconsumer waste).

10 9 8 7 6 5 4 3 2

DEDICATION

To all those who, over the last twenty years,
have shared in developing and applying
the processes described in the cases
in this book.

PARTICIPATION WORKS:
BUSINESS CASES FROM AROUND THE WORLD

James P. Troxel, General Editor

Preface	*Raymond S. Caruso*	xv
Foreword	*Antonia Shusta*	xviii

I. Defining Participation

Chapter 1:	A Time for Participation *John Burbidge*	3
Chapter 2:	Benefits Beyond the Numbers *James P. Troxel*	17

II. Increasing Productivity

Chapter 3: India	A Value-Driven Culture Widia (India) Ltd. *Judith D. Gilles and T. A. Sadasivan*	33
Chapter 4: Singapore and Malaysia	Excellence...A Journey Not A Destination Great Eastern Life Assurance Ltd. *Ann and John Epps*	53

III. Expanding the Customer Base

Chapter 5: U.S.A.	Transforming a Defense Research Organization: Can It Happen Fast Enough to Survive? Lockheed Missiles and Space Co. *Patricia Tuecke*	71
Chapter 6: United Kingdom	The Evolution of Customer Service in Hamilton Insurance Company Hamilton Insurance Company Ltd. *Alan Berresford and Femi Oguntokun*	95

IV. Maximizing Stakeholder Involvement

Chapter 7:   Integrated Company Teams Serving a Nation 113
Guatemala   Metacentros, S.A.
                 William and Barbara Alerding

Chapter 8:   Recovering a Culture of Participation
Russia   in Russia   131
                 Primorski Sugar Corp., Zostro Corp.
                 David Dunn with Alexey Kuzmin

V. Motivating the Workforce

Chapter 9:   Creating a Second Taj Mahal   149
India   JK Fibre
                 Cyprian D'Souza

Chapter 10:   Crisis: An Ally of Participation   165
Brazil   Mills Group
                 Nancy Grow

VI. What Makes Participation Work

Chapter 11:   Participation at the Grassroots Level   185
Canada   Hudson's Bay Company
                 Jo Nelson

Chapter 12:   Champions of Participation: 201
                 Organizations' Leaders
                 Gordon Harper

Chapter 13:   Cross-Cultural Leadership   213
Asia Pacific   DuPont Asia Pacific
                 Roy Stansbury and Chris Yates

Chapter 14:   Facilitation Skills in Action   229
Nigeria   Nigeria International Bank
                 Robert Vance

Afterword   *James P. Troxel*   245

Annotated Bibliography   249

CONTRIBUTORS

James P. Troxel is Senior Consultant for the Institute of Cultural Affairs in Chicago and has 25 years experience in community and organizational development and leadership training. He has conducted over 100 seminars in 30 states and 10 countries. Jim is one of the founders of the participative strategic planning process now installed in organizations worldwide and has pioneered many adaptions of ICA's technology of participation. Jim has facilitated training and planning sessions with private companies, national associations, local civic groups, and public agencies around the country. Recent clients include KPMG Peat-Marwick, Household International, City of Chicago Departments of Housing, Human Services, and Planning and Development, The American Public Health Association, and the Chicago Community Trust.

Institute of Cultural Affairs, 4750 North Sheridan Road, Chicago, IL 60640.

Barbara Alerding currently serves as Director of the Employee Training Skills Program, Training, Inc., Guatemala. She has led human development consultations in 16 countries during her 29 years with the ICA and has taught English as a second language in five countries for 15 years.

William Alerding served the ICA in Mexico, Spain, Portugal, and Singapore before going to Guatemala in 1984. He has facilitated hundreds of courses and training programs for organizations as well as community-integrated development projects in 25 countries for the past 26 years. Prior work experience includes teaching English and Social Sciences in Berlin, New Orleans, Singapore, and Chicago.

Instituto de Asuntos Culturales, 2 Avenida ``A'' -13-34, Apto. 4-C, Zona 1; Edificio El Callejon, 01001 Guatemala, C.A.

Alan Berresford is a professional facilitator specializing in strategic/operational planning, customer service initiatives, and change management. Prior to 1988, he spent 10 years with the ICA, four of those as Director for Europe. His career began with the U.K. Civil Service Department and National Westminster Bank. He has also led seminars in Europe, Africa, and Asia.

18 Ferncroft Ave., London N12 OLN, United Kingdom.

John Burbidge is Communications Director for ICA West, the Institutes's division serving the western U.S.A. Since 1971, his ICA work has taken him from villages in India to the European capital, Brussels. His articles have appeared in Australian, Canadian, and U.S. magazines and journals. He is editor of the book *Approaches That Work in Rural Development* and the newsletter *Initiatives*.

ICA West, 1504 25th Ave., Seattle, WA 98122.

Raymond S. Caruso, President of the Board of the Institute of Cultural Affairs, is currently President of Lord, Sullivan & Yoder, Inc., an advertising and public relations firm. Mr. Caruso has also served as a senior marketing communication executive at Red Lobster Restaurants, a division of General Mills Restaurant group; at Pizza Hut, a division of PepsiCo; and Backer Spielvogel Bates Advertising, a division of Saatchi & Saatchi Worldwide.

Lord, Sullivan & Yoder, 556 City Park Ave., Columbus, OH 43215.

Cyprian D'Souza is Co-director of LENS Services Private Ltd., a consulting company focusing on development of leadership and culture in bringing about organizational transformation. He has worked with ICA: India since 1974, and served as a member of the executive board of the ICA International from 1985-89.

LENS International, 25 Nav Jivan Vihar, New Delhi, 110-017, India.

David Dunn is a process consultant and writer who divides his time between Denver, Colorado and Moscow. Since 1991, he has traveled regularly to Russia to introduce ICA's technology of participation and to lead joint facilitating, training, and consulting projects with the Process Consulting Company team in Moscow, Siberia, and the Republic of Tuva.

ICA, 1741 Gaylord St., Denver, CO 80206.

Ann Epps is one of the originators of the LENS participation and implementation approach and has consulted in Europe, Indonesia, the Phillipines, U.S.A., Singapore, and Malaysia. In her nine years in Southeast Asia she has consulted with organizations on strategic planning, creative thinking, leadership development, and customer service.

John Epps is a director of LENS International in Malaysia and LENS Leadership in Singapore. He is one of the original designers of the LENS management approach practiced in 35 countries. He has worked with over 100 companies in Europe, North America, Australia, Indonesia, the Phillipines, Thailand, Singapore, and Malaysia.

LENS International, P.O. Box 10564, 50718 Kuala Lumpur, Malaysia.

Judith Gilles has worked with ICA's Corporate Services Division in Bombay, India, for seven years as a consultant on the process of organizational transformation. Other work includes a partnership in LENS International in Detroit, Michigan, and 22 years with ICA in Chicago, Chile, Mexico City, Cairo, and California.

. ICA, 13 Sankli St., 2nd House, Bombay, 400-008, India.

Nancy Grow is currently Director of Research and Publications for the ICA in Brazil where she develops programs for personal and group enrichment and the nurturing of the human spirit in organizational settings. She spent 15 years doing research and training in ICA's Chicago office, and another 8 years teaching participative skills in Europe, Asia, Africa, North and South America.

ICA, Av. Graca Aranha 416; Sala 1.116, 20030 Rio de Janeiro, RJ, Brasil.

Gordon Harper has served as Executive Director of ICA in Taiwan since 1982. He works with companies and government agencies helping people design and manage the process of individual, organizational, and social change. Prior experience includes ICA activities in India, Singapore, and Malaysia, as well as college teaching and a radio show he conducts on organizational leadership in Taiwan.

ICA, 6th Floor, 53-1 Chung Shan North Rd. Section 7, Tien Mou, Taipei 11136, Taiwan, Republic of China.

Alexey Kuzmin is Co-founder and Director of Process Consulting Company, one of Russia's leading OD consulting firms with a growing clientele throughout the former Soviet Union. An author of three books on creativity and problem solving, he also co-founded the Moscow Institute for Technical Creative Work in 1981 and later the Center for Innovation and Development in 1990.

Process Consulting Co., P.O. Box 71, 125183, Moscow, Russia.

Jo Nelson is an ICA trainer with Hudson's Bay Company. She consults in the private, public, and voluntary sectors all over Canada. Over the past 23 years, she has worked with ICA on six continents as an organization and community development consultant.

Hudson's Bay Company, Toronto, Ontario, Canada M5H 2Y4.

Femi Oguntokun is Director of Operations of Hamilton Insurance Company Limited in the U.K., subsidiary of Household Finance Company. He started his career with Price Waterhouse and Laurie International, then joined HFC Bank in 1990 as a project manager.

Hamilton Insurance, P.O. Box 889, North Street, Winkfield, Windsor, Berkshire, SL4 4EE, United Kingdom.

T.A. Sadasivan is the Division Manager for Training and Organizational Development for Widia (India) Ltd. in Bangalore. He is responsible for all training activities, from trade apprenticeship to management development. A mechanical engineer by qualification, he has been involved in training and organization development for 27 years.

Widia (India) Limited; 8/9th Mile, Tumkur Road; Post Bag 7300; Bangalore 560 073 India.

Antonia Shusta is a Group Executive at Household International where she manages the consumer banking, mortgage, and brokerage businesses in the U.S.A., and the banking operation in the U.K. Previously she held a variety of managerial positions in consumer and corporate banking at Citibank.

Household International, Household Mortgage Services, 2700 Sanders Road, Prospect Heights, IL 60070.

Roy Stansbury is an organizational development consultant for DuPont Asia Pacific. He has worked in the field of organizational change and leadership development for the past two decades. Prior to joining DuPont, he worked with ICA in the U.S.A., Australia, India, Kenya, Malaysia, and Hong Kong.

1827 West Touhy, Chicago, IL 60626.

Patricia Tuecke, principal of Pat Tuecke Associates, a management consulting firm, has over 20 years experience consulting with organizations seeking to address critical issues in participative and collaborative ways. Special interests are leadership development, continuous improvement efforts, and whole systems change.

Pat Tuecke Associates, 651 Scott #7, San Francisco, CA 94117.

Robert R. Vance is President of Strategics International Inc. in Miami, Florida. He founded the company with his wife and partner, Cynthia, and they operate as a consulting team. He has over 20 years of experience, specializing in strategic vision planning, customer service, focus groups, new product think-tanks, and consensus building.

Strategics International, 8245 S.W. 116th Terrace, Miami, FL 33156.

Chris Yates is Organizational Development Manager in DuPont Asia Pacific, working and traveling extensively in the countries of the region. He has worked in the Human Resource area in several industries, including: chemicals, retail, pharmaceutical, government, and agricultural; previous to this, he served in the British Intelligence Corps in West Germany.

DuPont Singapore; One Maritime Square # 07-01; World Trade Centre, Singapore 0409.

ACKNOWLEDGEMENTS

As General Editor, I would like to take this opportunity to thank the numerous people who contributed to and participated in making this book possible.

First, I want to say thanks to the team of contributors who labored through numerous rewrite requests. This book is theirs more than anyone's, and their collaborative efforts provide yet another testimony to the central message of this book.

Of course, the case companies themselves deserve a word of appreciation for allowing the contributors to highlight their stories, complete with successes and failures. These stories serve and will continue to serve as testimony to the creative power of group effort. Within each company we profiled, there stood one person who made it possible, and to this new breed of corporate leader, we also want to say thank you for allowing us to profile your own unique brand of leadership approaches to business problems.

More personally, I want to express my thanks to the number of "shadow editors" who served as sort of a kitchen cabinet to my own efforts as I planned this project. Thanks to Beret Griffith, Chuck Elliott, Laura Spencer, David Reese, and Linda Jones. My appreciation also to Nancy DuCharme of Sidley and Austin, Sally Fenton and Shirley Heckman for additional support, and to Eunice and Sherwood Shankland for their helpful advice from the initial stage of this project. I also want to recognize the support that my colleagues of the Institute of Cultural Affairs provided. The working environment of the staff team in Chicago and the encouragement of the Board of Directors propelled this endeavor forward during the lean times.

This undertaking began as part of my completion of graduate work for the School for New Learning at DePaul University in Chicago. To Dean David Justice, Catherine Marineau, Jean Knoll, Phyllis Walden, and David Shallenberger, thank you for providing the collegial learning environment that brought this book about.

To the staff of Miles River Press—Peg Paul, Elizabeth Katz, and Libby Schroeder—all I can say is, it would not have been possible without your unswerving belief in what the contributors and I had to say about what we knew. For collective capacity to see things we ourselves could not, and then to draw it forth from us, we want to say thanks.

Finally, I am grateful that this project became a family affair—with my son, Jonathan, serving as re-typist, and my wife, Karen, providing additional editorial support. Special thanks.

PREFACE

Over the past 30 years, a group of people working out of a common set of ideas and beliefs has honed an effective group of methods for working with organizations and communities. Organizing themselves as a unique network, this international group of professional facilitators is affiliated with a non-profit group called the Institute of Cultural Affairs (ICA), with offices in 20 countries.

Born out of fires of necessity in community development, ICA has its roots in Chicago's Westside neighborhood where it gained experience in organizational development as it developed its own unique approaches. ICA now uses these core methodologies within the private sector, as these accounts attest, as well as with the early clients in social service organizations, U.N.-affiliated bodies, community development associations, state municipal governments, and religious groups. In each case, ICA associates prepare others to be the principal agents of change in their own situations.

Our strategy is to use a process—a series of methods and skills—described generally as the Technology of Participation. Client organizations are able to harness employee strengths, craft a shared vision for the future, and determine the underlying or root causes preventing realization of goals. Then they are able to design a series of strategies to address those impediments in order to activate various employee taskforces and empower new configurations of personnel to implement those directions.

Our viewpoint is that organizations are of value to themselves, and have value in the larger society as well. The consulting facilitators turn this view into positive common sense and pour themselves into these organizations with an enthusiasm generally not found in most so-called "outside experts." Our approach is unabashedly affirmative. We believe, more often than not, that when a problem is well-defined, it is half-solved. Furthermore, we have experienced time and time again that when a group is permitted to examine the root causes of the issues it confronts, it finds the doorway to its future. These facilitators begin their engagements with the assumption that the key human resources necessary to transform the organization already exist within the staff, and that their task is fundamentally one of mining and harvesting that innate organizational power.

My own first encounter with participative methods occurred years ago when six of us in a small advertising agency participated in an ICA seminar called LENS (Leadership Effectiveness and New Strategies) to foster team building. Later in my career, when I became New Products Marketing Manager of McDonald's, I played a role in making it one of the first multinational corporations to apply participative methods. That story began when I helped to facilitate multilevel groups ranging from the senior staff (including Ray Kroc) to a cross-departmental taskforce to franchise owners' stakeholders meetings. Early on, the participants were careful to define what business the company was really in. Some influential voices insisted that we were only in the "hamburger business" and had no chance of being successful in selling breakfast. Using the participative process, the group paid attention to hamburgers being our predominant product, but decided that what we really provided to customers was convenience. Consensus created what looks obvious now: McDonald's is really in the *convenience* business. McDonald's added a breakfast menu, which generated significant real growth for five years.

Participation, then, is the strategy of accepting and affirming the latent potential in a group of people. To put it another way, we believe that management's quest for the perfect employee (and employees' search for the ideal boss) is fruitless. Not only are both non-existent, but ideas of perfection rarely address fundamental problems within a business, anyway. We believe that organizations today can best win by accepting and tapping the human resources they already have.

This book focuses on organizations in the private sector. What binds this collection together is the operational framework the facilitator used in performing services for each corporate client. So, while we have stories that range from North America to India, from South America to Africa, all are wedded by the similarity of methods—and the amazing similarity of results. Our contributors analyzed the strengths, weaknesses, opportunities, and challenges of these companies and proclaimed that each had what it takes to build its future.

The contributors to this book are all facilitators who have consulted with the companies in their cases. Levels of involvement and relationships vary from continent to continent, culture to culture, company to company. The contributors bring personal skills and talents to bear on their own cases. Some of them have lived and worked in one country for decades. Others have used one country as a home base and have traveled to other continents to help facilitate organizational change.

As they shared their experiences in using the Technology of Participation, ICA associate Jim Troxel grew enthusiastic about the results in the stories these facilitators told. He felt that a collection of these cases would be of more than passing interest to the growing number of companies as well as individuals now looking for ways to tap the human potential resident within their own companies.

We invite the reader, then, to read these case studies and marvel, as we ourselves did when the contributors gathered to share and learn from their individual experiences, at the collective power of the human mind, heart, and will whenever it is tapped and harnessed for useful collective purposes. We hope we provide here a testament to what businesses can do when employees work together to deal with today's complex business environment.

Raymond S. Caruso
President of the Board,
Institute of Cultural Affairs

President,
Lord, Sullivan, & Yoder, Inc., Advertising and Public Relations

FOREWORD

n an age when business management is treated as a science available primarily to the specially trained and anointed, the reader of *Participation Works* could not be blamed for feeling incredulous. The authors of these cases suggest they have found a "miracle" solution to virtually any organizational condition or situation, regardless of industry, economy, or culture. The results they document are truly impressive; clearly all who have been involved with the Technology of Participation through the Institute of Cultural Affairs come away from the association with deeply held convictions in the process. But it has been my experience that newcomers to this approach are most often won over by trying this process, participating themselves, rather than simply being told about it. The challenge undertaken in this book is to intrigue the reader enough to give it a try.

There is no end to the "how to" approach for managing all types of business today. Consultants, books, and business education programs can give advice on every imaginable aspect of management. The obvious question, then, is, What distinguishes this book from the multitude of others?

Virtually all managers look for solutions outside themselves and their organizations. In most organizations there is an implicit assumption that someone outside that group has an answer, or a better answer to questions and problems than anyone inside the group could possibly have. The "information age" is still the "age of the expert." The people described in *Participation Works* have found, and passionately believe, the answers they need are within themselves, not encompassed in an external authority. There is a major difference between this book and all the others you can find: it tells you simply that you can solve your own problems and inspires you with great stories of others who have done just that.

There is a baffling irony to the fact that managers hired to do a job, then turn to others to tell them how to do it, or to bolster their own confidence by affirming that they themselves are doing the right thing. Yet the industry of consultants spawned in the post-war economy has thrived due to just that mentality. The impact over time can be insidious: organizations as well as individuals lose confidence in themselves. This phenomenon has occurred at a time when managers around the world are better educated, both from formal programs and broadening work experiences, than at any other time since the industrial revolution. Against this background, it probably should not be surprising that people react with marvelous enthusiasm and energy when they try an approach that unleashes their own talents to produce results for which they are responsible and can have great pride. Using the participatory approach can be an antidote for the "overdevelopment" which has given us hordes of tedious, undermining experts.

I believe that organizations exist and thrive because people want to be part of something bigger than themselves. The Technology of Participation implicitly understands that hunger for involvement, and capitalizes on it. The movement in management theory toward a concept of empowerment also suggests this same outlook, if in a muted tone. Practicality more than idealism is behind this trend. The range of job skills and the break-neck pace of change mean that no senior leadership group in any company in any industry in any country can possibly have the personal experience and knowledge necessary for making all the decisions a company would need. As strange as it may seem today, there was a time not so long ago when it was possible and reasonable for a senior manager to have moved up the corporate ladder through a series of positions that reflected most, if not all, the experiences and skills essential in that company.

Today many organizations emphasize the need for formal training programs and lateral assignments to give leaders opportunity for growth. We want them to develop good judgment and maturity, as well as analytical, communication, and thinking skills. This training is important because we know that many job families and technical skills for doing all jobs will change dramatically every several years. The managers and leaders of today and tomorrow cannot possibly have firsthand experience with every aspect of the company, but they need to know how to learn, question, obtain input, assess and evaluate, and create a vision. Critical to these managers is the contribution of all the people in the organization who do the work at any given time so that good decisions can be made. Participation engenders empowerment, and today it is a necessity, not a philosophical ideal.

Reading over the cases in this book brought back to me numerous memories of the many circumstances since 1986 when I have applied participatory techniques. As a manager who gravitates to turnaround and start-up situations in the context of large corporations, I have personally used this approach in consumer and corporate financial services businesses in the U.S.A. and Latin America. Still, every time I feel that I am faced with some situation, whether it seems routine or intractable, I marvel about what happens when a group of people, regardless of their backgrounds or viewpoints, sits down together under the guidance of a professional facilitator and starts working on the issue at hand. By focusing on what we have in common, by focusing on what we want to accomplish, what our concerns and hopes are, we find we share a vision, a hope, a dream. Focused on that vision, we then work out in concrete detail what we have to do to reach that goal. Whatever our differences, real or perceived, the commonality of what we want to accomplish brings us together in ways that overwhelm whatever the differences among us. At the same time we use our individual talents and strengths in the tasks we undertake as we move toward our goal. It is a triumph—a little miracle—each time it happens.

And the triumphs continue. Generally people working directly for me who have participated as a group in the process of participation take the approach back to their employees and replicate the process. The experience is so powerful for many people that they are eager to take it back to their workplace. In fact, in the companies where I have worked, I have been amazed to find where and how it has spread. The ultimate case of this was a young manager in the U.K. who explained how he had used the process and began earnestly persuading me of its merits while completely unaware that I had introduced the process into the company some years earlier. After a group has worked together for several weeks, months, or years and seen the results of their concerted efforts grow into tangible financial and operating results, there is a lasting impact on the corporate culture.

The sense of ownership, responsibility, and accountability comes together with a recognition of the possibilities throughout the organization. That is certainly the kind of work environment which we all would like to have.

Whether or not the testimonials in this collection will persuade you to try participatory techniques, you will come away impressed by the hope, energy, and accomplishments of those who have tried them and count themselves as "believers." By the standards of even the most traditional and hierarchy-oriented managers, these people get results—outstanding results. With open minds and open hearts, all managers will find their way to participation. It is only a matter of time.

Antonia Shusta
Group Executive, Office of the President
Household International

I.

DEFINING PARTICIPATION

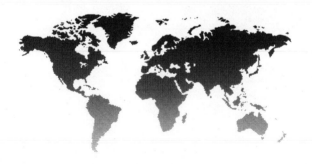

1. A Time for Participation

by

JOHN BURBIDGE

*Although participation is emerging as a dominant
theme in all facets of society today, it is the business
community that deserves much of the credit
for establishing it as a modus operandi.
It was in the offices, boardrooms, and production
centers of some of the more adventurous
global companies that participation
first caught a toehold.*

What do a Brazilian construction firm, an Indian machine tool manufacturer and a North American missile and aeronautics company have in common? Yes, they are all metal fabricators of one sort or another. And there are those rather fundamental issues of profit and market share. But in the case of these companies, the common thread runs much deeper. It can be summed up in a word—participation.

Faced with an internal financial crisis in the midst of a national and global recession, the Mills Group of companies in Brazil was forced to make some radical changes. After "trying on" participatory methods for over two years, management began to see not just the value but the necessity of these approaches. Quite literally, the walls at Mills came tumbling down. Open offices replaced private cubicles; information began to be shared across departmental boundaries, and everyone started eating in the same lunchroom. A new ethos still permeates the Mills Group today and the positive balance sheets reflect it.

In Bangalore, India, employee transport buses at the Widia (India) machine tool company arrived seven minutes late every day. An interdepartmental taskforce was put to work on the problem and came up with 25 reasons for the late bus arrivals. Honing in on the most serious causes, employees devised the following solutions: change factory timings to avoid peak traffic, reduce pick-up points, and bypass roads where traffic jams are common. Now buses are rarely more than a minute late. That's impressive in most countries, but doubly so in India, where people jokingly distinguish between "Indian time" and Indian Standard time.

When the U.S. national defense budget began to be slashed, workers at the Lockheed Missiles and Space Company in southern California understandably grew nervous. None more so, perhaps, than those in Lockheed's Research and Development Division where designing new products for new markets became a necessity. A series of participatory marketing workshops opened the door to new ideas and plans for new products began to flow— devices that allow computers to speak to one another, crises management centers to help cities deal with natural disasters, and low-orbit satellites for global cellular phone communication.

These three companies, along with the others featured in this book, are part of a groundswell of businesses which have come to see that when people have a stake in deciding the outcome of a process or product, they are more likely to be committed to its successful completion. The common denominator of all these companies is their intentional use of participative processes, notably the Technology of Participation (ToP) developed by the Institute of Cultural Affairs (ICA). The ICA is a global social change organization working since the early 1960s in community and organizational development. For a summary of ToP, please see the Preface.

The results of these companies' commitment to participative practices speak for themselves. They include:

- Increased performance and productivity;
- A more focused mission;
- Greatly empowered team implementation;
- More motivated employees in an improved working environment.

Clearly, participation as a mode of doing business is here to stay. And the reason is obvious—it works. And it works in an incredibly diverse array of historical, political, and business cultures. The case studies in this book are living proof of this fact—a Russian sugar factory, struggling to emerge from 75 years of a centrally planned economy; an Indian acrylic fiber company working against a backdrop of 44 generations of unbroken kingly rule, as well as the legacy of centuries of British colonial administration; and a Malaysian insurance firm set in a tricultural nation where respect for hierarchy and authority has always been the accepted rule.

The list can be extended. But in each case, when circumstances were ripe and corporate leadership was ready, participatory approaches to management were introduced into the company and eventually became the life blood of its operation. It is as if, below the surface of differences, there is a common water table which, when tapped, rises to the surface and transforms the situation, regardless of the setting in which it occurs.

In his chapter on Russia, organizational consultant David Dunn touches on this intriguing development. "Whatever the cultural context, there is in the Russian personality a natural affinity for participation and orderly progression of thought to a productive conclusion," he asserts. According to Dunn, the key is eliciting this innate human propensity out of people's consciousness as a "basic and natural way" of being human together.

Two observations should be added to this discussion. First, in today's global business community, there is an international "business culture" that often pervades, and sometimes supplants, indigenous customs. Not surprisingly, in a number of cases cited in this book, those responsible for initiating new modes of participation in their companies are the bright young men and women who left their home countries to earn their MBAs in the leading management schools of Europe or North America. Although products of different historical and cultural systems, these young people have bought into the values of today's global marketplace. One of those emerging values is increased employee participation in decision making.

Second, it seems that participation has been most effective where creative leaders have blended innovative participative methods with traditional cultural patterns. The Indian JK Fibre company discussed in this book is an excellent example. Its training program, Leadership Skills for Participative Culture, involves employees in both modern facilitation skills and in the ancient spirit practices of pranayama yoga and surya namaskar (greeting the sun). According to the author of the JK case study, Cyprian D'Souza, this "retooling of minds and hearts" combines personal and professional development in ways that are mutually reinforcing rather than divisive.

In the case of the Great Eastern Life Assurance Company of Malaysia and Singapore, participative practices did not eliminate traditional respect for authority. If anything, they may have reinforced it, while at the same time diffusing throughout the organization a sense of responsibility for the whole company. As consultants John and Ann Epps point out in the GE Life Case study, "Participation does not mean that every opinion deserves to be followed. Decisions must be made and designating the responsibility for making them proved important."

The growing acceptance and application of participatory methods around the world is one of the most intriguing aspects of the phenomenon. Indeed, it seems that more and more often, participation is no longer an option but a necessity. In the words of organizational development consultant Frank Powell, "Communities and organizations will either aggressively seek to enhance participation or they will see it happen in spite of their efforts to maintain control hierarchically. One way or another, it is happening universally" [1].

Participation, though, is not an isolated phenomenon. It is part of a wider circle of factors that define how human beings relate to one another in our times. It is a key component of the new paradigm of living in the 21st century, and as such, finds allies in other kindred disciplines such as conflict mediation, dispute partnering, and facilitative leadership, to name a few.

Note I said "discipline" in referring to participation and its allies. Many people often mistake participation for something that happens or does not happen, depending on the circumstances or the personalities of those in charge of a situation. But as Laura Spencer underscored in the book, *Winning Through Participation*, there is much more to the process of participation than first meets the eye:

Managers who are genuinely interested in participative techniques are no longer looking for a program.... They now seek a system, even an environment. They have learned, mostly by hard experience, that there are no 'quick fixes' for improving employee motivation and productivity [2].

She outlines four basic tenets of participation that apply across the board, regardless of the context in which participation happens. She explains that participation is:

- An ongoing, integrated, whole-systems approach;
- An evolving, organic, and dynamic process;
- A structured process involving learnable skills;
- A dynamic requiring a commitment to openness from everyone who is involved.

There is one other tenet I would add to this list—participation demands strong leadership. A contradiction in terms, you say? Surprisingly, no. Many who have tried to use participatory methods have discovered this but often too late. As the author and former editor of the *Harvard Business Review*, Rosabeth Moss Kanter, stresses in her foreword to Spencer's book, leadership is essential in making participation work.

"It is almost a paradox," Kanter observes. "Participation requires better leadership than a machine-like bureaucracy. The leadership tasks may be shared or rotated but they must be performed. And one of the leadership roles is to provide a structure for participative planning" [3].

The pivotal role of leadership in enabling participation to happen is underscored in many of the case studies that follow. Time and again, ToP methods have proven effective in transforming the culture of organizations where the leaders of those organizations have been committed to, as well as involved in, the process of change.

PARTICIPATION: A CORPORATE BUZZWORD

Although participation is emerging as a dominant theme in all facets of society today, it is the business community that deserves much of the credit for establishing it as a *modus operandi*. It was in the offices, boardrooms, and production centers of some of the more adventurous global companies that participation first caught a toehold. Drawing on the wisdom of the founding fathers of modern management, including William Edwards

Deming, Peter Drucker, and Robert Greenleaf, a new breed of managers began to emerge.

The word soon spread. Fueled by seminars on participatory management, books on organizational excellence, and videos on how to build more effective work teams, participation became a corporate buzzword. From New York to Tokyo, Bombay to Rio de Janeiro, companies began to shift both their corporate philosophies and everyday operations to allow for greatly increased employee participation in all aspects of their businesses.

At different points along the way, particular aspects of participation have taken root. The preoccupation with quality, manifest initially in quality circles and more recently in the total quality management (TQM) concept, is an example of this. At the book display of a conference of the Association for Quality and Participation, I counted no fewer than 25 books with the word "quality" in their titles.

In addressing that same conference, management author, teacher, and consultant Peter Senge noted that this current concern with quality suggests something profoundly amiss with American management systems today. In his analysis, the essence of management is the art of mobilizing the intellectual resources of everyone involved. But as Senge sees it, most American managers still operate out of the premise that "the top thinks and the bottom acts" [4]. For him, participation is fundamentally a thinking and learning process.

Others have emphasized different dimensions of participation. Tom Peters, in his book, *Liberation Management*, highlights the critical role that trust plays in participatory management. He refers to trust as "the missing x-factor," an essential ingredient in today's business environment, but one so often lacking in many organizations. It is trust that allows conversations to happen, conversations which form the basis of today's knowledge-based economy. To underscore his point, he refers to a federal prison where trust has been created between inmates and staff through regular town hall-type meetings and inmate surveys. It's a case of, "If it can happen there, it can happen anywhere" [5].

For CEO Jack Welch of the General Electric Company, trust is also critical, but for him the key is "boundarylessness," i.e., breaking down the barriers that divide employees and that distance companies from employees and customers. Welch calls for a willingness to listen and debate, then take the best ideas and get on with the job. "Exposing people—without the protection of title or position—to ideas from everywhere, judging ideas on their merits" is his message to the modern manager wanting to survive in the global marketplace [6].

Eliminating boundaries within the organization is a cry echoed by President and CEO of Levi Strauss and Company, Robert Haas. What he calls "the most rigid boundary of all"—that between worker and managers—must be redefined. Addressing the Commonwealth Club of San Francisco, he posed the questions:

Why can't some employees set production goals? Why can't they monitor plant efficiency? Why can't they hire and fire new workers on whom they are increasingly dependent? And why can't they benefit directly from their initiatives which result in higher profits? [7].

In Brazil, the machinery manufacturer Semco, S.A. has already gone a long way towards answering these very questions. The Semco experience has been a strong motivator for other Brazilian companies moving toward more participatory management practices, including The Mills Group featured in this book. Deciding that hierarchy was the single biggest obstacle to participatory management, Semco replaced its cumbersome pyramidical structure with three managerial circles and just four job titles—counselors, partners, associates, and coordinators—which included everyone in the organization. Furthermore, the corporation insists that certain important decisions are made by a company-wide vote.

Such was the case when Semco needed a larger plant for its Marine Division. Initially, it employed real estate agents to search for possible plant sites, but the agents were unsuccessful. So Semco's top managers turned the job over to the employees. In one weekend, they came up with three factory buildings for sale near the existing plant. The company then stopped work for a day and sent everyone to inspect the properties. Next, the employees voted and chose a plant site the counselors did not really want. Willing to trust the workers' wisdom, the company bought the building. Workers designed the layout and hired a top Brazilian artist to paint it. The result? In just four years, the division's productivity per employee increased 160% and its market share jumped from 54% to 62%. Commenting on the experience, Semco President Ricardo Semler said:

We accepted the employees' decision because we believe that in the long run, letting people participate in the decisions that affect their lives will have a positive effect on employee motivation and morale [8].

But dismantling unhelpful hierarchical barriers does not imply the absence of organization. Rather, it is the basic organizational unit that has changed, from mammoth departments or divisions to small, self-managing teams. One of the most dramatic examples of the effectiveness of working teams is the Ford Motor Company's Team Taurus. Faced with the challenge of the success of their Japanese competitors, Ford turned over the development of the Taurus to multidisciplinary teams that operated by consensus, without interference from top management. Working with amazing speed, the teams came up with a car which has outsold its competitors while giving a much needed boost to the American automobile industry.

Teamwork, boundarylessness, trust, and bottom-up thinking are but a few of the different faces of participation which are emerging in business today. There are others to add to the list. All are important and each is a doorway to a new participative mode of management, a new paradigm in business. But as Michael Ray, who conducts the New Paradigm Business course at Stanford University in Palo Alto, California, cautions, "New paradigm business is not a static template of criteria that an organization either has or doesn't have. It is a process that is in a constant state of development" [9].

UNIVERSALITY OF PARTICIPATION

While the private sector has played a leading role in introducing participatory concepts and practices, it is by no means alone in this regard. Its experience has been closely paralleled in a number of other fields—government, community development, rural development, education, and more. The universality of participation as part of the very fabric of our lives becomes more apparent by the day.

In the U.S.A., the 1992 Presidential election campaign heralded a new era as participation became a key word in the political vocabulary. Electronic town meetings or TV citizen forums became media tools for airing voter opinion. This type of town meeting bears little resemblance to the original New England variety; it has set a precedent for a whole new style of political leadership in which accessibility and listening are key factors.

Political candidates collecting citizen feedback electronically are not alone in this field. In 1987, a San Francisco nonprofit and nonpartisan media organization, Choosing Our Future, piloted a prime-time electronic town meeting with its local ABC affiliate television station. Designed to obtain instant public feedback on a critical political issue, the program combined a studio audience and panel with a preselected sample of citizens who phoned in their responses to questions which arose during the discussion. Six "votes" were taken during the one-hour show, which was seen by more than 300,000 people in the San Francisco Bay Area.

The Director of Choosing Our Future, Duane Elgin, sees this type of citizen participation as an essential ingredient of a healthy democracy:

> Involving citizens through electronic town meetings will not guarantee the right choices will be made, but it will guarantee that citizens feel involved and invested in those choices. Rather than feeling cynical and powerless, citizens will feel engaged and responsible for our society and its future [10].

Not only has participation come of age in highly industrialized countries. Much pioneering work on participation, both theoretical models and practical implementation, has happened in the so-called Third World. As far back as 1976, a United Nations (UN) conference in Nairobi, Kenya, declared that participation be put at the forefront of development. By 1990, it had climbed to the top of the agenda when the UN held another conference in Arusha, Tanzania, on Popular Participation in the Recovery and Development Process in Africa.

The World Bank, which earned a reputation in earlier years as a purveyor of large-scale, top-down development aid, has picked up on the necessity of participation in development. It has begun channeling funds to a number of non-governmental organizations working with grassroots organizations, and has embarked on a "learning process" regarding participation within its own ranks.

But these acknowledgments of the importance of participation from the development establishment came only after years of experimentation with participatory approaches on the part of development agencies and rural people themselves. In the early 1980s, the ICA co-sponsored a massive international project to define the key factors which had led to successful rural development worldwide. Known as the International Exposition of Rural Development, this three-year, global program documented over 300 projects in 55 countries.

Another large and growing advocacy group for participation has been educators from around the world who cry for more effective, more relevant, and more holistic education. Almost all reform proposals have included some component of increased participation on the part of parents, teachers, administrators, and students in the total education process.

The city of Seattle is a case in point. Facing a growing sea of discontent about the state of its schools, it decided in 1990 to launch an Education Summit to gain input and participation from as broad a cross-section of the community as possible. Over one weekend, more than 2,000 parents, students, teachers, business leaders, neighborhood activists, and elected officials turned out at 32 meetings to express their concerns and give their ideas about improving Seattle's schools. While many of the ideas generated in the summit were not unique in the educational field, the process used to elicit them was. It demanded and achieved inclusive participation from all those affected by the malaise in education.

The foregoing are but a handful of the many illustrations that could be given of participation in today's society. Certainly, the private sector has no monopoly on participation. What it has are the resources, marketing skills, and international connections that have popularized participation and made it accessible to a ready, global audience. At the same time, as Peter Drucker and other management analysts point out, the private sector still has much to learn from the human change institutions of the non-profit world when it comes to participation and other key dimensions of modern management [11].

One of the unique contributions of the ICA in promoting participation has been its use of participatory methods in all sectors and at all levels of society, across national and cultural boundaries. The success of this multidimensional approach only underscores the fact that there is something essentially human in devising ways to bring people together in an open and inclusive way. Participation builds common solutions to the never-ending challenges people face in their personal, community, and professional lives.

Scholar and management consultant Margaret Wheatley goes one step further. Drawing on the insights of quantum physics, chaos theory, and molecular biology, she makes a strong case that the universe itself is a participatory phenomenon. As she asserts:

> Nothing is independent of the relationships that occur. I am constantly creating the world—evoking it, not discovering it—as I participate in all its many interactions. Participation, seriously done, is a way out from the uncertainties and ghostly qualities of

this non-objective world we live in. We need a broad distribution of information, viewpoints, and interpretations if we are to make sense of the world [12].

PARTICIPATION: TODAY'S AXIAL PRINCIPLE

Futurologist Daniel Bell once asserted that a dominating idea or axial principle drives every major period of history. In the 18th century, it was equality. In the 19th, with the onset of the industrial revolution, it was rationality. For the post-industrial, information age in which we live, he named it to be science or knowledge. However, as Belgian management specialist Roger Talpaert pointed out, the axial principle of our time is not knowledge, but participation. "It is unthinkable today," said Talpaert, "for people to contribute to any form of collective action without being able to influence goals and choices" [13].

Be it in the poorest village or plush company offices, the cry to be part of the solution and not merely a victim of circumstances has become one of the defining characteristics of life in our time. As such, participation is not simply a luxury that only some people can afford. It is much more—a basic right of every citizen of the globe today.

Like any historical phenomenon, though, participation needs its champions. It has found those in many places, but nowhere so prominently as in the international business community. Led by men and women who have seen the end of the old order when authority, control, and power were wielded from above, this movement for change has rapidly gained momentum in recent years. A more inclusive, participatory ethic has taken root and there is no turning back.

At the same time, there is still much to learn about participation, even within the innovative walls of modern companies. One way to accelerate and enrich that learning is to examine situations in which participation has been applied internationally. The case studies that follow in this book are an excellent contribution to that effort. They are living proof that participation is truly enhancing people's capacities to live more fulfilling lives and to contribute to the betterment of their workplaces and communities, as well as to society at large.

References

[1]   Powell, Frank. "Training for Participation" in *Approaches That Work in Rural Development*. Edited by John Burbidge for ICA International Munich: K.G. Saur Verlag, 1988, p.167.

[2]   Spencer, Laura J. (ed.) for the Institute of Cultural Affairs, *Winning Through Participation*. Dubuque, Iowa: Kendall/Hunt Publishing Company, 1989, p.23.

[3]   Kanter, Rosabeth Moss. Foreword to *Winning Through Participation*. Edited by Laura J. Spencer for the Institute of Cultural Affairs, Dubuque, Iowa: Kendall/Hunt Publishing Company, 1989, p.xiii.

[4]   Senge, Peter. "The Learning Organization," Keynote Address to the 14th Annual Spring Conference of the Association for Quality and Participation, April 6, 1992, Seattle, Washington. A more elaborate version of his talk is contained in the article, "The Real Message of the Quality Movement: Building Learning Organizations." *The Journal for Quality and Participation*. 15 (March 1992): pp.30-38.

[5]   Peters, Thomas J. *Liberation Management*. New York: A.A. Knopf, 1992.

[6]   Tichy, Noel M. and Stratford Sherman. *Control Your Destiny or Someone Else Will*. New York: Bantam Doubleday Dell Publishing Group, Inc., 1993, p.246.

[7]   Haas, Robert D. "The Corporation Without Boundaries" in *The New Paradigm in Business*. Edited by Michael Ray and Alan Rinzler for the World Business Academy. New York: Jeremy P. Tarcher/Perigee Books, 1993, p.105.

[8]   Semler, Ricardo. "Managing Without Managers." *Harvard Business Review* (September-October 1989): p.79.

[9]   Ray, Michael. "Introduction: What is the New Paradigm in Business?" in *The New Paradigm in Business*. Edited by Michael Ray and Alan Rinzler for the World Business Academy. New York: Jeremy P. Tarcher/Perigee Books, 1993, p.8

[10] Elgin, Duane. "Revitalizing Democracy Through Electronic Town Meetings" in *Spectrum, The Journal of State Government*. 66 (Spring 1993): p.13.

[11] Drucker, Peter. "What the Non-Profits Are Teaching Business" in *Managing for the Future: The 1990s and Beyond.* New York: Truman Valley Books/Dutton, 1992, pp.203-215.

[12] Wheatley, Margaret J. *Leadership and the New Science: Learning about Organization From an Orderly Universe.* San Francisco: Berrett-Koehler Publishers, 1992, p.68.

[13] Talpaert, Roger. "Looking into the Future: Management in the Twenty-First Century." *Management Review* (March 1981), p.25.

2. BENEFITS BEYOND THE NUMBERS

by

JAMES P. TROXEL

To cope with the rapid changes in today's business world, executives are now working with all of their stakeholders and drawing upon their collective wisdom. By tapping the experiences of those already at hand in-house, corporate managers see participative strategic planning as an extremely efficient and effective way for organizations to solve their monumental problems.

Participation is becoming an integral part of organizational life. However, opponents of participative management approaches complain that increasing employee participation slows down decision making. Even worse than the time it takes, these critics claim, participation actually impedes an organization's ability to improve and grow. It takes the organization out of the hands of the knowledgeable few executives and gives undue control to the mass of less-qualified and poorly informed employees.

The case studies that follow are compelling stories of companies that profited because management opened up the planning and implementation process to a wider-than-ever segment of employees. Did this approach take longer to implement than earlier planning strategies? In some cases, yes. But the benefits of increased employee productivity and motivation turned this extra time into a good investment. In all these corporate cases, in rejecting a cynical view of their workers' capabilities, management recognized that their employees had highly valuable insights that could contribute to the well-being of their companies.

In fact, management discovered a chain of benefits that resulted from involving employees as stakeholders in the companies. Increasing the level of participation in planning, for instance, promoted a greater sense of employee responsibility for implementing the plans. Workers felt empowered to challenge the false assumptions and unreliable analysis upon which previous expert consultant plans were often built. This greater sense of ownership motivated employees to see that the new plans were carried out. Such an investment of confidence, in the long run, made the employees winners along with the company itself.

EXPANDED BENEFITS

This same notion of participatory involvement has always underscored the growth and preservation of the governmental institutions of democratic societies. But when it came to the "private sector," the belief persisted that wiserand, frequently, distantbusiness executives were the only ones capable of knowing what to do. However, the days of the aloof and autocratic business executive are past. To cope with the rapid changes in today's business world, executives are now working with all of their stakeholders and drawing upon their collective wisdom. By tapping the experiences of those already at hand in-house, corporate managers see participative strategic planning as an extremely efficient and effective way for organizations to solve their monumental problems.

When the contributors of the corporate case studies in this collection speak of increased participation, they mean something other than more frequent meetings in which a CEO or other executive recites the state of the business environment and proclaims management goals. They also mean something far beyond warm and fuzzy training events or rural retreats fostering emotional outbursts unrelated to business performance. The kind of participation illustrated in these cases involves a carefully designed and executed system of planning and learning events guided by professional facilitators from inside or outside the company. In each case, company leaders who are not defensive about sharing responsibility champion this involvement.

FOUR RESULTS OF PARTICIPATION

These contributors show that a culture of participation will take root in companies if planning sessions are held over a period of time sufficient to create a climate of change. These sessions must always be part of a coordinated business strategy. Performed in tandem with employee training sessions, ongoing use of these participative techniques fosters:

(1) Increased performance and productivity;
(2) Redirected business mission focus;
(3) Empowered team-based implementation;
(4) A workplace environment with motivated employees.

Because these cases come from ten different nations and represent diverse cultures, the success of these companies affirms the message that whatever the culture or environment, participation works, and introduces some very impressive results.

Result #1: Participation Increases Performance, Productivity, and Profits

Employing participative approaches in business planning yields real benefits, most importantly, a boost in profitability. All of the organizations discussed in these case studies realized such increases, which they attributed in varying degrees to increasing opportunities for employees to share in planning and decision making. Sometimes the results were dramatic. Increased profitability and market share grew naturally out of the performance and quality improvements promoted by participation programs. Remarkably, some of this growth took place in radically shifting business environments. For example, the Mills Group in Brazil was able to thrive in times of national economic chaos, while Lockheed's Research and Development Division was able to shift from being defense industry dependent to creating civilian uses for its technology research.

There is no guarantee that every company which attempts to increase participation will achieve such dramatic results. Many other factors, of course, contribute to the overall success of an organization. However, when participation programs have proper facilitation and are endorsed enthusiastically by the organization's leader, they will unleash latent talent, skills, and insights within a corporation. Increased and surprising performance often results.

Result #2: Participation Redirects Talents and Energies to Expand Customer Base

During the planning events described in the case studies, the companies refocused their basic business enterprises. Employees saw the need to jettison superfluous activities, and gained a clearer understanding of their company's market, and its changing demands. Clearly, successful business ventures do not result from managing a large number of variables and factors, but just a few. These variables may be the company's core competencies, the competition's weaknesses, or specific market niche identification. Focusing the collective energy of an organization on a few points of leverage, rather than scattering it across an array of options, will result, in the long run, in greater returns. The pathway to accuracy in finding these points of leverage begins with expanding everyone's understanding of the business, and drawing from the collective experience and wisdom of all employees.

Using participative approaches in business planning widens the world view of the participants. Employees gain a clearer sense of how they fit into the whole organization, are able to look at the whole company rather than its parts, and have a better understanding of the company's big picture. As active participants in company planning events, the employees learn to examine the company's inherent weaknesses and strengths, as well as its capacity to take advantage of market opportunities.

Some employees interviewed for the case studies talked about how their perceptions of the companies changed during participative planning events. For example, at Metacentros in Guatemala, employees came to understand that the company was not just dealing with business problems, but with the larger problems of Guatemala itself. Metacentros' mission, they discovered, centered largely on creating a business strategy that focused on meeting genuine human needs. This broad mission gave employees an even greater motivation to see their company succeed, and generated a battery of creative ideas to meet those human needs, even beyond the company's involvement.

Another objective of participative corporate planning is to ensure that everyone is "on the same page." In each case study, the company conducted a workshop to create a practical vision for the company's future. During these sessions, the participants clarified the philosophy, values, and mission of the company. At the same time a sense of alignment within the company became evident. As one employee participant said, "The `why' becomes more evident." An organization's need for a clear mission and vision is obvious, but creating them with widespread employee participation increases wider acceptance across the workforce. The individuals most involved in a business process have the knowledge and know-how to improve it, but frequently those persons are simply never consulted. Participative approaches require executives to listen to line employees. For example, at Widia (India), total quality management (TQM) meshed with participative techniques accelerated the learning capacity of everyone in the company.

Result #3: Maximizing Stakeholder Involvement

"Empower the workforce" is frequently recited almost as a mantra today in business. But with the hype stripped away, what does this motto really entail? One way to achieve an empowered workforce is to ask employees to take more responsibility for their work, their work teams, indeed, the whole company, i.e., for solving the business problems that affect them. Managers today often give lip service to this objective and would like to see it happen. But there is a catch. Empowering the workforce requires sharing some power previously reserved as the exclusive domain of the top-level executives. Executives, managers, and supervisors have been taught that their jobs are planning and control. The irony is that for executives to lead successfully, they will have to give up the notion of being in charge. Empowering the workforce requires the development of a new leadership role.

Empowerment starts with improved communication, which often begins in planning events where participants discuss the company's strengths, weaknesses, vision, blocks, and strategies. In listening to and learning from one another, employees begin to build communication channels which continue to function even outside the strategic planning events. Increased communication raises the level of teamwork needed to create and implement the plans for corporate change and improvement. Because the need to change is so obvious in business today, learning how to overcome resistance to change is very important. Generally those whose jobs are removed from the larger picture of the company have the least understanding of why or how the company should adapt to new directions or methods. Sometimes when executives hand down mandates stating there is a need to change, the walls of resistance go up. However, when employees actually participate in the process that identifies the need for change, they understand better why things need to be changed and are more willing to try new methods. This acceptance, in turn, increases each person's capacity to adapt to new business conditions and enables each employee to become ready to accept new ideas and technologies. In short, participation eases change.

Participation can also become a way of life for the company. Employees actively involved in designing business solutions and processes which affect their daily performance become motivated to acquire new skills, try new operating patterns, and even alter the way meetings are run. When these skills are shared with the entire workforce, everyone buys into reinforced business strategies. Creativity is then enhanced not just for its own sake, but as part of a coherent business plan. Intensive participative planning breeds intensive participative implementation and fosters an understanding of why experiments need to happen. It allows the employees to recognize why risks need to be taken to activate the larger business vision. We have seen repeatedly that when all the people affected by a plan actually help build it, they are more willing to take risks and experiment with new company ventures.

Result #4: Participation Motivates the Workforce

Corporate cultures of participation that produce the kind of results we are describing here take time to grow and flourish. However, when management pays attention to the human dimensions of the workplace, these additional corporate benefits gradually blossom. If participative planning events continue regularly throughout the company and then are augmented with training of the whole workforce in the same skills used by the professional facilitators, this new way of operating is ingrained as a company pattern. A greater sense of responsibility and ownership for the future direction of the company then becomes the standard. Since no one wholeheartedly implements someone else's plans, if a company leader wants greater employee responsibility for performance, the employees need to be part of the ongoing deliberations about those plans which affect their work.

In addition, regular use of participative techniques develops cooperation as well as trust; it breaks down walls that isolate. When productive manager/subordinate relationships take root, the language of hierarchy fades in importance, if not to irrelevancy. A greater level of trust is engendered. More often than not, goals set participatively are higher than those goals set for employees by their superiors. And, in turn, these higher goals result in higher levels of performance overall.

When the workers at the plant designated to be closed by the executives of the Mills Group came forward with their own proposal to keep it open, no one suspected that they would be able to achieve the impressive results they did. But because it was their plant and the company had trained them in participative approaches, these employees felt the confidence and courage to accept the challenge. In this case both the employees and Mills' leaders were winners because the workers were able to set goals higher than those that were handed down to them. Employees who are given this greater say, in turn, increase their commitment to their jobs and to their companies.

However, there is a subtle distinction between employee buy-in and ownership. Too frequently employee participation efforts are thinly veiled attempts to get employees to buy into a set plan that already exists in the minds of executives. Increasing genuine ownership, on the other hand, requires executives, managers, and all employees to begin together on a level playing field. When employees plan shoulder-to-shoulder with the rest of the company stakeholders, they are much more willing to implement and take responsibility for those plans. They become part of the larger team.

DISCOVERING THE CRITICAL FACTORS

The contributors of these case studies found that maximum stakeholder involvement helped to root a company's culture of participation firmly. The importance of such stakeholder participation is the first of a series of discoveries the reader will come to see as common to all the corporate stories. The second discovery is that a company's leader must be open to and supportive of the trauma and drama of corporate change. As strong participants themselves in this transformation, leaders cannot allow stakeholders' challenges and reactions to threaten them.

Adopting a participative company culture that works can be confusing and frustrating, especially at first. Readers will recognize this reality as the third discovery common to the cases. The fourth common thread revolves around time—having enough time and recognizing the proper moment for going forward with strategic change.

Discovery #1: Need for Maximum Stakeholder Involvement

Common to all the cases presented in this book is the recognition that putting into place a culture of participation is maximum stakeholder involvement. In other words, all the people affected by a problem need to be part of its solution. Of course, this has been a maxim of the field of organizational behavior for years, but as Margaret Wheatley stressed in her book, *Leadership and the New Science: Learning About Organization from an Orderly Universe*:

> We know that the best way to build ownership is to give over the creation process to those who will be charged with its implementation. We are never successful if we merely present a plan in finished form to employees. It doesn't work to just ask people to sign on when they haven't been involved in the design process, when they haven't experienced the plan as a living, breathing thing[1].

Simply put, not only do employees not fully implement someone's plans, they support more enthusiastically what they themselves create. This is simply part of the new common sense of organizational life today.

To be successful, business is discovering how to tap its human resources. Our cases have revealed that participation and learning are mutually inclusive and that participation will result in real learning opportunities, a sharing of knowledge and skills. Self-directed or self-managed teams become laboratories for group discovery if guided by trained facilitators who let these groups "know what they know," so they can tap into the incredible experiential base resident around the meeting table. This was especially evident in the Metacentros story from Guatemala where, when faced with the challenge to respond to a national economic development issue, the employees harvested their own experiences into a focused business strategy that serves the country and the company simultaneously.

---

[1]Margaret L. Wheatley, *Leadership and the New Science: Learning About Organization from an Orderly Universe.* (San Francisco: Berrett-Koehler, 1992), 66.

Our cases also reveal the power and integrity of people on the shop floors of industry and behind the retail counters. Those who perceived themselves as having customers, whether internal or external, are on the front lines of enhancing business performance. As the executive of a large municipal Department of Revenue claimed to his fellow workers, "There's those of you directly serving the public and then there's the rest of us." Frequently the problem is "they" are simply not asked what "they" think. The employees are not asked to share what they have learned from real business experience. Much could be gained in business today if its leaders were willing to listen and learn from their own people; successful leaders trust in the stored-up wisdom embodied in a workforce that for the most part wants to do the best job possible, but is frustrated over irrelevant and meaningless policies, procedures, programs, and plans handed down from the top.

One barrier to this kind of employee involvement, though, is management's distrust in its employees' abilities, experiences, and wisdom. This block is largely in the mind of the manager. For a company to harvest the collective wisdom of its own people, the manager must believe in the resident capacities of his or her own people. It takes a very self-assured manager to allow those who work with him or her to voice their opinions, ideas, suggestions, concerns. Insecure managers wilt because they do not think to seek out those nearest to an organizational problem who are frequently the ones best able to solve it.

Discovery #2: Importance of Leader's Support

Our contributors noticed that while much lip service is given to the claim that the human factor is a company's greatest competitive advantage, few leaders really believe it. Their actions profess a different attitude. Once the General Editor and an associate were asked to facilitate a strategic planning session with a division of a Fortune 500 company, its executive claiming he wanted total commitment to the plan, and understood the importance, therefore, of the participatory approach we would be using. However, midway through the process, he walked his team through 125 overhead slides of the new corporate plan that he had been working on; he said he wanted everyone's opinion of his plan. Though he did not get an honest reaction, he left the meeting nonetheless convinced he had achieved their commitment to it. He even thanked us for our assistance.

A great disservice has been done to a generation of leaders trained to think that because they are assigned the leadership role, they are expected to have all the answers, know all the right moves, make the right decisions. The times we live in do not give us such a simple world and many current leaders are not prepared to come to terms with their inability to always know what's best. On one occasion the General Editor was sought out by a company's employees to convince management to convene the group in a participative planning session. The senior executive allowed the session to proceed (in an attempt to placate them), but did not participate. The session allowed a venting of frustration, but did not enable the organization to make any significant breakthrough in thinking, organization, or action. The executive in charge came back at the end of a session and essentially torpedoed the group's few creative suggestions.

This behavior is symptomatic of insecure leaders, those not capable of allowing people "under them" to offer any insight, for fear it might expose the leader's own shortcomings. Simply acquiescing to scene ritualized group process meeting, management did not really take workers' sentiment seriously and fundamentally did not believe in the usefulness of the process. Just like W. Edwards Deming will not institute his TQM approach without the top executive commitment, participation should not be approached unless an organization's leadership champions its cause.

Business is at risk unless it can be set free from the notion that its leaders are above mistakes and have a clear solution for every complex issue they face. The problem is not a character flaw in leadership, but over-expecting market forces that need a sense of security out of reach in today's complicated world. The real leader of the future will be the one who is secure enough in his or her own sense of self-worth to reach out for input and feedback from others, even from the newest employee on the line.

To maximize its investments in its human resources, a company must be committed to altering the basic organizational paradigm that managers have the knowledge, and workers are just supposed to comply with leadership's thinking. The participative imperative we propose in this book requires a fundamental transformation in the way business leaders think and act. This transformation is first and foremost a change of heart and mind rather than a change in organizational structures. This transformation will require managers to surrender some of what they were taught was one of their main functions: control. A manager will probably be unable to achieve the enhanced business performance that increased employee participation can bring if he or she insists on dominating the processes.

Discovery #3: Participation Can Be Chaotic

A third discovery is that there will be a certain amount of confusion at first as old patterns are replaced and new ones tested and adopted. When first introduced, participation can be messy. Organizational leaders can be comforted in knowing, though, that creative new patterns often emerge through such upheaval, not from a logical, linear extension of old patterns hoping to respond to new situations. The Mills Group story, for example, shows that company's capacity to increase the level of workforce involvement while at the same time accepting that "crisis was their ally." This gave them the perspective and patience necessary to weather the economic turmoil of the Brazilian economy and prevail.

Discovery #4: Participation Involves a Matter of Time

Another key to success common to the case studies is having enough time at the right time to implement participative work arrangements. Participation is not a quick fix, though the search for quick fixes seems endemic to our society. We long for no-risk investment returns, fantasize about winning the big contract to escape our problems, employ the "technique de jour" to solve our business problems. Slowly, however, the message sinks in that our times require a fundamental reexamination of basic operating principles upon which business was founded. The problem is that no one business school, no one book, no one management consultant can possibly deal with all the factors that require examination.

In business, people are impatient with things that do not bring instant gratification, results, and feedback. Following through a process of full stakeholder participation takes time. Initially it might mean more meetings rather than fewer. But as our cases have witnessed, increased results do materialize. Consultant D'Souza's insistence that JK Fibre suspend financial measurement of his injection of participative methods reaped dramatic rewards in the long run.

Our cases revealed that there is a time to use participation...

THE RIGHT TIME

(1) At the beginning of a new venture or undertaking (as illustrated by the JK Fibre story);

(2) When a new direction is required with an existing venture (as with Widia (India) and Great Eastern Life Assurance, Ltd.);

(3) Soon after new leadership is in place (depicted with the story of Metacentros);

(4) When the lack of productivity and profits, the rock-bottom morale, or high employee turnover can no longer be tolerated (portrayed by the account of Hamilton Insurance);

(5) When the external forces of the competition, the new technology, or the national economy are so powerful that the company must respond in brand new ways (seen both at the Mills Group as well as Lockheed Missiles and Space Company).

... and a time to avoid it.

THE WRONG TIME

(1) When there is no apparent need to do things differently;

(2) If the leader does not champion it;

(3) When people want a quick fix to a deep problem;

(4) If participation is performed around a non-issue or merely a surface issue—that is, when the focus is to "straighten something out." Participation works best when it alleviates the core issues of a business.

Once a company establishes the best time for introducing a culture of participation, the work has only begun. The contributors begin to see the internal dynamics necessary to sustain successful culture transformation after the initial idea of major participation is introduced. Nearly all the case study companies began the change process with a strategic planning retreat (or the LENS seminar as some called it). These were highly participatory in nature. Widia (India) began with a half-day planning session which then convinced senior management of the need to do a three-day planning retreat. Lockheed employed the "off-site" as a principal means of participative planning and used these sessions to help integrate TQM with participative management. A central activity in each of these inaugural participative planning sessions was the formation of the company's vision, mission, values, and purpose, usually accompanied by an examination of root causes blocking the fulfillment of the vision. Strategies then were designed to overcome constraints.

After an initial burst of enthusiasm for this new way of operating, our contributors discovered the need to conduct small group demonstrations of the new corporate culture through such activities as TQM projects. Frequent references to project action teams punctuate our cases. Great Eastern Life Assurance, Ltd., began with computerization and eventually moved to a point where task-forces became a way of life. When the Mills Group's directors reported to the employees of one plant that it had to close for the overall company profitability, the workers, having become skilled in the use of team approaches, suggested another direction. They wanted to remain open as a demonstration of the new work ethic required to pull the company out of the country's deep recession. As the case reported, "They won, and the company won."

Next the contributors saw that a period of training is needed to transfer group process techniques necessary to sustain a participatory environment. An in-house team of facilitators was trained at Great Eastern so the company would not be dependent upon the external consultants over the long haul. At Metacentros, constant training, including a focus on new thinking skills, was a key to business success. Mills reported that training in participative techniques took root best when it was coupled with participative approaches used in their strategic planning processes. JK Fibre combined training in participative techniques with a focus on personal development.

Last, it was obvious to the contributors that there needs to be within the company internal interchange wherein groups share approaches that work. Widia (India) used cross-departmental communication to break down walls between isolated departments. Moving from isolation to collaboration was considered key to success at Lockheed, using at first a division-wide newsletter. Later, as Patricia Tuecke reported, they found "getting the whole system in the room" was critical to maintaining forward momentum. JK Fibre started by having managers meet daily rather than monthly, and then moved on to have an employee "sabha" (company meeting) periodically to show how the company's big picture related to its game plan. Mills, too, reported that participative interchanges were vital ingredients in their approach, beginning with a ten-minute intercom company "news flash," which informed employees of the volatile business conditions they were working under.

Having all four of these dynamics integrated is critical to an organizational transformation process. Sherwood Shankland, a consultant with long experience in organizational transformation, made a salient point about personal resistance to change. "There is no cure for resistance, but if there is clarity on the dynamics of the big picture, commitment to it is enhanced and outweighs the resistance."

This chapter has analyzed how participation leads to celebration when the company's leaders, as well as its stakeholders, rejoice in the benefits of the transformation they helped create. The success factors we present here add up to a kind of model a company can use to ensure a productive transformation. But the voices that speak best about how participation works are those of the contributors of the case studies that follow. Their stories tell of the frustrations and struggles, as well as the commitment and inspiration, that helped corporations from around the world achieve the benefits of participation.

II.

INCREASING PRODUCTIVITY

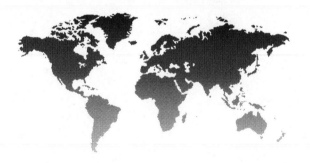

WIDIA (INDIA) LIMITED

3. A VALUE-DRIVEN CULTURE

by

T.A. SADASIVAN AND JUDITH D. GILLES

*"Quality is a thought revolution and our
endless desire for quality will make life
worth living (including making a profit)."*
R. Srinivasan, Managing Director,
Widia (India) Limited

To visit Widia (India) Limited's factory in Bangalore, India, is to experience a different kind of environment from the usual engineering plant in India. Most manufacturing operations are poorly lighted, full of greasy machinery, and littered with discarded materials. At Widia (India), the machines are placed in orderly patterns with work areas clearly delineated. Neatly trimmed grounds, numerous flowering shrubs and trees reflect the image of Bangalore as India's "garden city," and as one of the fastest growing industrial centers in Asia. At lunch time music plays in the canteen, while lively conversation buzzes around the tables. It is an inviting place, more like a university campus than a factory.

Widia (India) Ltd., a financial and technical collaboration of Krupp Widia GmbH, Germany, produces a wide variety of metal cutting and forming tools and special purpose machines for domestic and export markets. The annual turnover is approximately U.S. $30 million. In German, the words, *wie Diamant*, or diamond-like, are put together to form the name, Widia. Heavy-duty mining drills are one of the products which are manufactured at a smaller unit in Hyderabad in southern India. In fact, because few places in the world manufacture these specialty tools, Widia (India)'s engineers have developed and indigenized the process for many of their products. The company's symbol of three interlocking triangles which form a "W" is symbolic of the triangular insert tips that are used in each cutting tool.

TOP OF THE LIST

The Confederation of Indian Industries (CII), which is spearheading a quality consciousness drive, placed Widia (India) at the top of their list of Indian corporations progressing the fastest to change organizational culture and attitudes toward quality. As Sarita Nagpal, CII Quality Division Director, puts it, "I was impressed by how far ahead of other companies Widia (India) was in getting people involved in thinking through its systems for everything."

It was not surprising that, in February, 1992, Widia (India) was the sixth company in India to receive ISO (International Standards Organization) 9001 certification. This is the most comprehensive award for consistent adherence to procedures and processes stipulated in the ISO standards. An ISO label does not certify product quality. It merely testifies officially that a company's systems are in order. ISO 9000 certificates became mandatory for companies exporting to European markets, beginning in January, 1993.

The company employs 1,400 people of whom 1,000 are unionized workers and 400 are officers and executives. Everyone, including the managing director, wears a blue uniform. Women employees wear blue sarees. Widia (India)'s Managing Director, R. Srinivasan, is on the shop floor daily interacting with people and listening to their concerns. "When that happens," affirms a supervisor, "a worker has a very special day because of it."

POISED FOR CHANGE

In the mid-1980s, Widia (India) was poised for rapid financial growth, but complacency had set in. "We were not being responsive to the market," recalls H.R. Gupta, Executive Director of Production. "Internally, we were too compartmentalized. Each department was out for itself, often at cross-purposes with other departments. People were not completely involved with their work."

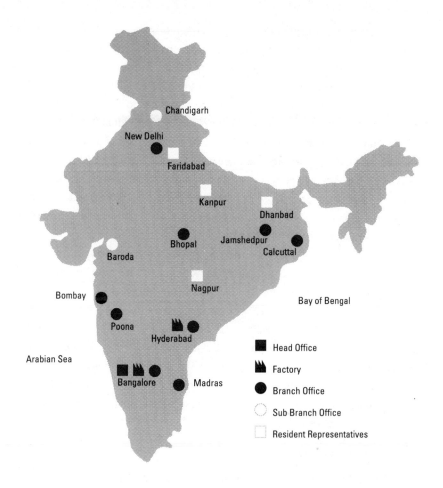

Chandigarh

New Delhi

Faridabad

Kanpur

Dhanbad

Bhopal   Jamshedpur

Baroda   Calcuttal

Bombay   Nagpur

Poona   Bay of Bengal

Hyderabad

Arabian Sea

Bangalore   Madras

■ Head Office

🏭 Factory

● Branch Office

◯ Sub Branch Office

☐ Resident Representatives

In 1986, Widia (India) came in contact with Richard and Gail West of the Institute of Cultural Affairs (ICA), who were assisting several manufacturing units to clarify the company's mission, purpose, and values in sessions with senior managers. These consultants continued with follow-up programs which included strategic planning and leadership development skills, such as time management and communication prowess. "We hired them," said Gupta, "and they suggested we hold a half-day participatory workshop for senior managers on the company's future and the issues it faces, to test the process. What sold us was the facilitative style that had us interacting with each other."

The senior managers decided to carry the process further and over a three-day period drafted company purpose, mission, and operating values statements for the company, with the help of the consultants. It was during this time that senior management resolved to adopt 12 values as a first major step towards the shift in corporate culture they wanted to put into practice. These values included respect and care for every individual associated with Widia (India), commitment to excellence through perfection and consistency, and according top priority to customer needs through prompt and appropriate response. These values provided the benchmarks of daily work practices and personal styles of interacting with other employees, customers, and suppliers. Operating values are just that—one believes in them and uses the principles to demonstrate effective working practices.

Today, all Widia (India) officers and executives carry in their shirt pockets a small notebook containing the company's purpose, mission, and values statements. At the start of every company meeting, the 12 operating value statements are read aloud, a ritual that gives everyone a common starting point. The entire managerial staff of the company was involved in the process of discussing and refining these statements. During the annual sales conference of 1988, when all the officers and executives met for dinner, the purpose, mission, and value statements were officially adopted by reading the statements aloud in chorus. At monthly senior management meeting, individuals relate illustrations of how the values are being put into everyday practice.

DRIVE FOR QUALITY

To survive today every company is faced with the question of how to produce quality products and services. Achieving ISO certification is but the tip of the iceberg. "To achieve total quality management (TQM), one has to go through total organizational change," asserts Srinivasan. The acid test is changing work attitudes so people will not want to produce anything but quality. Widia (India)'s case study illustrates over a five-year time span how a TQM process operates in an organization which is simultaneously changing its own corporate culture. This case study addresses two questions:

(1) Is putting a participative culture in place a prerequisite for the success of TQM?

(2) What role do operating values play in changing organizational culture?

Probably no topic has been as hotly debated in management circles worldwide. Numerous consultants from the U.K. and other parts of Europe and America offer their services to Indian companies on how to implement quality concepts at every level in organizations. Japanese success in quality manufactured goods is driving Indian companies to reorganize operations to produce world-class quality goods and services. The rush to get ISO 9000 certification is epidemic worldwide. But the larger question of consistent quality goes far beyond meeting ISO certification standards. Each company, unique in its history and culture, is faced with determining what a quality conscious culture path looks like. Cautious managers are quick to point out the poor track record of Indian companies that have tried to transplant Japanese concepts like teamwork or consensus to Indian soil, only to see attempts fail to take root. Indeed, the case can be made that to achieve total quality, each individual in the organization has to adjust his/her own behavior before quality can become a way of life.

Meanwhile, the Indian government's gradual relaxation of trade barriers and easing of financial restrictions signal the opening up of India to global market competition. Increasing the percentage foreign companies can own in Indian businesses makes it easier for investors to make and transfer monies in and out of the country. Attractive incentives encourage non-resident Indians to invest in India. All these measures result in a dramatic increase in Indian dollar and gold reserves. For Indian industries, the competition and joint-venture (technology licensing) partners are requiring that the Indian business community produce world-standard quality. Customer demand for quality is pervading every market and forcing the business environment to be more flexible, quality-conscious, and responsive, yet competitive, profitable, and growth-oriented. Government liberalization policies now pave the way for multinationals looking at India's 850 million people as a potential market for products. Recently, this can be seen by the explosive interest of giant telecommunication companies in the Indian market, the new battleground of Pepsi and Coke for market share, and the establishment of joint ventures between Indian companies and high-tech organizations such as Apple Computer, Inc., IBM Corp., and Sun Micro Systems.

Yet, operating in an Indian business environment includes many factors that mitigate against a quality culture. A prime stumbling block is a militant and divisive labor/management situation in many companies. Labor union leaders, who often operate outside the factory premises and who have strong national and local political ties, negotiate with management over quality procedures. Quality then becomes a bargaining tool. Quality circle programs may be killed if relations between union leaders and management are turbulent. The author of *Thresholds of Motivation*, V.S. Mahesh, in talking about his extensive human resource development experience in India with labor unions in both the manufacturing and service industries, reports:

> Whenever organizations took care to make work interesting, and gave freedom and space for employees to think for themselves and to innovate, the more entrenched union leaders felt threatened. There have been many occasions when my advocating of humanistic policies in corporations has led me into confrontations with entrenched union leaders, for they were afraid that their popularity, and need, would be eroded. The higher the stakes for their continuing in leadership positions, the happier they were to let some amount of unhappiness and unrest continue among their members. Not only has human labor, but also human misery, become a commodity for trade [1].

Another major constraint to quality is poor productivity. Many companies greatly overstaffed, largely because of the government's emphasis on employment schemes, feel fortunate if they can get as much as six hours of actual, productive work for eight hours of pay. Even today, because of the Indian government's protective labor laws, it is extremely difficult to dismiss an employee. High absenteeism, a poorly-educated workforce, and lax discipline standards only add to the difficulty of getting goods produced. Nationally, an underdeveloped infrastructure of poorly constructed and maintained roads results in delayed or damaged shipping and receiving of manufactured goods. Power outages are frequent. Bangalore, located in the south of India, is rapidly becoming the "Silicon Valley" of the sub-continent.

Yet, Karnataka, the state in which Bangalore is located, is not even close to providing an adequate power supply for plants to operate at full capacity. An overburdened and unreliable communication system in many parts of the country further frustrates business operations.

Many Indian manufacturers have to deal with a proliferation of spurious goods. For instance, a customer may unknowingly purchase imitation replacement parts or spares that will fail after even limited use. The govern-

COMPARISON OF TURNOVER*

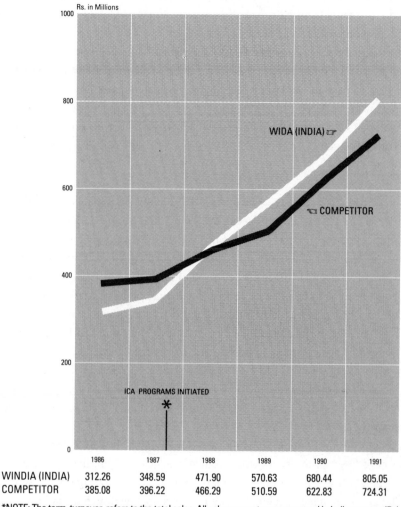

	1986	1987	1988	1989	1990	1991
WINDIA (INDIA)	312.26	348.59	471.90	570.63	680.44	805.05
COMPETITOR	385.08	396.22	466.29	510.59	622.83	724.31

*NOTE: The term, turnover, refers to the total sales. All sales amounts are measured in Indian rupees (Rs).

ment's policy of allocating exclusive manufacturing rights to the small-scale sector often leads to poorly produced components. An otherwise quality product, e.g., a well-designed office swivel chair, may fail to function when the rubber casters split because this important part was produced by a supplier in a separate shop with little accountability for quality standards to the major furniture manufacturer.

Another issue concerns spare replacement parts. Often dealers will unknowingly buy fake, branded goods that later fail to perform because they were not manufactured to standard specifications. Although not universal, frequent and widespread practices of corruption and bribery permit non-quality goods and services to reach customers. This is commonly seen in substandard construction materials where officials are paid off to allow shoddy work to pass inspection. Add to this an inherited British bureaucratic mind-set that tends to push decisions up the organization ladder and one begins to see a small part of the complex picture of what companies are up against in trying to produce quality.

LEADING THE CHANGE

From the company's inception in 1967, until 1981, expatriate Germans were Widia (India)'s chief executives. A highly centralized, autocratic leadership helped set up the company and enabled it to take roots. The first CEO encouraged innovation and self-reliance in technology. Under the leadership of the second CEO, focus shifted to marketing and customer service. The company came to be known for its technological innovation and concern for customer needs, particularly for the attention paid to special orders.

In 1981, management made a bold move and promoted R. Srinivasan from within the company to become its first indigenous director. This was a rare practice among Indo-German companies. Srinivasan joined Widia (India) as Works Engineer in 1966 after receiving extensive training on hard metals in Germany for several years with Krupp Widia. Taking control of the company as Managing Director in 1981, he saw that Widia (India)'s major strength lay in a young, dynamic workforce which thrived in the environment of freedom to experiment and innovate, especially in the area of product and process technology. Under Srinivasan's encouragement, Widia (India)'s technicians explored many new technologies, such as carbide cutting tools. Specialty machines, designed and developed in-house to meet the company's own needs, soon became a separate division filling orders for "one-of-a-kind" products for an expanding client base.

At this time frequent informal interaction took place among the senior executives of the organization and a fairly well-defined organizational structure existed. But the individual departments worked in isolation, many times promoting departmental achievements which were at cross-purposes with the

Purpose

Our purpose is:

to enhance the productivity of industries by being the leader in supplying high technology, quality engineering products and services,

— by being responsive to the needs of customers, employees, business associates, shareholders, the community, and society at large.

— through an organization of committed, highly skilled, motivated and satisfied people striving for innovation and excellence.

and

to achieve continual growth in sales and profits through fair means in all dealings.

Mission

We will:

1. be responsive to customers' needs and develop, manufacture and supply high tech, quality products and services to enhance their productivity and reduce costs;

2. train, motivate and provide a growth-oriented environment to our employees and encourage team work, mutual co-operation and support team members to achieve peak performance;

3. encourage innovation and creativity to stay ahead of the competition;

4. give necessary support to suppliers; subcontractors and business associates, to enable them to meet our requirements on a continual basis;

5. be systematic and cost effective in our working and ensure adequate profits to satisfy shareholders and provide resources for continuous growth;

6. control pollution and environmental deterioration for improving quality of life; and

7. meet commitments to the Government, community and society at large.

Operating Values

We believe in:

1. according top *priority for customer needs* through prompt and appropriate response.

2. *team spirit* through mutual co-operation and support and participative decision making.

3. clear, crisp, *frank* and effective oral and written communication.

4. disciplined and *systematic working* with well defined responsibilities and *accountability*.

5. *training* our employees for *peak performance* and developing them to their *utmost potential*.

6. *respect and care* for every individual associated with us.

7. growth of an individual through *objective evaluation* of performance.

8. commitment to excellence through perfection and *consistency*.

9. encouraging innovation and creativity by *welcoming* challenges and suggestions and by *accepting risk*.

10. cost effectiveness by optimum utilization of *time* and other resources.

11. being responsible good corporate citizens.

12. dissemination of information.

larger interests of the company. For example, the Production Department focused on meeting monthly targets and did not pay much attention to delivery dates. The Marketing Department was not concerned with forecasting, and therefore the Production Department was in the dark about the fluctuation in demand for products. Quotations to customers for special items, which involved coordination among various departments, were subject to inordinate delay. In short, teamwork was absent. Leadership style was highly autocratic and centralized. Systems were haphazard.

Interaction between the corporate officers and the executives was very limited during working hours, with no significant informal mingling occurring outside the workplace. "You could hardly believe how isolated people were!" commented a supervisor. "People would come and go and not even acknowledge one other." Among workers it was much the same. A worker might have few close friends. A tool plant driller, Anthony Lobo, described his work in those days as monotony. "You just picked the pieces up and put them down. There was nothing to show that you did anything. People didn't enjoy being on the machines. Everyone was working to catch the boss's eye."

At this time Srinivasan was very concerned. Although the growth of the company in the early 1980s was fast, by 1985 total sales began to flatten out. No matter how well Widia (India) performed, its competitor did better. Management saw a dangerous plateau. After a great deal of thought, Srinivasan brought the senior managers together for what was to be the beginning of regular meetings to try to resolve the dilemma. Together they reached the conclusion that one of the fundamental blocks to the company's programs was isolated working patterns which hampered interaction between people of various departments.

In their search for a solution to this issue, Srinivasan and the senior management executives met and discussed various articles and books on management topics. The book, *In Search of Excellence*, by Tom Peters and Bob Waterman [2], convinced the entire group that establishing their own company values, evolved out of their own experience, could help. A common set of values would give a sense of direction, which would help bring people together. The coming together of Widia (India) and ICA in 1986 to develop purpose, mission, and values statements launched a seven-year journey of transformation.

TASKFORCES: A WAY OF LIFE

Once the values were spelled out and beginning to give a sense of cohesion, the management team decided again to draw on ICA's experience. Beginning in 1988, a series of strategic planning sessions occupied a large part of the shift in company culture from isolated patterns of working to a highly integrated system. These workshops, conducted by Richard and Gail West, who had first worked with Widia (India) in 1986, produced group consensus around the company's future vision, issues, and strategic actions. The program generated taskforces to carry out the strategic corporate actions identified in the workshops. For the first time the Executive Director of Finance found himself on a taskforce developing performance appraisal systems; and the Marketing Director was part of a taskforce promoting teamwork throughout the company.

By 1989-1990, a matrix of cross-departmental taskforces turned working relationships around. This approach of getting group involvement definitely brought about a shift in the management style of the members of the senior management group and throughout the company. Middle management and supervisors began to hold strategic planning sessions with 20 to 25 employees. Overall, 350 people had direct participation in contributing their ideas and forming taskforces to implement them. This was an important turning point. The walls between departments crumbled like the Berlin Wall. People from different departments started talking to each other and began to understand each other's problems. "The ICA process is the most powerful tool for pulling down barriers between departments and people," remarked Srinivasan. As a result, mutual trust and respect were developed across the senior management group.

In-house facilitation teams developed as an adjunct dimension to the planning process. With so many people involved in programs, there was a need for co-facilitators from senior management who could work with the ICA team for each of the groups of 20-25 employees. As a result, one-half dozen senior managers developed facilitation skills as well as gained insight into the pulse of the organization; they listened to employee participants at mid-management and supervisory levels describe their own visions for the future and the way to resolve the blocks and hindrances they experienced. For instance, dismantling the previous autocratic style of telling people what to do, instead of inviting their suggestions and ideas, released a great amount of enthusiasm for self-disciplined work patterns. A tool plant driller described the shift "from one of arrogance on the part of management, to one of listening to workers more and becoming involved in their work issues." This core facilitation prowess is frequently sought after by other organizations who have witnessed Widia (India)'s approach.

The movement away from hierarchical to participatory management created a climate within Widia (India) that ensured the success of the taskforces that were formed. Taskforces regularly train managers in the art of brainstorming and asking questions. Resolving problems by local decision making guarantees buy-in since people are acting on the issues that they are most passionate about. For example, one of the taskforces working on the development of teamwork decided that all employees of the company, including the managerial staff, should wear the same uniform. This decision was implemented within a period of three months.

Forming all these taskforces now necessitated face-to-face coordination. The senior management group started meeting once a month away from the plant to discuss all activities having interdepartmental ramifications. Every department started holding meetings to discuss and set priorities and to tackle problems. While the sales department held meetings daily at the start of the day, other departments held meetings weekly, biweekly, or monthly, depending upon their felt need. Specific taskforces tackled many issues and carried out a wide range of activities as the following list demonstrates:

- **Performance planning and appraisal:** Employees were told what their jobs were, how they could achieve their goals, and precisely how they would be appraised.
- **Updating and upgrading information systems:** Putting together data, for instance, monthly sales figures, used to take up to one month, with the result that sales figures were always outdated. After the company bought a minicomputer for 10 million rupees, statistics were more quickly accessible to all. Now statistics of the previous month are available by the tenth day of the next month.
- **Getting timely quotes out to customers on special items.** It was taking from two to three months to complete the quotations on special items. After the taskforce began a daily 11:00 a.m. cross-departmental meeting, quotation time was reduced to several days.

- **Having information accessible to everyone:** In every department white bulletin boards displaying current production targets, achievements, rejections, and rework were placed. For example, "achievements" ranged from receiving positive letters from customers and suppliers to meeting monthly targets and achieving production schedules ahead of time. "Rejections" that were prominently displayed listed what product was rejected, why it was rejected, and what must be done the next time to correct it. The "rework" list outlined information that helped employees know what needed to be done to improve goods and services.

  A first-line supervisor, Francis Zavier, commented that "the display boards really improved workers' attitudes toward targets. For the first time the goals were clearly stated and up there for everyone to see." A recent innovative program on information-sharing brings all employees together for one-half day sessions to explain the company's financial picture, profit and loss, future plans, etc.

  "Mere sharing of information has brought us tremendous results in terms of trust and commitment to goals," says the Executive Director of Production, H.R. Gupta. "You have to create a credible environment in which you are not changing your colors all the time."

- **Housekeeping and machine maintenance being everyone's concern:** A group is appointed to monitor space use and levels of cleanliness throughout the factory. Shrubs and potted plants are tended year-round. In the Maintenance Department, the assistant manager has his team enthused about the Japanese "5 S's" method which teaches employees a self-monitoring regime for workspace cleanliness. The Assistant Manager, Mr. Banaji explains:

  > If you have only five minutes, you sort, systematize, summarize, use spic and span maintenance, and self-discipline to keep your table, workspace, and tools clean. Now people do not even have to think about it. It is a much safer environment than before.

- **Employee suggestions:** Getting employees to submit suggestions became more effective when 35 committees were formed to screen all written suggestions. Within 15 days, a contributor

Company Profile

Name of company	Widia (India) Limited
Name of holding company	Krupp Widia GmbH, Essen, Germany
Headquarters location	Bangalore, India
Company product focus	Tungsten carbide metal cutting and forming tools
Case study plant location	Bangalore, India
Leader and title	R. Srinivasan, Managing Director
Last fiscal year-end sales	$30 million
Profit percent on sales	6.32%
Number of employees	1,400

receives notification about the feasibility of the suggestion, along with an initial cash award given to anyone who takes the time to write up the suggestion. With this change in procedure, response to suggestions went from a meager 0.1 suggestions/employee-year to 1.0 suggestions/employee-year. While this increase is still quite low by Japanese or Western standards, it indicates a trend toward bridging the gap between workers and management.

"Forming a taskforce has become a way of life," remarks N. Banaji, Assistant Manager of the Maintenance Department:

> If you want to solve a problem, form a taskforce. Before, that kind of group thinking was not a part of the company. You were left on your own to figure things out. But now, everyone knows that anything that gets done, happens after one talks in groups.

TQM IN ACTION

To be sure, these seven results were not the only changes at Widia (India). Far more fundamental was the change in management style. Up until 1989, the top management fixed targets which had to be met by various departments and executives. H.R. Gupta calls this management by objectives. Orders flowed down from the top without any discussions involving those employees having to meet the targets. Gupta recalls:

Then we switched to 'management by quality policy deployment,' a systematic matrix process of action steps. This tool now connects the entire way the company operates. Targets are fixed after mutual discussion with managers and engineers, and the means of hitting the targets are worked out jointly. What we are working with has to do with process, not just results.

After attending a one-week quality program in Japan in 1989, Gupta was convinced that Widia (India)'s focus on values and participative task-forces was the right direction. He explains:

The whole thing became clear to me. All the work we had done during the past two years was preparation for a total approach. I saw how TQM could become the umbrella under which we could do everythingquality, involvement of people, new products, everything. We learned from ICA the importance of the role of the facilitator in this process. That's been the real learning for us.

By 1991, style and role questions, particularly among mid-management, began to surface. Involving greater numbers of people in planning and implementation intruded on previously held roles of managers. As managers faced the need to change their styles of operating, many welcomed the change enthusiastically, some took it as a temporary fad, and some were confused. A program, led by Judith Gilles, an American ICA consultant living in Bombay, used the theme of a "learning organization" from Peter Senge's book, *The Fifth Discipline* [3]. The focus of this program related disciplines, such as Senge's techniques of personal mastery or team learning to the issues on the Widia (India) shop floor. Mid-level managers developed skills in leading workshops and focused discussions so that management involved workers in analyzing product defects, or in generating ideas, for instance, scrap reduction to cut costs. These skills will become even more critical as the company moves closer to expanding the operating values and increased involvement in quality circles, i.e., focused groups centered around specific quality problems, to the entire workforce.

"I see a gap," states Gupta, "between mid-managers and the workers. There is a boundary that shows up in a 'we/they' attitude." The ICA experiences in initial programs with union leadership have helped to break down some of the barriers, but the trade union 'confrontation culture' is still very much alive. The old patterns of mistrust, fear, and win/lose thinking are there under the surface, waiting for opportunities to strike back across the negotiation table. A 'learning organization' assumes that individuals and the organization as a whole learn from everything that it is doing. Much of the effort in dealing successfully with the shift from a confrontation culture to a learning organization falls on the shoulders of mid-level managers because of the communication role they play between senior management and workers.

Today at Widia (India) there are 25 quality improvement teams and 10 quality circles actively working. Significant improvements have been made in the short period of three years since the introduction of the Widia (India) TQM program called CONQUEST, an acronym for customer and organizational needs through quality employees and strategies. As a result of this program the following positive changes occurred:

- Inventory levels of stores and consumables, a measure of good planning systems with less money tied up in supplies, dropped from 138 days in 1989 to 90 days in 1991. The 1992 target was 60 days.
- Gross profits increased from 9% to 11.5% of turnover, or total sales.
- Return on investment increased from 24% to 31%.
- Work in process, the time it takes for people and resources to manufacture any product from start to finish, was reduced from 90 days to 68 days.
- Scrap in tool plant was reduced from 6.8% to 3.8%.
- Variable expenses were reduced from 29% to 22%.
- The average number of hours of in-house training per employee has increased from 16 hours/year to 32 hours/year.

When CONQUEST was launched, there were three important changes in mind-set required for successful implementation:

(1) Concern for prevention of defects rather than detection of defects;
(2) Continuous prevention of defects until zero level of defectives is reached;
(3) Concern for quality rather than production.

The primary requirement for this transformation is that all defects must be exposed. This is possible only in an organization where people are concerned about what is wrong, rather than who is wrong. Thus, TQM only thrives in an organization that believes in teamwork results, participative style, customer orientation, and product innovation. Such an organization will cherish values of mutual trust, openness, care and respect for individuals, as well as commitment to excellence. In these companies, people will not hesitate to expose problems, but instead will develop the habit of solving problems immediately, on the basis of data. Such a transformation can only happen when people celebrate success, live out of meaningful values, and experience their life goals and company goals as one. Widia (India) has established the necessary changes required for TQM to take root and flourish.

The company today is poised for becoming an important player in the global market. Helped by its parent company, it has ambitious plans to export to Japan, Korea, Taiwan, and other countries in the Pacific Rim. Meeting and surpassing international standards of quality are the keys to export markets. To excel in these markets, Widia (India) has many challenges ahead. In a span of about five years, the company has transformed itself from a reactive organization to a proactive one by establishing a set of values for the organization and then living by them; by promoting teamwork and a participative style of management; and by establishing clear goals for everyone and tying them to company goals. In the words of Srinivasan, "It is a continuous journey, a journey with a shifting goal line; once one is on that journey the commitment increases to accelerate the pace."

CONCLUDING THOUGHTS

Transformation is a word that is easy to talk about but difficult to document. Statistics alone can indicate a change, but not necessarily a transformation. Likewise, transformation is a journey with stages of incubation, growth, adoption, and recommitment. Clearly something dramatic has happened in and to Widia (India). People are taking notice. Perhaps, transformation can be best summed up by the shift in spirit. There is a new spirit evident in the company. Today Srinivasan is convinced "that there is a tremendous potential in people waiting to be unleashed, if only enough opportunities can be provided for them."

References

[1]   Mahesh, V. S. *Thresholds of Motivation: The Corporation as a Nursery for Human Growth.* New Delhi: Tata Mc-Graw-Hill Publishing Co. (1993) p. 27.

[2]   Peters, Thomas J. and Robert H. Waterman, Jr. *In Search of Excellence.* New York: Harper & Row, Publishers (1982) pp. 279-291.

[3]   Senge, Peter. *The Fifth Discipline: The Art and Practice of the Learning Organization.* New York: Doubleday (1990).

Great Eastern Life
We take care of you for life

1908

4. EXCELLENCE...A JOURNEY NOT A DESTINATION

by
ANN AND JOHN EPPS

*In November, 1992, The Singapore Business Times in an article
headlined "The Secret of Great Eastern Life's Success"
observed that, "Dedication to training, efficient use of
automation and information technology, and a people-oriented
management philosophy are responsible for the success
of The Great Eastern Life Assurance Company Ltd."*

Great Eastern Life Assurance Company Ltd. (GE Life) was one of five Singapore companies to win the prestigious National Productivity Award of 1992. This award was granted in recognition of GE Life's "efficient use of automation and information technology," "people-oriented management," and "outstanding efforts in training." In the high-powered Singapore business environment, high productivity is assumed; to win an award in that arena is a major accomplishment.

Formed in 1908, GE Life operates in a few countries, including Singapore and Malaysia, and is a leading life insurer in both nations. In Singapore, approximately 450 people are full-time staff members; in

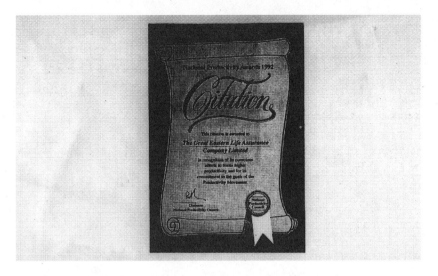

Malaysia, the figure is above 600 (figures do not include agents). The staff reflects the cultural and ethnic mix of the two nations: Chinese, Malay, and Indian.

How did GE Life come to win the 1992 National Productivity Award, and what was unique about the company's journey toward excellence? These are the questions explored by this case study, which focuses primarily on the award's second arena of merit for GE Life—people-oriented management.

SINGAPORE'S BUSINESS ENVIRONMENT

The city nation of Singapore has a remarkable business atmosphere. Its record of economic growth over a relatively short period of time is universally acknowledged as a major achievement. What was at the end of World War II a defeated, occupied British colony has now become a developed, high-tech business center boasting world-class industry, commerce, communications, and transportation. As a part of its ongoing campaign for increased efficiency, Singapore has achieved a worker productivity ranking of number two in the world, second only to Sweden. While much of the Western world is experiencing economic recession in the early 1990s, Singapore continues to show a 5-6% Gross National Product growth.

Malaysia, too, is on the developmental fast track. With the year 2020 established as the target date for achieving "developed nation" status, rapid industrialization is in full swing. Signs of a new affluence are everywhere; glittering boutiques, fashionable condominiums, five-star recreational and resort facilities, and even the perpetual traffic jams attest to a newfound access to wealth. Although the majority of the population still lives in rural areas, people have increasing access to urban amenities and have become accustomed to factory life. Both Malaysia and Singapore actively solicit and receive foreign investment, and multinational companies dot the landscape. In both nations, the style of business is fast-paced, and highly competitive. Although the legendary service and courtesy of the East are highly visible, no Westerner should ever mistake these cultural niceties for a lack of business acumen.

This rapid pace of development has been enhanced by streamlined organizations and strong leaders. Since all three of the cultures (Chinese, Indian, Malay) that make up the society have a tradition of respect for those in positions of authority, the hierarchical approach to management has been a natural fit. All that is now changing. Young people in companies are highly skilled, well-educated, and often reflect a heavy dose of Western-style individualism gained from overseas schooling and/or TV. These people have multiple job opportunities and are willing to leave a company whose policies seem to be too stifling. Furthermore, business activities are becoming too complex and detailed to be controlled by one person or even a few at the top.

In this setting, the top-down style of management is slowly giving way. A more participative approach to decision making is clearly in order, if two pitfalls can be avoided: confusion and time-consuming procedures. People in this business culture expect leaders to be decisive and visionary, but also to be open to input and to the honoring of contributions from throughout the organization. People want to "own" their work, to have some voice in how it is carried out. And they also want action. They are impatient with the red tape and procedural gyrations of some consensus-building

Company Profile

Name of company	Great Life Assurance Company Ltd.
Primary company locations	Singapore and Malaysia
Founded	1908
Commercial focus	Life insurance
Leader and title	Allen Pathmarajah, Director and CEO
Full-time staff	In Singapore: 450 In Malaysia: over 600

processes. The Technology of Participation (ToP) techniques, as described in the Preface to this book, provide some of the methods for avoiding the traps that erode staff initiative.

The life insurance industry in Singapore and Malaysia is still growing. At the present time, only about 53% of the population in Singapore and about 14% in Malaysia hold life insurance. In spite of substantial and compulsory government "Social Security" savings schemes, and reliance on families for supporting the elderly, there is an increasing awareness of the benefits of life insurance. These are fertile grounds for aggressive marketing.

What does it take in this environment of opportunity to create an organization capable of seizing the advantage and growing with the economies?

(1) Leadership that promotes a clear and compelling vision;
(2) Programs which balance emphasis on technology, staff, and customers;
(3) Participative methods of operating that generate and use insights from staff;
(4) The conviction that one's product or service meets genuine human need.

All four dynamics are apparent in the GE Life story.

VISIONARY LEADERSHIP

"Excellence is a journey, not a destination" is the motto of Allen Pathmarajah, GE Life's Director and CEO, who came to the organization in 1984 from a consulting company (owned by a number of companies in the OCBC Group); he was also assistant to the Chairman of the OCBC Group. In his initial contact with GE Life, he quickly initiated a three-pronged approach to seizing the opportunity for expansion in both Malaysia and Singapore: computerization, empowerment, and training. Combining a focus on high-tech with one on high-touch has made this a leading company in the life insurance industry.

In November, 1992, *The Singapore Business Times* in an article headlined "The Secret of Great Eastern Life's Success" observed that, "Dedication to training, efficient use of automation and information technology, and a people-oriented management philosophy are responsible for the success of The Great Eastern Life Assurance Company Ltd."

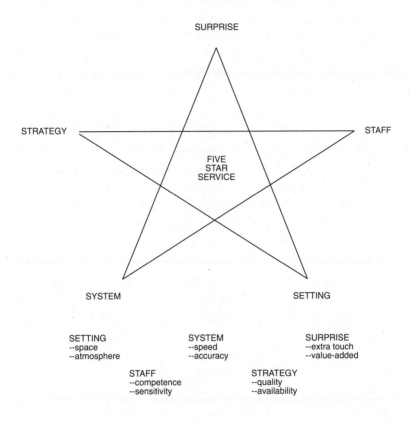

PROVIDING CUSTOMER DELIGHT

SURPRISE

STRATEGY

STAFF

FIVE
STAR
SERVICE

SYSTEM

SETTING

SETTING
--space
--atmosphere

SYSTEM
--speed
--accuracy

SURPRISE
--extra touch
--value-added

STAFF
--competence
--sensitivity

STRATEGY
--quality
--availability

When asked about his leadership "secrets," Pathmarajah responded that two elements were necessary: having a vision and displaying leadership by example. But vision in this sense has little to do with volume, bottom-lines, or being number one. As Pathmarajah explains:

We never talk about money or being number one as our goal. Goals, bottom lines, get old after a while; values never do. And when you become number one, there is nowhere to go. Money and status will take care of themselves if you show respect for individuals, provide the best in customer service, and are excellent in everything you do. That's where we have to focus. If you focus on money, you will cut corners. Profit comes as the consequence of praise from customers. Life insurance is a beautiful business; we must do it with beauty.

A critical, if little practiced, role of the CEO is to be a symbol of the company—to manifest in personal style and operation what the company stands for, to be a sort of walking logo for the organization. The popular stereotype of the CEO, however, is of someone who is aloof, distant, who passes along generalized mandates, and is too "busy" to get involved with the company's practical operations. The resistance to "top down" management is, in part, a reaction against this perversion of the leader's symbolic function. Pathmarajah grasps this symbolic role of leader as a crucial function in the new environment of participation. He stays in hands-on contact with the staff in carrying out business, while still providing the distance and objectivity required to view the overall company picture.

Pathmarajah spends many weekends meeting agents in branches throughout Malaysia to keep abreast of developments and to talk with staff. Even as early as 1987 during the first of many strategic planning consultations led by Ann and John Epps, Pathmarajah, or AJP, as he is affectionately called, extolled the values of participation and encouraged staff to say anything they wished about the company and their work during these sessions. Speaking out is not a normal practice in the Asian culture, so, initially, participants in these sessions were slow to respond. But as they realized that this was a serious invitation, candid and constructive comments began to flow. The upshot was a frank and healthy discussion that resulted in a solid consensus about the company direction.

As an involved leader, Pathmarajah never fails to reiterate the company mission and philosophy. Although session participants have heard it all many times before, his sincerity of delivery and obvious commitment to a participative company culture give his statements an appeal that is highly motivating. His belief in the importance of life insurance and his respect for individuals within the organization are visible and genuine.

In an address to the Singapore Group Sales Managers in September, 1990, Pathmarajah commented:

Had I said a few years ago what we're doing now, people would have said it was impossible. But positive thinkers are those who see everything as having potential—all pain, frustration, prob-

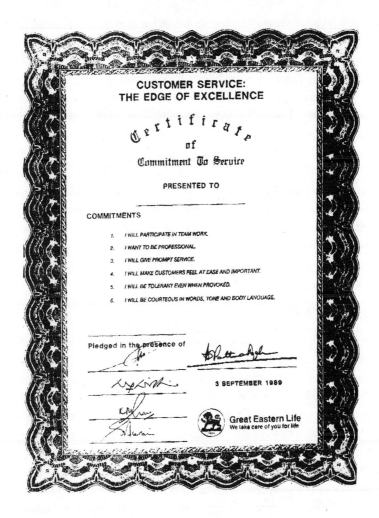

CUSTOMER SERVICE:
THE EDGE OF EXCELLENCE

Certificate

of

Commitment To Service

PRESENTED TO

_____

COMMITMENTS

1. I WILL PARTICIPATE IN TEAM WORK.
2. I WANT TO BE PROFESSIONAL.
3. I WILL GIVE PROMPT SERVICE.
4. I WILL MAKE CUSTOMERS FEEL AT EASE AND IMPORTANT.
5. I WILL BE TOLERANT EVEN WHEN PROVOKED.
6. I WILL BE COURTEOUS IN WORDS, TONE AND BODY LANGUAGE.

Pledged in the presence of

3 SEPTEMBER 1989

Great Eastern Life
We take care of you for life

lems, as having potential.... Everything in the world begins with a dream. Never stop dreaming. If you believe in something strongly enough to give it all you have, it will come to pass.

One of his initial acts was to formulate three basic values to guide the company. Not being one to reinvent the wheel, he chose to adapt the values made famous by some successful companies. These became the three company goals: Respect for the Individual, the Best in Customer Service, and Excellence in Everything We Do. The three were successfully communicated and modelled at the initial strategic planning program in Malaysia in 1987, during which managers decided to conduct a contest for designing a poster that best displayed these three values. Now the winning poster is prominently displayed throughout the offices of the organization. More importantly, the values actually function as guidelines for company policies and practices.

Pathmarajah also holds down another symbolic function—interacting with the scions of business. He is a sought-after speaker in the international insurance industry, having addressed various life insurance conferences in Singapore, Malaysia, Australia, the U.S.A., and South Africa. Though this international exposure provides him access to the latest and best in management practices and industry development, his solid grassroots presence provides renewed commitment to the real service of the company. The two personal approaches are mutually reinforcing, and have produced an impressive company momentum. Yet, he says, "One should never be satisfied, or even state that things are going well. They can always be improved. Excellence is a journey, not a destination."

COMPUTERIZATION

The GE Life journey began with computerization. According to Pathmarajah, the company is willing to invest in whatever leading edge technology exists, if it will enhance service to customers. Computerization helped to initiate GE Life's rapid growth. The company could not expand its market aggressively until the infrastructure was in place to handle the increased work; the capacity of GE Life to handle information was already strained. As recently as 1985, "master premium cards" were still used to record premium payments and other policy status information manually. As the business grew, the difficulty of this system became not only obvious, but also intolerable.

Installing a computerized system of managing company records was a major forward step, but playing "catch up" is not the game of excellence. So the company went further and invested in a system to put its branches "on line real time," as they put it. This new capacity vastly reduced the time required to service a request, and greatly enhanced communication in the organization. Inquiries could be handled by front-line staff whose terminals were linked to the mainframe. Soon agents began using laptop computers on sales calls; then forms, quotations, and applications could be generated and modified on-site. GE Life has since kept up with the continuing advances in information technology.

In 1990, a Phone-Link System was installed at GE Life in Singapore so that agents could obtain up-to-date information regarding their clients' policies and other required information. With this system, an agent can immediately access the latest information on policy status, policy values, agent's productivity, clinic locations, etc. This has saved countless hours of waiting time for agents and detail work by staff in accessing necessary information. The result is higher productivity of both the agents and staff. "But," Pathmarajah is quick to add, "we have never retrenched anyone. Staff members whose work was taken over by the system were reassigned, not released." The company is concerned with developing its human resources, not minimizing them. "Each person," says Pathmarajah, "has a spark of excellence; the question is how to find and ignite it." Currently a new imaging technology is being developed that will make possible another leap forward in the company's capacity for speed and accuracy in attending to its customers. Previously, questions involving a policyholder file made it necessary to extract the file itself from the records storage facility. With the new technology, the relevant information can be obtained on the screen.

PEOPLE-ORIENTED MANAGEMENT

But GE Life does not have a one-sided infatuation with the computer. Pathmarajah and the management team have launched an emphasis on empowering people, a focus that has turned the organization into a participative, innovative, and high-spirited company. In a traditional hierarchical organization, an individual employee's influence is limited to his or her job, and everything is closely scrutinized by "superiors." In a culture of participation, staff members are respected, and both permitted and expected to make a significant contribution to the whole company. As a result, respect and permission are evident at GE Life.

One example of showing respect for the individuals who make up the GE Life team occurred after the company received the National Productivity Board Award; a card of congratulations was sent out to everyone in the company including over 3,000 agents. Each card, personally signed by Pathmarajah, included a pen. Asked about other times when he recognizes people, he says:

> Whenever we finish a major project of any sort, like the computer project, for example, we have a celebrative dinner and good

fun. We believe in recognizing people; our morale is up because of the new incentive scheme for everyone—back room, front line, from top to bottom, including the messengers. We also reward merit on an individual basis.

The GE Life management team has found that the use of the ToP techniques fits in effectively in supporting its people-oriented management style. When they first encountered ToP in 1987, the management team found that these techniques proved valuable in forming a consensus on future directions and strategies. The participants in the planning session initially expressed multiple viewpoints over where the company should go. But when they listened carefully to each other, they saw that the views seemed to be complementary, and that they contributed to a larger picture. Participants found a unity among their diversity that was unexpected. They also realized that the participative approach, instead of releasing a Pandora's Box of contention, actually disclosed a deep-rooted consensus within the company. And being entrepreneurs, the management team reckoned that if the approach could work for the central office, why not give it a try among the agents?

Life insurance agents are generally left to their own devices to make it or to fail in the business. Companies often provide technical and sales training, and occasionally offer a motivational event for the agents. But somehow the sales people never see themselves as participants in the broader company strategy; consequently there is a high turnover rate in the industry. GE Life perceived that the ToP approach might provide an answer.

They then arranged for an in-house team of facilitators to be trained in the approach and to work with the sales agents in Malaysia. The LENS International consultants, Ann and John Epps, conducted a Facilitator Training session for selected staff members, including the senior managers from Malaysia who resolved to put the new methods into practice. Their first hands-on experience with the ToP method was a strategic planning session with group sales managers jointly facilitated with the LENS team. It resulted in a new level of communications and cooperation between company managers and sales agents, and confirmed their intuition about the applicability of the participative approach. After that experience, the in-house team went directly to agents.

They adapted the ToP approach to strategic planning, renamed it "SLAP" (Strategic Leadership Action Process), and began conducting four-step sessions for agents and their leaders. The four steps referred to vision, contradictions, strategy, and action. The SLAP program activated some basic shifts in corporate style. Weekends are rarely used for work in this culture. But the designated in-house team travelled to agencies in small towns throughout Malaysia on weekends for many weeks to get agents involved in developing their personal strategies for success. The first year this program was undertaken, the CEO himself went to the weekend sessions as a further symbol of affirmation and assistance. The results were very encouraging; the company's growth rate far exceeded the industry average. These SLAP programs have been conducted annually since 1988, and the growth rate has remained very satisfactory. When people have the power to plan their own strategies, they are remarkably prone to carry them out.

After a year, the team developed SLAP II, and went back for another round. This time, they took the individual performance records of participants for the previous three years, and used the records as a basis on which to build their vision. "Are you satisfied with your accomplishments? What would you like to achieve?" are the initial questions asked in SLAP II sessions. The responses reflect a realistic vision, analysis of personal obstacles, strategies, and actions that will help ensure personal success. This time around, they built in a monitoring system which subdivided action plans from the year, to the quarter, to the month, the week, and even to the day; then the plans were put on a computer, both in the field and at the central office. As a result of this process, the company now has a systematic, objective, and participative way to keep agents motivated. Some have achieved membership in the Million Dollar Round Table, and the company growth rate still leads the industry.

In conducting these programs, a team of six goes out on weekends. The team consists of the SLAP facilitators, two support staff members, and an editor—all of whom manage to produce the results of the session on site for the participants. There is a rotation system for conducting these programs, but there is no problem getting team members to sign on. People want to be where the action is.

The effects of the participative approach go even further; the members of the facilitation team itself have become highly motivated role models for the company. In addition to conducting SLAP sessions on the weekend and holding down responsible positions in the company during the week, several of the team members have gone for advanced insurance courses. As one put it, "After seeing the agents so concerned to better themselves, I thought I should do the same." The SLAP Program, initiated in Malaysia, has been conducted for agents and agencies in Singapore as well. Both the company and the individuals have profited tremendously from these sessions.

In Singapore, the company began using ToP, as provided by LENS International, with the head office staff. Senior managers went through a Customer Service Seminar in 1989 and subsequently arranged for similar seminars to be conducted through to the junior executive level. Then a group of managers and executives learned to become facilitators to take the program throughout the organization, engaging clerical staff in suggesting ways to improve customer satisfaction and staff performance.

The Singapore National Productivity Board cited this employee suggestion program as one of the major reasons for GE Life's winning its 1992 award. The management philosophy behind this scheme involves a shift of responsibility for identifying and solving problems—from management to both management and staff. This shift is accomplished through a team approach. Action plan teams are formed to find ways of reducing costs, making their work more efficient, and improving overall productivity and profitability. The team leader, usually a manager or an executive, is responsible for discussing the action plans in detail with the teamworkers, formulating action plans, and following up on implementation. Every member of the company, from the CEO to the clerical staff, is involved.

Once again, results of the participatory process have been noteworthy in the Singapore offices. The company followed up on employee suggestions by providing uniforms for front-line staff, staying open for business during lunch hours by using a rotation system staff themselves developed, redesigning the reception area, and greatly improving their telephone service. With senior managers' support, a new level of teamwork and enthusiasm has emerged.

In the work culture of Singapore, people tend to concentrate on productivity directly, sometimes to the neglect of the "fizz and mischief" that sustains it. The Singapore GE Life managers cum facilitators are an exception. They have been innovative and resourceful in adapting to the participative approach, and have filled it with engaging bits of humor and fun. They have developed role plays to demonstrate different office styles, developed promotional posters for in-house courses, designed and led successful workshops with participants, and have even made their own video entitled "What Went Wrong?" to highlight what could happen if there were no teamwork. During workshops, they also initiated the practice of giving out simple gifts to staff members as a reward for good ideas.

The enthusiasm of the Singapore manager after the first round of workshop sessions was high, as energy was released throughout the organization. At a lunch with Pathmarajah celebrating completion of the workshop, they reveled in stories of experiences during the course of their facilitation. The participative style of GE Life gets staff involved in their work projects to the point of using hidden talents to succeed. The projects then "belong" to those who carry them out; and this sense of "ownership" then permeates the organization.

TECHNICAL TRAINING

Subsequent to Pathmarajah's appearance, staff training took on a more proactive role as GE Life placed a major focus on skill enhancement and innovation. The company established new training centers for agents in Singapore and in Malaysia, and equipped them with the latest in advanced audiovisual equipment and other training aids. With a focus on selling skills and insurance product knowledge, the Singapore center boasts three large training rooms which are in constant use. The staff has also produced video-based self-study kits for new agents to prepare for their licensing examinations.

The in-house trainers conduct regular staff seminars on such topics as telephone courtesy, customer service, communications, and team building. In addition, department heads have been given the authority to approve external training programs for their staff members, up to a given annual budget. Staff members are given generous incentives to pursue advanced professional training certified by insurance institutes based in the U.S.A., the U.K., and Australia. According to GE Life's Personnel Manager in Singapore:

> The role of participation and training has been significant since
> LENS International became involved in 1989. Before that we
> didn't do in-house training as an annual program. The staff suggestion and participation scheme highlighted by the National
> Productivity Board is derived from the ToP method, and we have
> adapted it for our clerical people.

In the arena of research, the company sends managers overseas for attachment to innovative companies so that they can learn new approaches to be adopted at home. When a clear, relevant benchmark is found, wherever it is located, a team is formed to look into the matter and adapt it for GE Life or a representative of the benchmark company is invited to Singapore for a presentation and/or consultation. The company has sent representatives to the U.S.A., the U.K., and Australia to pursue leading edge innovations in insurance products, human resource development, and technology. These international contacts result not only in company improvements, but also in establishing ownership among managers, the very people who are committed to making them work.

Continual innovation is fostered by continual learning. According to Pathmarajah, "Continuous improvement is what all GE Life staff are striving for. Our work attitude is to learn from the past, live today, and plan for the future." The company has recently entered into a strategic alliance with two major banks, one in Malaysia and one in Singapore, to offer insurance policies to the banks' customers. It has also developed and launched new products to meet the needs of the rapidly developing markets. In addition, GE Life was the first company in Singapore to introduce a Student Plan and a College Plan for funding education, the first to offer "Living Assurance" for financial protection against ten major illnesses, the first to offer an insurance savings plan, and the first to offer a group dental plan. "Our role is to give customers what they want, not to force them to make do with what we have," says Pathmarajah.

In addition, GE Life has developed a long-term community service project supporting underprivileged children. For its unique efforts, the company won the 1990 Special Merit Award from the Community Chest of Singapore presented for meritorious service to GE Life by the President of Singapore. These efforts were again recognized by the Community Chest in 1992 when the company won the Special Event Award. The Institute of Public Relations of Singapore named the company winner of its PRISM Award (Public Relations in the Service of Mankind) in 1992 for its role in the Sharity Gift Box Project.

CONFRONTING PROBLEMS

As with all journeys, the progress of GE Life towards excellence has faced some difficulties. It became necessary early on to clarify the lines of authority, even in this highly team-oriented organization. Despite a strong consensus established in the initial planning consultation, it proved important to designate formally and officially which position was to be the dominant authority. Participation does not mean that every opinion deserves to be followed. Decisions must be made, and designating the responsibility for making them proved important. That was done with sensitivity, and with no demoralizing loss of face.

In the high-powered work environment of Singapore and Malaysia, staff turnover is generally high, especially at the clerical level. Great Eastern Life has not been immune. Although people are not let go, many members of the clerical staff leave for other jobs, which are plentiful. Dealing with this changing situation requires a constant intake of new faces and orientation of newcomers into the company.

Among managers, however, turnover is negligible. As one manager put it, "When you're working for the best, why would you want to move?" Even for the electronic data processing staff, who are among Singapore's most mobile, turnover is low. They say that the work is challenging and innovative; they feel they are well-recognized and appreciated for their efforts. The company's participative style of management, enhanced by effective group process techniques, has also contributed to staff satisfaction. As Pathmarajah notes:

> You have to get a sense of belonging and a kind of 'ownership' of everyone to make it work. So we took every department in the Singapore office through the Customer Service program using the ToP method. Other managers have noticed a significant change in staff attitudes since participation became the company *modus operandi*. As one manager notes, "Before, it was 'It can't be done'; now it's 'Why not?'" There is much more positive thinking, fewer complaints, and the staff is passionate about its work.

It becomes clear, after analyzing the company, that GE Life manifests all four criteria for growth: leadership with vision, a balanced program, a participative method, and a belief in its product. Great Eastern Life has a compelling vision, although not one which is easily quantifiable. The company is out to provide an essential financial service through embodying its three values. While this may sound absurdly "soft" to managers more accustomed to bottom lines and numerical targets, GE Life has shown this vision to be capable of generating results that impress the most hard-headed of the competition. The vision moves into human motivation, commitment, and attitudes, the three most frequently mentioned barriers to company success. But make no mistake, GE Life managers are not at all hesitant to pose challenging targets. These challenges, however, are presented in a participatory manner so that everyone understands why these targets are desirable, and how they fall within the framework of the company vision. It makes a big difference.

So fine is GE Life's balance among its three-pronged approach of technology, human resources and development, and customer service that it is impossible to discern a logical sequence. The three have become intertwined in the culture of the company. Since all three are necessary for success, any imbalance will skew the momentum. Barriers among people and individuals at different staff levels are continuing to fall; more open communication is occurring; decisions are made consultatively; teamwork is a prime emphasis; and things are becoming, according to Pathmarajah, "more pleasant and much easier in terms of human relations." Pathmarajah continues:

> The ToP process is simple but effective. Many people can generate brainstorms of ideas, but often they then select some and reject others. This leaves some people feeling rejected. This ToP approach clusters ideas and then moves to a consensus on what they mean. This way everyone owns the outcome. It helps people figure out where they want to go, identify obstacles in their way, and decide how to get there.

Perhaps there are some companies whose products and services are questionable in their benefit to humanity. If that is the case, then those organizations will have great difficulty in transformation. But more likely, when one raises the question, "What's it all for?" one has only to look deeply enough to find a satisfying answer. Certainly, GE Life has no problems convincing its personnel that its service benefits humankind. And because that benefit is so tangible, they are constantly developing new products to deliver it, procedures to support it, and ways to promote it.

In consequence of this belief in what they are doing, GE Life has developed an effective barrier against burnout. Perhaps the company is embodying the old Confucian tenet, "Whoever loves his job never has to work a day in his life."

III.

EXPANDING THE CUSTOMER BASE

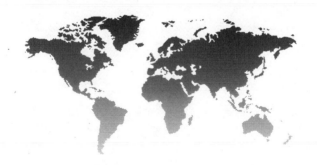

≡☆Lockheed
Missiles & Space Company

5. TRANSFORMING A DEFENSE RESEARCH ORGANIZATION: CAN IT HAPPEN FAST ENOUGH TO SURVIVE?

by
PATRICIA TUECKE

How does a defense industry organization survive with peace breaking out all over? How does an R&D organization deal with dramatic post-Cold War challenges and change its culture to a more flexible and participative operation that will respond rapidly to its current situation? For Lockheed Missiles and Space Company's Research and Development Division, the overriding question was if they could make these shifts fast enough to survive the decline in defense spending.

uriosity was in the air as 52 managers of the very successful Research and Development Division (R&DD) of Lockheed Missiles and Space Company (LMSC) gathered in April, 1991 for an unusual meeting. Given the recent dramatic shifts in the defense industry business climate, the leadership of R&DD felt they had to make a quantum leap forward to remain in the forefront. The company had just experienced its first lay-offs in ten years, which, not surprisingly, were creating growing apprehension at R&DD. The division leaders were unclear and uncertain about the future, and about how the research labs fit into the line of business strategy at LMSC. If their work were not relevant to the future business, would they or their people be vulnerable to lay off? People felt that "somebody" knew; they felt their future was dependent on "somebody's" budget and were waiting for a signal. Some senior managers, however, understood that to keep the company viable, their research labs funded, and maintain their jobs, they themselves were going to have to find new markets and create products to meet civilian and commercial needs. Taking such a proactive role was a new task for most of them.

To meet these needs, the managers were participating in an off-site planning conference to look at their entire division, create a shared vision to guide their future work, and embark on a plan of Continuous Improvement (CI) in their business. At this off-site meeting, the division managers had to consider how a defense industry organization could survive with peace breaking out all over. No one knew for sure. But they were certain of one reality. The companies that learn to reinvent themselves, who quickly seize the opportunities and creatively confront the dangers in the current crises, will survive. This is an immense challenge with no well-known maps for navigating the voyage and no guarantee of success.

Today, whole industries are experiencing major upheavals caused by new technologies, sobering economic realities, new political alignments, and the growing global marketplace. The defense industry is a prime example of this trend. For decades defense corporations such as Lockheed have had one major customer, the U.S. Department of Defense (DOD), with its large budget and desire for newer, more powerful, and more effective weapon systems. The Cold War had fueled this industry's growth and the need for highly sophisticated defense products. Now, the post-Cold War defense budget is shrinking rapidly; one estimate shows the total U.S. defense expenditures will be down $93 billion in four to five years. The industry anticipates that, in four years, only a handful of aerospace companies will remain in the U.S.A.

The defense industry is responding to the crisis with "right-sizing" consolidation (a euphemism for massive lay-offs), selling unprofitable businesses, merging, and restructuring. Significant potential targets for these cost cutting measures are the research and development (R&D) laboratories. The old "ivory tower" approach to managing the R&D function, with scientists and engineers choosing their research, on the basis of personal expertise and goals rather than on company goals is over. Corporate management is applying the same kinds of cost-benefit criteria for R&D programs as they use with other investments. At the same time that funding for R&D has declined across the U.S.A., R&D is seen as a vital link in some defense companies' long-term competitive strategies of "conversion," the industry term for transforming military technologies to commercial applications.

Since that first planning meeting in 1991, Lockheed's R&DD managers have shifted their way of thinking about the business of the division. Previously, each lab went about its research projects expecting that funding would come to it without much effort on its part. Managers would worry only about how to get money from the General Manager's budget. Now, each lab considers itself a business, not a "kept" lab. They realize that the only pot of money available to fund their work is in the pockets of their customers. The challenge then is for every person in the division to "think marketing." Before, most managers focused only on their own area of work and left the responsibility for the division to the General Manager and his senior staff. Now, managers see that they are all responsible for the organization; they have a picture of the whole organization, and the overall health of the division. They are thinking like teams, and no longer talk about "my" project but about "our" project. In the past, according to one manager:

Every department did its own thing, had its own turf....Now, we're really doing things together. We're making marketing plans together, talking to customers together. It's like we all work for Lockheed. It's a good feeling. The troops really like this. In many cases the technical people were working together before anyway, on their own time; it was at their initiative. Now [that] the company is behind them, it's really rolling. Everyone believes we're going to end up making some more money and winning more contracts.

How did this shift in attitude occur? What caused it?

DEFENSE INDUSTRY LEADER

The huge Lockheed Corporation, headquartered in Calabasas, California, is a very diverse, successful, and established corporation, with 1990 revenues of over $9 billion and over 70,000 employees working in several locations. In 1990, for the first time, LMSC in northern California's Silicon Valley generated over one-half of the annual revenues; previously the aircraft-building operations in Georgia had been the revenue leaders. Because of cuts in defense spending, Lockheed has already laid off thousands of aircraft workers.

LMSC is the developer and builder of the Polaris, Poseidon, and Trident submarine-launched ballistic missiles and a major supplier of advanced satellite systems for both the military and the National Aeronautics and Space Administration (NASA). The company's success with these systems has made LMSC an industry leader. Its Palo Alto R&DD, one of the country's largest research labs with a thousand employees, provides advanced scientific capabilities support to the current and prospective operations of all the LMSC product divisions. Here scientists are designing cryogenic cooling systems, robots, supervised autonomous control systems, methods to control advanced space platforms, laser systems, infrared optical systems, advanced space platforms, artificial intelligence systems, and space science exploration.

At the beginning of 1991, several major challenges faced R&DD.

- The division had to shift from primarily developing technologies and applications relevant to the Cold War to creating technologies with diverse peacetime applications as well as military applications, i.e., dual-use technologies. For example: composite materials—lighter, more durable plastics first developed for military usage in aircraft, missiles and satellites—now are used for commercial airplanes and in the future, will be used for construction projects.

• The division had to end its heavy dependence on one major customer, the DOD, and rapidly create a diverse customer base. At LMSC they were counting on R&DD to be in the forefront of this new marketing effort.

• The division was forced to increase the effectiveness of its business operations, and expand beyond their scope of just doing good research to becoming technical business people. They had to go beyond their own jobs, lab, or directorate, and begin thinking about the whole division, working as a team to create more effective work processes.

• The isolated, individualistic style of operation in the division needed to expand to a more collaborative mode. Both the CI thrust, and the need to develop new markets and products rapidly, called for a more participative mode of operation. No longer would it be effective for a few people at the top to have all the data and answers. Everyone's creativity was needed to win. Division employees would need to share information and collaborate on projects to achieve their goals.

How does a research and development organization deal with such dramatic challenges and change its culture to a more flexible and participative operation that will allow it to respond rapidly to its current situation? For Lockheed Missiles and Space System's R&DD, the overriding question was whether they could make these shifts fast enough to survive the decline in defense spending. To deal with this question, Joseph B. Reagan was named General Manager of R&DD in January, 1991. Most managers felt the change in leadership was a sign of hope for the division. One of his first decisions—to involve all the division's managers in planning a continuous improvement effort and in responding to the challenges—was a concrete example of this positive outlook.

DECISION, DESIGN, AND LAUNCH

At the time of his appointment, Dr. Reagan had been with Lockheed Corporation for over 30 years in their Research Division. He knew from a long-term and very practical perspective how R&DD worked, its capabilities, the challenges it faced, and its need to change to meet them successfully. During the previous year, the entire Lockheed Corporation had embarked on a quality improvement effort, required by the Pentagon of all defense contractors. Well-known quality programs had been used mostly in manufacturing settings; however, there was little precedent for total quality management (TQM) in research environments. The R&D Executive Committee was considering how to launch its participation in this effort. In Dr. Reagan's opinion, the division's goal was to strive to become the best R&D lab in the country, which meant continually improving the quality in their own R&D processes and products. He recalls:

> I knew what we needed to do, but I didn't know how to bring about the changes. I knew we had to open up the communication between R&DD and our customers and between departments and labs, but I didn't quite know how to make it happen quickly.

Coincidentally, at this time, Dr. Reagan heard from two industry colleagues who had successfully initiated CI in their companies by using the planning approach of LE Associates, a consulting firm in California. In the words of one colleague, Allen Atkins, Vice-President and General Manager of McDonnell Douglas Technologies, Inc.:

> This planning approach integrates all the key elements of TQM and participative management into a real working program with which the workforce can identify and be party to the end results—the state that I think we all want. [This] unique approach allowed our team of approximately 14% of the entire company to quickly, and with consensus, reach clearly stated visions and formulate real result-producing actions.

Dr. Reagan decided to explore how this approach might be used at R&DD. After talking with Lee Early and Patricia Tuecke, consultants with LE Associates, he invited them to facilitate a February, 1991 meeting with his senior executive team. He asked them to focus on the critical issues the division was facing and to design a way to involve the entire management team in dealing with these issues.

At the beginning of this February meeting, Early and Tuecke asked each of the 13 directors and managers to talk about highlights of his work at Lockheed, which for most, spanned more than 20 very successful years. Some of them mentioned working on the early space exploration payloads and the space shuttle. Next, the consultants involved the executives in a workshop which demonstrated some of the Institute of Cultural Affairs (ICA) Technology of Participation (ToP) techniques used in planning with large groups. The executives individually listed the critical issues they felt were most important. In discussing these, the executives saw much overlap, and identified three major arenas of concern: corporate strategy, operational decision making, and organization culture. The consultants then described a planning approach which would involve a group of company representatives

R&DD's PRACTICAL VISION

TOWARD IMPROVED EFFICIENCY			TOWARD CUSTOMER-FOCUSED PERFORMANCE		TOWARD BUSINESS DOMINANCE			
STABLE FINANCES	EFFECTIVE COMMUNICATION	OPERATIONAL EFFICIENCY	WORK ENVIRONMENT	LOCKHEED RELEVANCE	CORPORATE RECOGNITION	WORLD-CLASS REPUTATION	NEW BUSINESS	TECHNOLOGY INNOVATION

R&DD's MISSION

Vision

Recognized leader in technologies relevant to Lockheed's programs

Highly-qualified and motivated staff, oriented to customer needs

Dynamic, productive environment which promotes superior technical and business performance, innovation, and professional growth

Goals

Excellence in key science and technology areas

Timely and efficient application of technology to Lockheed's products and services

Enhanced personal and team productivity, innovation and professional development opportunities in building a common vision, discerning contradictions to that vision, formulating new strategies to address the contradictions, and creating tactical plans to show rapid, concrete, and visible results in the short term. The senior executives next formulated the following focus question that would guide the planning work: How do we expand, improve, and implement the R&DD vision, mission, and strategy? This question would open for broader participation the vision, mission, and strategy statements for R&DD that Dr. Reagan and his senior executive staff had just previously created.

The executive team then decided that the focus question needed answering immediately, and though they had formulated the question, they could not answer it alone; all 52 division managers needed to be involved. They checked their calendars and set a date in April when the 52 managers would meet for a planning conference at a location away from the labs. Consultants Early and Tuecke were invited to design and facilitate this planning conference that would launch R&DD into their CI effort.

At an orientation meeting preceding the off-site conference, the 52 managers talked about the purpose of the conference and their expectations for it. Some commented that it would be worthwhile it if they could:

"Create a plan to make R&DD labs relevant to the company lines-of-business."

"Increase communication and get rid of extra forms."

"Improve business operations."

"Have less management and more leadership."

"Have specific goals that will kick-start our CI effort."

"Increase the quality of what we are doing."

"Build a new management team with leaders who will do differently than in the past."

"Develop ways to measure and assess how we are doing over time."

"Have longevity, once we have buy-in, and practice what we preach."

"Figure out ways to better support our customers."

Remarking about the significance of the planning event to the company, some managers said:

"If we're not to die as an organization in these times, we need to rejuvenate ourselves."

"This is a milestone for R&DD. We haven't taken a strategic look at ourselves. Now is a critical time."

"We've had a change in leadership. We can develop ideas about how to bring our ideas to fruition (provided management listens)."

When the April conference actually took place, much high energy, involvement, and excitement surrounded the discussions and planning as the 52 managers created a shared vision to guide them for the next five years. They began by looking at the focus question developed by the executive team. Then, dividing into four small groups, they individually listed concrete images of what they wanted to see in their future. Each person shared these ideas with his/her own team; then the team created a list of unique images of what they wanted to see in place in R&DD in five years. The individual teams brought this list to the whole group plenary session where an animated exchange took place as similar ideas were combined in clusters of data to form nine arenas that described their desired future.

In the conference's second session, using a similar process, the managers identified the major contradiction arenas, which would block them from achieving their desired future if left unattended. Confronting the current reality of their situation and discerning how they participated in it took courage; as a result, discussions in this session were sometimes pointed and passionate. However, when the managers saw that the process used was not about blaming anyone or finding fault, they were willing to set more negative perspectives aside. They searched instead for those points where structural and operational policies, procedures, and patterns inhibited or frustrated their movement toward the vision state. They identified seven major blockages or contradiction arenas including unrewarded collaboration, fragmented planning processes, and unbalanced long-term/short-term goals. Once named, these contradictions become the focus for a burst of creative energy, as ideas of how to deal with the contradictions began to come forth.

In the third session, teams proposed new strategies to deal with the seven contradiction arenas and focused the myriad of proposed ideas into three new directions that would deal with the contradictions and move the teams toward the future they wanted:

(1)   Meeting the customers' and R&DD's needs; .
(2)   Motivating the R&DD people;
(3)   Providing the policies and tools for success.

The managers then chose a strategic mix of 13 proposals within these broad directions to begin working on immediately. Some of the proposals they chose were: involving R&DD in Lockheed's business planning, organizing a joint Lockheed trade fair, and creating a new policy for proportional credit for sales and sign-ups. The next day they divided into 13 cross-functional taskforces for the last two sessions and wrote charters for the taskforces, selected key implementary actions, and built a 90-day implementation calendar with assignments and accountability checkpoints. The entire group assumed responsibility to see that the work was done.

At the close of the final session, the managers were a bit awed by their accomplishment and by the level of consensus among them. One manager said, "The technique for taking a broad range of inputs to obtain a focused consensus in each session was impressive." Another after finding out that other managers had a vision similar to his, exclaimed, "Their aims, goals, and frustrations were the same as mine!" Several managers were pleased with the opportunity to spend time with the other managers, shaping opinions together. One said, "In my 25 years at R&DD this [interaction with all managers simultaneously] has never occurred. Truly a major milestone." Addressing the group at the closing dinner celebration, Dr. Reagan said:

> We started into this continuous improvement effort, recognizing that we were probably at least a year behind our compatriots down in the other divisions. I have the feeling that we have probably caught up and may have exceeded them. I've never experienced anything like the kind of concentrated progress we were able to make in a short period of time.

Following the planning conference, the hard work for the division began. The enthusiasm of off-sites does not easily stand up to the force of long-term behavior patterns and structures, the 'way things are done around here' attitudes, and the grind of daily operations. Integrating the new plans into the division's ongoing work and continuing to communicate across the barriers did not happen automatically. It took consistent, conscious, creative effort to work collaboratively across labs and implement the initial planning.

For example, at R&DD a taskforce established a new list of key indicators that would actually indicate the state of health of the business. The change in thinking here was to consider the indicators like the instruments on the dashboard of a car, which signal the fuel level, brake condition, engine temperature, mileage, and give a quick picture of the current state of the car's critical operations.

The taskforce chose 17 items that would demonstrate R&DD's current state of operation; among them were:

- bid win/loss ratio
- number of late contract reports and customer satisfaction reports
- number of technologies transferred to the product divisions
- number of papers published, patents and awards received
- task cycle time
- number of environment, safety and security violations.

Managers now track, report, and openly discuss these indicators of how business is going.

As a result of this conference, the division is reducing the cycle time of those business processes which, assessment showed, previously took too long. To reduce cycle time for product development meant that formerly isolated and independent labs, engineers, managers, departments, and directorates had to interact in new ways. Previously, it took three weeks for a purchase request from a lab to go through the approval cycle and move on to a procurement. A time-saving effort called "Fast Buy" was initiated through joint effort between the Information Services and the Finance and Procurement groups. One manager explains how the Fast Buy works:

> Where we save time is that the engineers and quality people that used to review paperwork can now electronically pull up the information on their computer screen, approve, disapprove, or ask questions, and get on with other things. It prevents backlogs and gets people on to other activities. Fast Buy customers have their purchase requests processed error free in three and one-half days as compared to paper purchase requests which take 15 days to process, plus corrective action time.

A SHIFT FROM LABORATORY TO MARKETPLACE

Most scientists and engineers are not experienced at marketing, especially in the commercial arena. Some scientists felt intimidated at the prospect, a few more entrepreneurial souls were anxious but excited by the opportunities; most would just as soon not bother. Yet, their future success depended on technologists becoming more customer-oriented and developing marketing savvy. It became apparent that the directorates and labs needed some immediate and relevant help in reaching the major goal of expanding into new markets. One part of the solution to this situation was a series of marketing workshops held early in 1992. Designed by a consultant and a group of R&DD managers, the workshops enabled a group of interested people to work as a team to identify and pursue various current and potential contract research and development business. These contracts with organizations outside LMSC, such as NASA and several universities, enabled labs to expand their technology and revenues. Working as a team to build a marketing plan made the task seem less formidable to the scientists and engineers.

The Cryogenics Marketing Workshop was the first one held. It pulled together people working with cryogenics, the science of low-temperature phenomena, which is a key technology for many different R&D products such as cooling systems for spacecraft and various kinds of measurement instrumentation in satellite systems. These products account for a sizeable fraction of the R&DD business. Representatives from various labs which use cryogenics clarified the roles and responsibilities involved in winning new business, and made plans to improve coordination among departments in cryogenics marketing. They prioritized a potential opportunities and customers list that helped generate creative ideas for possible new products. To keep the creativity flowing and the momentum going, they created a New Business Council, dubbed the Customer Solutions Cadre, which meets every two weeks.

The Intelligent Structures Marketing Workshop was held three months later. The participants were an interdisciplinary group representing four R&DD departments and the Missiles System Division (MSD) and Space Systems Division (SSD) departments that use intelligent structure technology in their projects. This workshop launched an interdivision cooperative effort in getting new business and created a tighter link to the long-term LMSC strategy. A manager in MSD remarked, "The Palo Alto Labs (R&DD) are taking the lead in learning how to market R&D." A number of "conversions" of products from military to commercial use have come from the ideas flowing from more than 14 of these marketing workshops. These are all opening new markets. One example now under development is a device that decodes and recodes computer languages almost automatically to enable old software to be used on new computers. Now R&DD is offering this service to such commercial software users as banks, insurance companies, etc.

In summing up the new commercial directions R&DD adopted, Dr. Reagan maintains, "It's no longer enough just to do good research. We must go beyond that and become good technical business people." To do just that, managers initiated another innovative project, The New Business Strategy. According to Dr. Ernest Littauer, Assistant General Manager:

> This strategy involved taking a look at the way we tackle new business ventures. We concluded that, at times, it wasn't as well structured as it should have been, so we have now got in place a Bid Structure Review. This has been quite effective in helping us define which are the targets of opportunity and where to put our resources. The purpose is to look at and understand the bids, not to control them. We don't say, "Do not bid it." Sometimes we say we don't think it has a good chance as it is and give some ideas on strategy to win.

Another part of the New Business Strategy is the Proposal Management Center (PMC), which gathers, in one place, the people and resources needed to put together winning proposals. The manager of the PMC, explains:

> We've created a culture of going after new business. In the first quarter of 1992, 38% of all proposals and 85% of all dollars bid went through the PMC. These are tough times so there is lots of energy and enthusiasm to go after this new business.

A manager chuckled as he reflected on the success of the Center:

> I must admit I was very pleasantly surprised. It was an instant success, mainly because the PMC organized us and made us get to work, optimizing our time and probably saving the company a lot of money.

After the opening of the PMC, the number of proposals going out doubled in six months. With the assistance of a professional proposal consultant, the quality of the proposals has also greatly improved. In one lab alone, there was a 20% increase in proposal wins in 1992. During the first half of 1993, R&DD won about half of all the competitive proposals decided by customers, a significant improvement over past performances. A large number of proposals are still undecided, but if customers continue to select at this rate, R&DD will have a healthy backlog of research business to carry it through the difficult times.

A SHIFT FROM ISOLATION TO COLLABORATION

Employing a thousand people, R&DD comprises seven large groups called directorates with over 40 sub-unit laboratories or departments. The five science directorates each encompass several laboratories performing work in related disciplines: Physical & Electronic Sciences, Engineering Sciences, Materials Sciences, Information & Computing Sciences, and Electro-Optical Sciences. There are also three support services directorates: Planning & Development, Finance & Management Controls, and Laboratory Operations. Before 1991, people in this huge organization seldom worked with others outside their specialized labs. Now they are finding ways to reach out and collaborate across structural boundaries as they learn to become more customer-focused and business-oriented. The interdisciplinary marketing workshops are an example of this new approach.

The R&DD has made few formal structural changes in the division. However, many informal changes in the organization and operations of the division have happened in several ways. For instance, the division managers have decided to meet for one hour weekly. One manager said:

> The "Manager Only Meetings" have been a most successful way to
> get in touch with the kinds of problems and things going on in the
> labs that we don't necessarily hear about because we're so involved
> in the day to day activities of running our own department.

Meetings are informal; occasionally the General Manager or a director will stop by. Managers find these small meetings informative and supportive and they consider them to be time-savers. The directors now hold a similar meeting for themselves.

Another informal innovation is the creation of Customer Solutions Cadres created by the Marketing Workshops. The Cadre, an experimental team approach to leadership, meets every two weeks, with a rotating chair, and provides continuing oversight and coordination of all the new efforts growing out of the Marketing Workshops. The Cadre assumes the responsibility for allocating bid and proposal funding to possible projects, a task formerly carried out by a director or the General Manager.

Several other moves away from isolation towards collaboration have also been successful. The first interdepartmental event held was the R&DD

Expo, a 'trade fair' for the internal customers of the R&D division, and lab personnel. This was done to increase R&DD communications with the two LMSC product divisions, MSD and SSD. The Expo also was an occasion to provide recognition to the engineers and scientists at R&DD. Most people in R&D did not really know what else was being done outside their own laboratory or project. Over 800 people came to the Expo in two days, an exciting and visible first step in opening up communications.

Another effort to increase communication—this time with the customers—took place when the support services directorates (Planning & Development, Finance & Management Controls, and Laboratory Operations) decided to find out how well they were providing support to their customers, the labs, as a first step to improving their processes. They created a campaign to become a Five Star Service Organization and focus on Service, Team, and Reputation, building on the Lockheed corporate logo of a star. They wanted to know how the technical people perceived them and the service they provided. The directorates then used the feedback as a basis for involving their customers in developing realistic actions to address real needs.

This feedback initiated two customer-responsive programs. The Support Services "Yellow Pages" and user-friendly "How To" Manual is a two-part single-source reference guide provided to the labs. It describes the various service capabilities and gives lab personnel concise, helpful guidance on how to most effectively use the services. The purpose of the "Walk In Our Shoes" program was to improve the way the technical and operations organizations understand each other and work together. Lab managers were invited to visit the office of Planning & Development, as well as the Finance & Management Controls and Laboratory Operations offices. During the visit, they received a customized tour of the Directorate, visiting specifically requested departments, and heard an explanation of the steps involved in providing particular support services. The technical lab personnel and administrative support staff both learned something about each other's jobs, and what each expects of the other in order to do his/her best work.

The science directorates also used the concept of the "Yellow Pages" directory to reach out to the R&DD customers in Missiles Systems and Space Systems. A manager involved in a taskforce aimed at improving customer satisfaction describes the project:

We sent survey questions to every manager at Missiles Systems and Space Systems to find out to what extent they used us [R&DD], and what their satisfaction level has been. And, if they have not used us, we asked, Why not? We found out that clients who used us spoke quite well of what we do. We found out a significant number hadn't used R&DD because they either didn't know what we did that was of value to them, or they didn't know whom to contact. In response to this we put together the "Yellow Pages," as a capabilities book that lists all technical expertise available in the labs and the key individuals to contact.

One scientist in the MSD reacts to this attempt to tap sources of customer satisfaction information:

Relationships between the Palo Alto Labs [R&DD] and MSD continue to be good. They've [R&DD] always been open to being approached. I'd say they're more responsive now. There's a growing recognition on Palo Alto's part that we're all in this together. We've attended, as invitees, two of their workshops.

Another reach-out effort is the CI newsletter, "From The Labs." Published bi-monthly, the first issue rolled off the press in September of 1992. It is a forum for the active exchange of information and ideas, and reports significant accomplishments in the CI program to all employees.

Seeing the wide range of responses R&DD has made to communicate and collaborate more actively, it is obvious that communication channels have opened up. What often took months to do before, now takes hours because people know whom to talk to and they make direct contact. They had never done that before. An R&DD director comments:

Departments are not just exchanging technical information and ideas, but are getting different perspectives from people very different from them in background. Taskforces are springing up around very specific areas. People are learning what their strengths are and how to sell their strengths. A lot of these are interdisciplinary as a result of being together, across departments and across directorates. Now, collaborating to go after new business is the norm. Taskforces are creating new policies and systems to support this as a way for labs to share credit for sales in cross-directorate projects.

Another director agrees:

> The most important thing that has happened as a result of CI is the greatly increased communication at all levels. The formal introduction to CI (the CI Planning Conference) had a great effect of breaking the barriers down in a natural way. Managers got to know and respect each other.

How did the CI Planning Conference, the formal introduction that this manager speaks of, break down barriers? What was unique about this off-site planning retreat that launched these kinds of shifts in their thinking, organization, and action?

The structure of the planning conference and the procedures used were carefully designed to ensure participation of everyone and give opportunities for managers to work with others outside of their lab or organizational unit. For the first three sessions, the assigned teams were a cross-sectional mix of people from different functional areas. On the last day, the participants self-selected into taskforces to do the implementation planning. These groupings gave the managers two opportunities to work with people they may have never worked with before, or perhaps with those whom they did not really know.

The design of each working session allowed real communication to happen between individuals and between groups of managers. The initial questions they were addressing in each session were open-ended ones to which everyone had an answer. Participants were given time to write down their own responses before sharing them in small groups, thus giving individuals the opportunity to access their own wisdom and creativity before entering the discussion. People, who might have been reluctant to speak out in the large group of 50 persons, were willing to discuss their ideas with two or three others, and then in a group of six or seven persons.

In the large group plenary, individual ideas, written on large cards and placed on the front wall of the meeting room, became part of the data pool, with no names attached. Teams made decisions about where their data related to data from other groups. People did not have to defend or attack ideas for the task was to discover the common ground represented by the data. This made a safe environment for dialogue to take place and differing opinions to be heard. Even the way the chairs and tables were set contributed to the easy exchange of information and dialogue about ideas. In the large group, participants sat around team tables, so they could easily huddle together and make decisions as a team. The room was arranged so that everyone could see the front wall of data and could hear everything said.

This new way of working was continued in many of the follow-up planning meetings. At 90 days following the off-site, the whole group came together to report on the accomplishments of the taskforces and to plan for the next quarter. Each of the directorates held its own "Action Planning" events. Lee Early trained a group of employee volunteers to help facilitate these workshops. The participative and collaborative procedures used continued to break down the communication barriers and then led to consensus-based decision making. People began to feel more comfortable with this mode of planning and strategic thinking. Managers began to see the difference in effectiveness when trained facilitators were invited to help plan and facilitate their meetings, using this approach. It was also important to the effectiveness of this CI effort to involve everyone in the division at some point. The initial CI planning involved only the 52 directors and managers. The Directorate Action Planning included personnel from the several labs in each directorate. Then the departments began to hold their own planning events and included all of the hourly employees, group leaders, and managers.

A REFLECTION ON THE JOURNEY SO FAR

An organization's transformation journey begins when it can no longer deny the reality that things are changing or must change. Sometimes there is a gradual awareness; sometimes it is abrupt. It usually begins with a few people and spreads throughout the organization. Finally the energy that flows from this awareness gathers enough momentum to fuel the transformation. Though several factors have influenced R&DD's journey, the obvious driving force behind the change at R&DD has been the economic crises, the drastic decline in defense spending, and the decision to find ways to survive in spite of this. Because everyone's job is uncertain, this fear stimulates incentive that is overcoming cynicism and reluctance to change by both managers and employees.

The guiding force for change in R&DD has been the vision and wisdom of the General Manager, Dr. Reagan, who said that the transformation was possible. He put his career on the line by trying some new ways of man-

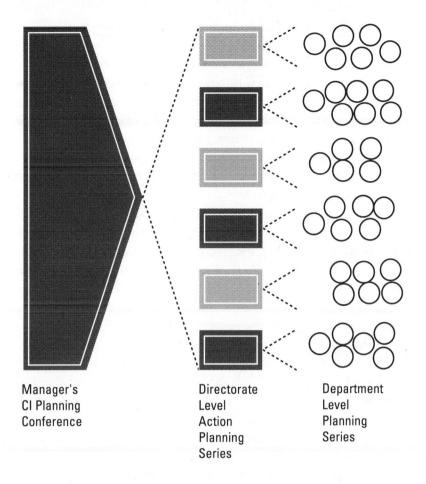

Manager's
CI Planning
Conference

Directorate
Level
Action
Planning
Series

Department
Level
Planning
Series

aging and operating. In launching the CI effort that involved the whole division, he made a commitment that declared that the participation and involvement of everyone were critical to reaching the company potential he knew was possible. He was willing to let taskforces make mistakes and learn from them. Dr. Reagan displayed a stance of real faith in the potential of the division if it could learn to work together to solve its problems and leap forward together. These dynamics were crucial in moving the division along on its journey.

In his work with the division after the initial CI off-site launch, consultant Lee Early's experience and objectivity as an outsider helped the division maintain momentum and move through obstacles. When the division as a whole needed a new way to approach a situation or decision, Early designed a format or process that led the division to a breakthrough to another level of action. For instance, the managers knew it was crucial to create new markets for their products and services. However, being inexperienced in marketing, they found it difficult to quickly move ahead on this. Early designed the marketing workshop that helped the groups in defining their products, describing their products' benefits to customers, brainstorming customer possibilities, and creating market strategies. This sequential design of a marketing strategy opened new ways of looking at opportunities most lab groups had never thought of before.

In an organization the size of R&DD, not everybody makes the transformation journey at the same rate. There are always those people and departments out in front of the rest, leading the way, anxious to change things. There are, however, always those who resist any changes. Most people are somewhere in the middle. At R&DD, there was always one manager, lab, or directorate that "pioneered" the first new workshop or process and helped convince others to move forward.

Other aspects of this journey of transformation were critical to its success. The design of the April, 1991 managers' off-site conference launched the CI effort beyond R&DD's expectations. Getting the whole system into the room, even representatively, and looking at the whole system and mission from many differing perspectives, created commitment and community. Creating a shared five-year vision, naming the underlying obstacles, and formulating new strategy gave the managers new ways to think about their organization. The conference experience hit the group of managers with the message that things will be different and that together they can create the future they want.

Once people have experienced a new way of relating, even for a short while, the possibility remains for them to operate this way in the future. Beginning with the CI conference, people discovered that it was not necessary to defend or attack ideas and positions in meetings, because the group process built upon the diverse ideas of individuals and developed from them consensus-based decisions and plans. Though there were disagreements, this focus on finding common ground transformed the energy of the meetings. The organizational units began to learn together new ways to think and work, fostering CI in many aspects of their mission. This change illustrates an aspect of what Rosabeth Moss Kanter said in an editorial in the *Harvard Business Review* [1]:

> Shared disciplines facilitate teamwork and allow organizational flexibility. People can get to work faster—and more easily work together in new groupings—when they share a methodology, or planning and problem-solving framework....People can stop wondering about how to get started, or arguing about whose way is better, and just get on with it.

The action planning and taskforce meetings gave a structured way for implementation to happen. The follow-through to planning at every level was not left to chance or good intentions, but structured in as part of the overall design, thus avoiding the "plans on the shelf" dynamic that aborts many change efforts. Some organizations try to force change through training. People are trained in new skills and concepts whether they sense they need them or not. But R&DD decided to go another way. They provided training when it was obvious that division members needed new skills. With this approach, the people took the training with enthusiasm.

Transforming organizations is not easy. According to Michael Beer, in an article, "Why Change Programs Don't Produce Change" [2], organizations that are successful in transforming themselves do not rely on programs such as quality circles or training. Instead, they mobilize energy to deal with the real, external pressures facing the company; top management then supports the changes with resources and personnel. One approach to creating change in organizations is to change the organizational context, put people in new situations, and create new responsibilities and relationships that require new behaviors and attitudes. This is the path that R&DD chose.

The challenges that R&DD faced in January, 1991 are still there, but not to the same degree. A transformation journey is not a short trip. There are no well-known maps for charting this journey. Companies have to discover their paths to future viability for themselves. Though its transformation is not yet complete, Lockheed's R&DD has traveled far in two years. The labs are seeking a balance of military and commercial applications for their technology. They have a customer-focused consciousness now, and are learning to find new markets and to develop new technology to satisfy them. It will take additional time to determine the effectiveness of their marketing efforts, but the confidence level is continually rising. The shift to a participative style of management is happening across all directorates. A comment heard often is, "We can never go back to the old ways."

References

[1]   Kanter, Rosabeth M. "Discipline!" *Harvard Business Review* (January-February 1992): 7-8.

[2]   Beer, Michael, Russel Eisenstat and Bert Spector. "Why Change Programs Don't Produce Change." *Harvard Business Review* (November-December 1990): 158-166.

CARES AND PROTECTS

6. The Evolution of Customer Service in Hamilton Insurance Company

by

ALAN BERRESFORD AND FEMI OGUNTOKUN

Hamilton Insurance Company Limited is a wholly-owned subsidiary of HFC Bank plc, a United Kingdom (U.K.) consumer banking business. HFC Bank, in turn, is wholly-owned by Household International Inc., a major U.S. provider of consumer and commercial financial services. Although separate legal entities, Hamilton and HFC Bank are interdependent and rely on each other to operate effectively and efficiently. In addition to sharing office premises with HFC Bank, Hamilton also shares support functions such as training, human resources, information technology, and marketing.

Focusing on the customer is not the norm within the United Kingdom (U.K.) insurance industry. Indeed, the insurance industry is not noted for being "customer friendly." In fact, most customers want to have as little contact as possible with their insurance company and hope that the event for which they are insured does not happen. Yet it is exactly when that event does happen, that the customer needs good service. When the claim is for loss of employment, sickness, or injury, the customer may well be upset, confused, angry, or despondent. It is at this time that the customers require sympathetic treatment as well as efficient handling of their claims.

Hamilton Insurance Company's chance to display this caring attitude towards customers arose when a young couple who had purchased credit protection insurance from Hamilton was involved in a car accident. The woman who was pregnant died in the crash. The next day an HFC Bank employee spotted the newspaper account of the horrific event and immediately notified Hamilton Insurance. The Hamilton claims staff, realizing there was sufficient evidence to verify the loss, processed the claim before it had been submitted. So when the customer arrived home from the hospital, he found a letter waiting for him explaining that the company had heard the sad news, offering their condolences, and informing him that the car loan had been paid off from the insurance. In this case Hamilton Insurance employees had not followed standard procedures laid down in the manuals. Instead, they had combined their good judgment with an opportunity to exceed customer expectations.

Customers' experiences with their insurance company during the critical period when they need to make a claim will influence their assessment of the company for the future. Not only will they make a judgment about the company for themselves, but will also tell their friends. If the experience has been favorable, they may well encourage others to become customers. It is easy to see that the quality of service to the customer has a very large impact on the company's future business and on profitability. Customer service has to permeate every aspect of the business, even the budgeting process, as the following story shows.

BUDGET CONSIDERATIONS IN CUSTOMER RELATIONS

It was time once again for the annual budget preparation. All the departments of Hamilton Insurance Company were required to deliver a very tight budget for 1993. Indeed, the expectation was that 1993 expenses would be below 1992's in real terms. Mike Varlow, the Claims Manager, who was preparing the budget for the Claims Department, knew that every line would be scrutinized by senior management and he had better have his planned employee headcount well justified. He was also aware that members of his staff were taking more time over claims assessment than they had in the past. To justify this increase in claims processing time, Mike prepared a bottom-up production plan which broke down the tasks involved in claims assessment and attached standard times to

Company Profile

Name of company	Hamilton Insurance Company Limited
Name of holding company	HFC Bank, plc.
Headquarters location	Winkfield, Windsor, Berkshire, U.K.
Company product focus	Insurance products, such as credit protection, term life, critical illness protection policies, etc.
Company insured customer base	250,000
Number of employees	60, in addition to the 700 sales representatives selling insurance products through the 150 HFC Bank branches
Per/annum contribution to parent company	U.S. $27 million

each task. Where previously the standard time allowable for processing a new claim was ten minutes, Mike insisted that it would be beneficial to customers and the company if an average time of 15 minutes per claim were allowed. When Mike presented the production plan to the Senior Management Group, there was great debate. Everyone acknowledged that this was a tough budget round and several people argued that production costs must be cut. Mike's plan to increase new claim processing time ran counter to that cost-cutting push.

Eventually, however, everyone was swayed by one argument in favor of Mike's plan: the longer standard claims processing time that he was proposing would ensure that claims would be processed properly. That, in turn, would mean the company would get it right the first time, saving time and money, while at the same time giving outstanding service to its customers. The Management Group adopted the proposal. How was this emphasis on customer service in the company's culture achieved? To get a fuller picture of the company's financial concerns, it is important to go back and look at the challenge that Hamilton was facing.

FINANCIAL CHALLENGES

Until 1988, the HFC operation in the U.K. had produced the highest return on equity of any Household unit. Like many other financial companies in Britain, HFC Bank profited from the rapid and massive expansion of consumer credit in the 1980s. All this changed, however, as the U.K. economy plunged into recession. Many people lost their jobs, and rising interest rates increased the cost of borrowing. Those homeowners who had bought houses in the boom years found themselves saddled with high mortgage repayments, and as house prices fell, they were faced with negative equity in their property. Consequently, payment arrears and bad debts spiralled for the lenders. The HFC Bank was not exempt from the effects, and registered net losses of U.S. $2.7 million and U.S. $24.1 million in 1989 and 1990, respectively.

CUSTOMER SERVICE: A COMPANY CORNERSTONE

Faced with this dramatic decline, Household needed to bring some stability to the situation, and to tighten controls on both lending decisions and the collection of overdue loans. Larry N. Bangs was appointed as the on-site Managing Director. A widely experienced Household veteran, Larry embarked on a program of improving quality within the U.K. organization. In addition to improving the quality of credit underwriting, collections, and management, Larry took the opportunity to gain an advantage over competitors on the customer service front. He saw quality customer service as a cornerstone of the group's strategy, as this statement from the 1991-1994 HFC Bank Strategic Plan reveals:

> The foundation of the strategy over the planning horizon 1991-1994 is the explicit recognition that the most important single factor affecting HFC's performance is the quality of the service we provide relative to our competitors. The aim, therefore, is to deliver a level of service that, as perceived by the customer, will differentiate us from competitors with similar product lines.

Larry's stand was a challenge to his executives to make this vision a reality. Andy Marchington, Managing Director of the Insurance Business Unit, took up the gauntlet. He knew from experience that effective change requires leadership and that leadership must generally come from the top. Indeed, the whole Executive Group must be convinced and committed to change. The issue was how to gain such commitment.

In many ways the culture within Hamilton seemed to be right on target with the desired profile of an effective company. The staff was small, so everyone knew each other. There was a pride in the name and identity of the company; the in-house newsletter was popular and company social events well attended. But there were some signs that everything was not right. There was friction between departments. People were nervous about contacting anyone in the company outside Hamilton. They would rather send a memo or form letter than pick up the phone to speak to someone in accounts or in a branch. Within the Claims Department, morale was particularly low, with a spate of resignations in 1991. The reasons staff members cited for leaving included the oppressive atmosphere in the workplace, and what was perceived as a detached and insensitive management. For example, there were two teams in the Claims Department, both dealing with the same type of claim. This arrangement encouraged competition, but it was an unhealthy kind of competition. The two team leaders did not get along with each other, and the members of one team would often criticize the work of the other team. Moreover, the members of one team felt they were regarded by others as lazy and incompetent.

Employees constantly complained about the difficulties of working with branch offices and of the time spent rectifying mistakes. And customers? Customers were looked upon as insurance applications to be underwritten, claims to be assessed and processed, and complaints to be dealt with. Consequently, letters were full of jargon, forms were difficult to complete, and processes were bureaucratic. Some staff members even believed that because they did not meet the customers face-to-face, customer service was not their problem. Customers contacting the company with a request or complaint would be moved from one department to another, with no one taking responsibility for them. Promises were made and broken, particularly about the time when a problem would be resolved. Members of the Senior Management Group were aware of these difficulties, but saw them more in terms of line management issues rather than the actual consequences of their own management decisions.

In an attempt to get the senior managers involved in solving these problems, Andy Marchington convened a special session of the nine-member Executive Group. To facilitate the session, he called in Tim Casswell, an outside professional consultant with expertise in interactive cycles of behavior. Using his skills in group dynamics, Tim helped the executives understand how their interactions with one another affected their feelings and behavior. The "opening up" yielded valuable insights into the perennial question of why people behave the way they do. The finding, in turn, put the focus on how their own interactions with their employees affected those employees' own attitudes and behaviors, which then influenced responsiveness to the Hamilton customer.

REVIEWING MANAGEMENT'S APPROACH

For example, it became clear that it was not enough just to talk about customer service. If a manager's emphasis is on numbers, so that the only measurement of a team's performance is how many cases are completed, then quality of service becomes unimportant. Managers who convey to their team members the idea that complaints are a nuisance prevent their staff from learning from those complaints and improving performance. And managers who do not value the staff will discourage those same employees from valuing customers and colleagues, alike. In contrast, a manager who listens and responds to staff suggestions, who seeks to learn from staff experience and customer complaints, and who finds ways to gauge customer satisfaction, will tend to motivate the staff and encourage better quality service.

The Executive Group became excited about the potential of this approach. They realized their own responsibility for creating a customer-focused culture in the company and decided that the next step was to hold a special session with the managers who report to them. This event was planned in a similar way to the earlier Executive Group session and the result was just as positive.

For example, Mike, the Claims Manager, took the opportunity to review his own management approach. He recognized that there were severe problems in his department, and he began to reflect on what was causing them, and what could be changed. One of the department's two team leaders had by this time left, but Mike's relationship with Nancy, the other team leader, was still strained. Mike realized from considering the cycles of behavior that he was at least contributing to that tension by holding a very tight rein on Nancy's management of her team, and by being closed to her suggestions. So he decided to relax his own management to create more space for Nancy to try out her ideas. His new approach met with a good response from Nancy, who clearly had been carrying out some analysis of the situation herself. This new relationship helped to ease the tensions in the department and improved the working environment, so that the staff could concentrate full time on the work, rather than on petty bickering.

EMPOWERING EMPLOYEES

Not surprisingly the Management Group wanted to take things further and create a learning experience for all Hamilton Insurance employees. Suddenly there was a strong sense of urgency about the whole new approach.

The Executive Group was galvanized into action. They knew that one facilitated planning event by itself could not change everything, but they felt it necessary to have some way of allowing all staff members to have an insight into good customer service, why it is important, and what it entails. And, most importantly, they wanted to empower employees to champion the cause of the customer themselves. They wanted to create a company environment in which employees would constantly see the customers as their point of reference. Employees would then be asking themselves:

- How can I write this letter so that it conveys the information clearly and concisely to the customer?
- What reasonable expectations can I set for the customer about how long it will take to resolve their complaint?
- How can we reduce the number of phone calls we make to the customer or to the branch staff to check details?
- How can we carry out the necessary checks on claims without unduly delaying payment of genuine claims?

Andy appointed a Core Team of the Executive Group and asked an expert facilitator to assist them. They embarked on designing a training process which would allow employees to immerse themselves in the service delivery process and ignite a transformation in attitudes and behaviors.

To feed ideas to the Core Team, the facilitator worked with Hamilton's Production Director, who combined a good knowledge of company operations with an understanding of customer service and enthusiasm for improvements in the company. The combination of the Production Director's inside knowledge and the facilitator's objective input proved to be the basis of a creative partnership. They wanted to provide some way of making this customer service orientation come alive. Many hours were spent, including weekends over coffee and cake, challenging each other's views and probing the desired transformation. In the end, a framework for learning emerged, based on the principle that people learn (and therefore change) when they experience a set of conditions which is different from their normal point of view. Now all that remained was to plan the logistics for this "learning event."

STRATEGY SESSIONS FOR ALL EMPLOYEES

The Core Team considered various options for the event. Should this be a single event for all staff members? If so, it would have to be on a weekend, in order not to close down the company's operations. But such an approach might give the impression that customer service had nothing to do with everyday activities of the staff. So the Core Team decided to set up three one-day events at a nearby site away from the company's offices, and have one-third of the company at each one. They decided that all employees, including managers, would attend one of the days, and that there would be a mix of people from the various sections in each group.

The Core Team saw that the key to improving customer service is allowing staff members to see for themselves the importance of good service. This approach often requires them to change their point of view: they must see the service being offered from the customer's perspective. To dramatize this insight, during one of their sessions, the Production Director and the outside facilitator invited the Core Team to get up from their chairs and actually stand on the tables to take a look at the room from a new perspective. This was an "Ah-Ha!" moment; they were actually able to see things differently from a different point of view.

Another consciousness-raising activity used by the facilitator was to have staff members relate to their own experience of being a customer, and recall what it feels like to be at the receiving end of service; they need to remember what they actually thought and how they reacted, both when a company's service disappointed them, and when it delighted them. Everyone is a customer of several organizations, and everyone has experience with both poor and good quality service. And once a person has recalled such experiences, it is surprising how strong are the associated feelings and actions. The key is then to make the transition from the employee's personal experience to understanding the likely effect of the service which they themselves provide to their own customers.

To effect this perspective and attitude change, the Core Team designed a day with three sessions:

Session 1:	Understanding why customer service is important
Session 2:	In small teams, using case studies to examine in detail three key Hamilton business processes from a customer's perspective: — Handling new business — Processing claims — Dealing with complaints
Session 3:	Identifying actions to improve quality of service.

The Core Team next took an important step—they tested this preliminary session design by setting up and running the day with members of the Executive Group as participants. The outside consultant led the facilitation team which included Patsy from the Planning Department and Dennis from the Training Department. This test run not only demonstrated management's commitment to the whole process, but also gave the Executive Group a chance to give valuable feedback to the Core Team about the design of the day.

Using this information, the team adjusted some of the timings of the sessions; they tightened the procedures and clarified the questions the facilitators asked. In particular, participants pointed out that because the case studies used in the test run had been invented, certain events they were to react to were unrealistic and would not happen in practice, so that the exercise seemed artificial. So for the actual events, the team found case studies based on real examples from the company's files with names, addresses, and other identifying details changed.

With everything finally in place, the Core Team set up and ran the three one-day events. In the first sessions, participants described many examples of both poor and good service they had experienced from restaurants, garages, shops, banks, and hotels. They discussed the effect of these experiences on their relationship with the company concerned. Turning to their own experiences as employees of Hamilton, they then made a rough estimate of how much providing poor service could cost the company to rectify a mistake and to absorb the loss of customer business. The result was several hundred pounds, or in some cases thousands of pounds, per customer. On the other hand, they recognized that good service gains the customer's commitment. And in the insurance business, where products are very similar, it is often superior customer service that gives a company its competitive advantage.

ADOPTING THE CUSTOMER'S PERSPECTIVE

The second session was the heart of each day. At this point, the group divided into three teams, each of which looked at one of the three business processes in detail. Each team comprised a mix of people from the department concerned, who knew the process well, and people from other departments, who would look at the process more objectively. Each team took a different scenario through the actual company process by re-creating every activity and experiencing events as they unfolded. They then stepped back and looked at the process from the customer's point of view, and identified the poor customer service aspects.

One team looked at the process for handling customer complaints. Their scenario concerned a woman who had been a long-term Hamilton customer. She and her husband had taken out a loan from the HFC Bank, which included Credit Protection Insurance from Hamilton. She had suffered an accident and was home from work for several weeks with an injured wrist. When attempting to claim, she was informed by the HFC Bank branch that sold the policy that under the terms of the policy only the first signatory to the loan was covered; being the second signatory to the loan agreement, she was not insured.

She then contacted Hamilton to complain about what was, to her, a technicality which she maintained was not brought to her attention at the time of purchase. She wrote to Hamilton Company:

> Over the years you've had a lot of money from me, and to be
> told this after all these years, I don't think much of it. My hus-
> band has said, when we finish in October, we will no longer do
> business with you again.

The team mapped out the process for dealing with the complaint and was amazed to discover how may people contacted the customer to ask her information about the complaint; the Complaints Section, the branch, the Regional Manager each called the injured woman, as though each one was checking the story. They found that procedures within the company were thorough and careful. However, it became clear that no one person took responsibility for keeping the customer informed of what was happening, and for setting reasonable expectations of when the complain would be resolved.

The second team considered the claims process. Their scenario concerned a bus driver who had submitted a claim for a sickness benefit; a liver complaint had prevented him from working for several weeks. However, information from his doctor indicated that the claimant had first consulted him before the policy was purchased. A standard letter was dispatched stating, "Dear Sir" (rather than being addressed to the customer by name), and explaining that the claim was being turned down on the grounds that the illness was a "pre-existing condition," i.e., that the claimant was suffering from the complaint and had seen a medical practitioner prior to taking out the policy.

It was a rather confused customer who wrote back pointing out that the company had paid a claim the previous year on the same complaint. Upon further investigation it was revealed that the first visit to the doctor had been for an unrelated ailment and that the liver condition did not pre-exist the date of the policy. Looking at this scenario, the team then considered the impact of this process on the customer and his wife. Because of the illness and the delay in settling the claim, the couple's loan account was now in arrears. The customer's job was low-paid, and so the team realized that the customer was no doubt in some distress about his financial position, let alone his medical condition. Any claims department must be vigilant against fraud, but the team recognized that more careful investigation at the beginning could have avoided some of the distress. In addition, the team recommended improving the form and tone of letters used in the claims process to make them more personal and applicable to the particular case.

The third team re-enacted the procedure for accepting, checking, and setting-up on computers, a new insurance proposal for Payment Care (an income protection product). The process was traced from the branch office completing the sale with the customer, to sending the Payment Care proposal to Hamilton, to internal processing by Hamilton, and finally on to the "Welcome" letter to the customer. A number of "fail" points were exposed. For example, in this case the Hamilton Administrator and the Underwriter both contacted the branch office to obtain missing information. The branch in turn contacted the customer on two separate occasions to request the required information. It became obvious that it would be far better to check the form in its entirety and make requests for further information at the same time. Another issue was that the branch salesperson had to look up the appropriate premium rate from a set of premium tables listing 1200 individual rates! Not surprisingly, the salesperson in this case had identified the wrong premium, so that it had to be corrected by the Hamilton

Administrator. The team looking at this process recommended using a more reliable system which has since led to the introduction of computerized quotation for insurance products.

As each team replayed its particular scenario and identified shortcomings, individuals would ask why things were done that way. The usual response was, "That's the way we do it." A good example of this approach was the experience of a customer in Norwich who had submitted a claim. The staff in the Claims Department spent three months collecting information about the claim, and then declined it. When the customer questioned why the decision had taken so long, the manager investigating the complaint discovered that there had been sufficient data on the original claim form to decline the claim on the first day. He then asked why the staff needed to collect all the extra information. "We always do that," one staff member explained to him. "Because if there is another claim in the future, we then have all the information there." Shifting from a company process perspective to a customer perspective is the only way to question this kind of perverse organizational logic. Happily, this particular procedure has now been changed. After reviewing this scenario in the session, one participant reacted quite openly, "But we've never been allowed to look at it that way. Do we now have permission to suggest doing things differently?" Such comments were clues to the Executive Group about the changes they needed to make in the company culture. Quite clearly, staff members did not feel encouraged to suggest changes to improve the service they offered customers. The Executive Group took notice, and following the event, they began to find ways of listening to staff feedback.

STEERING GROUP FOLLOW-UP

During the third session the participants brought together the 60 or so actions they had identified in their teams as ways to improve customer service. These actions were sorted into related topics and then given to small mixed staff teams to research and follow up. The overall Steering Group set up to oversee the work of the teams consisted of one member of each team, together with three members of the Executive Group. Eight months later, the Steering Group reviewed the progress of the teams. A number of significant changes had been achieved. What is particularly noteworthy is that the great majority of actions taken to improve the quality of customer service also benefited staff members. For example, the Claims Department was reorganized into two sections, one to deal with unemployment claims, the other to deal with claims for accident and sickness. This new arrangement benefited the customers by ensuring that the person handling the claim knew the procedure in detail and was less likely to make errors. The new approach was a source of satisfaction for staff members in allowing them to become experts in that area. To alleviate the possibility of rigid job specialization leading to boredom and a feeling of being in a dead-end job, a program of cross-training has been put in effect. As a result, morale in the section has increased dramatically. For example, where formerly employees working in the same department but different sections would hardly speak to one another, the atmosphere is now buzzing. Unprompted suggestions for improvement are now raised and acted on. One staff member commented on how she now reviews her own letters and mentally puts herself in the customer's shoes.

More and more staff members now ask themselves how what they are doing affects the customers. And they look for improvements. Commitment to the customer is not an overnight conversion. Changing to a new orientation is a matter of seeing things differently, of altering priorities, of applying new values. But it takes a great amount of practice to apply this new vision to everyday operations and to the constant small crises of business life. It also takes colleagues who recognize and support the need for change, and encourage it in others, until people reach a point where the new viewpoint is seen as natural. That is the point where a Management Group starts to make new decisions.

KEY RESULT AREAS

The following changes were a direct result of actions suggested during the three one-day events:

- **Complete review conducted of all letters, which are the company's main channel of communication with customers**. Now Hamilton will compose more personalized, clear, and direct letters. A letter writing course has been set up to train staff to write more effectively.
- **Improved communications with other parts of the company** has reduced errors in dealing with customer details.
- **Redesigned forms to capture all required information in the first communication, thereby eliminating the need for follow-**

up requests. Forms were all made much clearer, and a simple "How to Claim" booklet was produced, explaining how to complete the form, as well as informing customers about what to expect from the process.

- **Each case of long-term disability was investigated and, where appropriate, claims settled in full**. This procedure avoids customers' having to give evidence every few months that they are still disabled.
- **Reorganization of the Claims Department into two sections, one for unemployment and one for sickness and disability**. This rearrangement has reduced harmful competitiveness and unhealthy rivalries, as well as engendered a pride in each section's specialized knowledge and increased efficiency. As Mike reports, "No more glum faces can be seen; you can even hear occasional laughter. A satisfied staff is the first step towards satisfied customers."
- **Complaints procedures have been reviewed and simplified**. Complaints are resolved more quickly and fully, and customers are kept informed of progress.
- **Individuals are much more supportive of their colleagues;** greater trust and participation are evident. There are now regular team leader meetings providing forums for testing ideas, making suggestions, and giving feedback. Team leaders take an interest in their individual team members, demonstrating that staff members are wanted and valued by the company. In addition, on the shop floor, it is no longer taboo for members of teams to talk to each other; when there is a particularly sticky problem, two people may work together on it for a time to resolve the difficulty.
- **Procedures have been streamlined**. Long-standing backlogs have been cleared. In many instances, claims can be processed in one day—this quick turnaround was thought to be impossible only two years ago. When a new filing system was recently introduced, the staff worked through the night to complete the changeover.

Having achieved these results, Hamilton Insurance Company Limited has successfully completed its first phase on the journey to provide reliable, consistent, and superior service. A year later, the second phase has already commenced, though many challenges lie ahead. There are various facets to measuring customer service, and many questions to be answered:

- Are the right parts of the process being measured?
- How does the Executive Group know it is making improvements?
- How are middle managers to be coached and empowered to support the transformation process and encourage initiative and creativity in their staffs?
- How is the whole approach kept vital and alive and not allowed to become mundane and out of focus?

These are serious challenges, but not insurmountable. They can be met by a company like Hamilton which has renewed its commitment to its customers at all levels.

IV.

MAXIMIZING STAKEHOLDER INVOLVEMENT

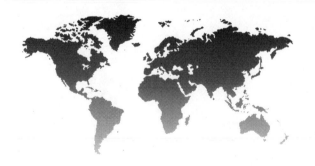

metacentros, s.a.

7. Integrated Company Teams Serving a Nation

by
WILLIAM AND BARBARA ALERDING

*Dr. Rodolfo Paiz, President of the Paiz Organization, believes
that the words which best capture the aspirations of his group
of companies are on a wall tablet in St. Paul's Cathedral in
London, England. Dedicated to Christopher Wren, the famous
cathedral's architect, the words are: "If you want to see his
monument, look around you." Dr. Paiz, too, wants to lead an
organization driven by the same pragmatic spirit. The real
estate and architectural arm of his organization, Metacentros,
has created a new socioeconomic environment to improve the life
of all Guatemalans. One can look around Guatemala and find
within the retail landscape, the dynamic monument of Metacentros.*

Metacentros, S.A., the real estate and architectural division of the
Paiz Organization's family of companies, along with the Paiz
Organization as a whole, is transforming the development of
retailing and commercial projects in Guatemala. It has surpassed
all of the older established competition and has become the
largest and most efficient supermarket and department store
chain in Guatemala. The country's ten million inhabitants live mainly in

rural areas, where the indigenous and poor are the majority. One million of the people living in the capital city are in the middle and low-income groups with one-half million constituting the high income elite, and the rest, the marginal poor.

The presence of the organization seems to be everywhere as Guatemalans are seen walking along the streets carrying bags of groceries with the familiar Paiz logo. One of the largest private employers in Guatemala, the Paiz Organization is a family of companies with its activities integrated into a network of four company groups: Real Estate, Commercial, Financial, and International. Although the Commercial Group is the largest, with estimated annual sales of U.S. $300 million for 1993 from some 40 supermarkets and discount stores, this case study focuses on Metacentros, S.A., the leading company in the Real Estate Group, a technical team of 100 young professionals undertaking a vision-driven strategy for change.

STRATEGY FOR CHANGE

How have Metacentros and the Paiz Organization managed to carry out this successful strategy in such a small and poor country? First, they have created a new retailing concept, the metamercado (metamarket), a modern, privately operated market selling popular products. In some places, these have become a substitute for the deteriorating and unsanitary traditional governmental markets; in other places, these complement older retailing styles.

The concept is not a new invention, but a different understanding of how to order reality. Imagine driving into any town or neighborhood in Guatemala and becoming bogged down in traffic snarls, which occur around every open market in the country. These markets are no longer adequate and all the surrounding streets are clogged with individual vendors and small retail shops, completely blocking off traffic. It is necessary to walk and push one's way through, trying to avoid the ever-present thief. What is pioneering about the metamarket is that it combines all the markets in one large area, including retail outlets, necessary services, and sufficient parking space. This is a transformation in urban design.

In the traditional Guatemalan shopping center, the anchor store is a department store; in a metamercado, the anchor store is a form of the traditional market located alongside a Paiz discount store called "Despensa Familiar" (family discount store). The metamercado is complemented by

Company Profile

Name of company	Metacentros S.A., the leading company in the Real Estate Group, one of four company groups of the Paiz Organization
Headquarters location	Guatemala City
Industrial focus	Real estate development, commercial projects, shopping centers.
Leader and title	Dr. Rodolfo Paiz, President
Estimated 1993 sales	U.S. $300 million
Net profit for 1993	U.S. $3 million
Number of employees	5,000 - Paiz Organization 100 - Metacentros

multiple popular outlets and retail stores. All parties win in this retail arrangement. Low-income population groups are served by modern and efficient retailers who provide low-cost food and basic items. At the same time, Paiz finds a profitable opportunity for itself and for Metacentros, which gets the work and the return as the developer.

Another example of a successful retail strategy is a massive project called Metaterminal del Norte (Northern Super Terminal). This project, which will become the first major, private distribution area for markets in Guatemala, is a sorely needed innovative enterprise. All cargo and passengers from the northern regions of the country will stop at the metaterminal instead of continuing into the congested heart of the city. Presently, the only major distribution terminal for all cargo entering the city is located in the heart of Guatemala City. Overcrowded, jammed with noisy traffic and many outdoor stores, it is considered to be one of the most dangerous areas of the city. The metaterminal will offer a very large retail shopping area of indoor stores with a wide diversity of products and sizeable warehouses for massive quantities of wholesale merchandise. It will also contain a major depot, convenient medical services, and a hotel for passengers travelling into the city. The whole complex will be well-organized, clean, and safe, and will provide the infrastructure that does not exist in the overcrowded, chaotic central distribution area. Guatemala needs more public markets for the people, but the government cannot afford to build them.

It is a fact that throughout the country more shopping for food, clothing, and housewares is done in the public markets than in individual stores outside the market area. Metacentros, then, is providing for the city badly needed retail services which the government cannot continue to offer as the population grows. To understand the real impact Metacentros is having on the socioeconomic development of Guatemala, one needs to look at how the Paiz Organization:

(1) Developed its spirit and purpose;
(2) Restructured itself to provide growth and profitability, while making a significant socioeconomic contribution to the development of Guatemala;
(3) Continues to develop innovative concepts in design;
(4) Exemplifies a flexible organization which has the capacity to adapt to change.

"INTRAPRENEURSHIP" IN A FAMILY ENTERPRISE

The spirit of this innovative organization comes from Dr. Rodolfo Paiz, a man of extraordinary vitality and vision. He has a dream of improving Guatemala, a country with a high rate of poverty and illiteracy. Dr. Paiz obtained his M.B.A. and Ph.D. in Business Administration from Harvard University. Between 1967 and 1976 he was a member of the faculty of the Central American Institute of Business Administration (INCAE) in Managua, Nicaragua. In 1976, he returned to Guatemala and started Metacentros, a new company within the larger Paiz Organization, which had been founded in 1928 by his father, Carlos Paiz, Sr.

Even as early as 1974 when writing his doctoral thesis, Dr. Paiz explained his new concept of retail food distribution in an economically developing environment:

> For developing societies, the poor performance of the traditional retail structure that serves low-income communities of urban areas constitutes an administrative problem of broad economic and social implications. Inefficient retailing can decrease the welfare of the majority of the population, hamper the performance of the entire food marketing system, and slow down economic development in general.

His thesis documents how in the early 1970s, the Paiz Organization began a small supermarket called, Mi Super (My Supermarket) in a low-income neighborhood of Guatemala City. This experiment was not profitable and eventually failed because the local residents could not purchase enough of the higher-priced items to make it a lucrative enterprise. From this experiment, Metacentros learned that merchandising concepts cannot be automatically transferred between socioeconomic groups; for example, a supermarket cannot simply transfer a high diversity of products to a poorer neighborhood and sell only a few items at lower cost. What the Paiz Organization and Metacentros did to transform a failing situation was to start the chain of "Despensa Familiar" stores which offer a limited assortment of 750 basic items, like rice, beans, bread, dehydrated milk, and sugar at lower prices for the economically disadvantaged. This financially viable venture has greatly increased the quantity of food people can afford to buy. Its profitability comes from the high volume of sales and high turnover of inventory achieved within a very low-cost structure of operation. Metacentros is a rare company in that while it focuses on socioeconomic change, it still makes a profit.

The first major project that Metacentros designed for the Paiz Organization was the Montserrat Shopping Center, the first large shopping center built in the lower-income suburbs of Guatemala City. At that time, there were no large commercial centers for the nearly one million people spread throughout this western section of the city. Now the local people enjoy shopping at the large Paiz supermarket, as well as in the 141 retail shops spread throughout the complex. Shoppers can find any household product they need at reasonable prices in a clean and safe environment. The local residents are excited when they get lost in the huge area that has so many corridors twisting and turning among the labyrinth of shops. Montserrat became such a popular shopping area in this neglected part of the city that it pioneered the way for other businesses to locate in the same complex. Hundreds of new businesses opened their stores so that today this zone contains an array of commercial ventures.

Another major Metacentros project was the Vista Hermosa Shopping Center in the newly developed upper middle-class area in the eastern section of the capital. This shopping center combines indoor shops with a high-rise apartment building. For the first time in Guatemala, people had the convenience of shopping in the same building in which they lived.

Dr. Paiz continued to guide Metacentros into pioneering projects that he felt were making a difference in the socioeconomic development of his country. For instance as the years passed, he also started a company of employee services for the Paiz Organization; served as President of both the Rotary Club and the Guatemalan Management Association; and obtained another Master's degree from Harvard's John Kennedy School of Government. Because he wanted to do even more for his country, he entered politics as the nation's Finance Minister serving from January, 1986 through October, 1989.

It did not take long before he found that being the Minister of Finance was a full-time job, and he could not continue to be the guiding light of Metacentros at the same time. Although he selected an experienced manager to replace him, unfortunately the manager was unable to communicate effectively with the larger Paiz Organization and chose to leave. Three other managers came and left in rapid succession during these years, and Dr. Paiz's vision of Metacentros was held in limbo. The company simply flattened out and conducted "business as usual" with very few innovative, pioneering projects. When Dr. Paiz finished his term as Finance Minister in 1989, he spent a year as a Fellow at the Harvard International Program, and returned to Metacentros as President in January, 1991. At this time, he realized that the company needed to recharge its batteries to once again be a decisive force in the development of the country.

RESTRUCTURING METACENTROS

At this point in 1991, Dr. Paiz hired a number of young, intelligent employees, many just out of the university, involved them in training programs, and sent them to study other projects in Mexico, Colombia, and the U.S.A. He wanted Metacentros to develop projects which would have an impact on Guatemala's socioeconomic development, and knew that the real power of his organization lay in the participation of all of his employees, not just those at the managerial level. Because he recognized that managers are only as effective as their employees, Dr. Paiz wanted everyone involved in his dream for the country. He reorganized Metacentros into 12 smaller business units to spread the decision making and responsibility across the board. Each group was responsible for its own "company." Then he invited consultants from the Institute of Cultural Affairs (ICA) in Guatemala to help facilitate a one-week Thinking Skills Course made up of short, practical work-shops to help motivate the entire staff. No one was left out of this course, including the security guards and maintenance staff. This personal touch is characteristic of the way the Paiz Organization works. During the week of this first course, the ICA staff employed the Ten Basic Thinking Skills of Dr. Edward de Bono, along with a series of presentations on how the human brain learns, the Multiple Intelligences framework of Dr. Howard Gardner, and the Four Styles of Learning of Dr. Bernice McCarthy[1].

The entire Metacentros staff broke into small groups to apply the different thinking tools through various exercises. The course was highly participative and helped create a more cooperative ambiance among the Metacentros staff members as they saw each other in their new roles as thinkers. Because they all believed in the dream of Dr. Paiz, they saw that they could use their new thinking skills to find alternative ways to enhance their work, broaden their options about their various projects, and improve their interpersonal relationships. They appreciated the way these tools widened their perspective before making a decision and how these skills opened up more possible solutions to a problem. The participants saw more alternatives, possibilities, and options; they also learned how to analyze new ideas, consider all the factors before making a decision, and how to look at the long-range consequences of decision making.

Shortly after this course ended, ICA came in again to facilitate a strategic planning program, a two and one-half day workshop which involved the entire staff of Metacentros in the creation of a two-year strategic action plan for the company. During this program, the staff created a document which included various proposals and tactics for the execution of ten innovative projects: four metashopping centers, two renovation projects on established complexes, one industrial condominium, two monumental metaterminals, and a major administration building for the organization. The document also spelled out a master plan for coordinating all project activities and teams. The plan created 12 teams which would meet together weekly to plan and review their interdepartmental projects. A monthly information bulletin would be published. In addition, the workshop document included creation of a human resources department to completely overhaul administration of

---

[1]Breadth, The CORT Thinking Program. (New York: Pergamon Press, Inc.), 1986.

promotions, salary schedules, and evaluation procedures. They even produced an exhaustive list of training programs for all personnel. The document also set out a plan to computerize all departments, as well as a design to raise funds for financing all their projects.

During this period of corporate restructuring, the staff became clear about their company objectives and how they as employees could best work together as a unit. They realized that they had been lost in the particularities of each team's work and had not clearly seen their work in relationship to the whole. The strategic planning program also helped each employee come to know other company employees and to understand the special roles each played in the entire organization. The older employees appreciated the way the two and one-half day process aided them in their struggle to adapt to a new, nonhierarchical structure in which they no longer needed to punch a clock, but which demanded more personal initiative and responsibility. After this initial planning session, the ICA consultants facilitated follow-up meetings every 30 days to monitor the progress of the practical actions the staff had created during the workshop and to make any needed midpath corrections.

The follow-up process was so motivating that the teams have decided to continue meeting every quarter as part of their general corporate *modus operandi*. Each of the 12 action teams prepares a report to present to the company's general assembly and then shares its plan of work for the next three months. All the team members observe the work of other teams, evaluate each, and then see how their own work fits into the overall design of the company. During these meetings, the staff celebrates birthdays and provides entertainment to show off the various talents of staff members.

From the organization's beginning, the senior Mr. Paiz had encouraged his employees to become shareholders; this policy continues today. In fact, an employee representative is a permanent member of the Board of Directors and is elected by the employee shareholders each year. The Paiz Organization continues to be well known for extending various benefits to more than 5,000 of its own personnel. These benefits include a 10% discount on personal purchases, medical insurance, a retirement plan, training programs, and recreational facilities for vacations. Everyone in the organization has the satisfaction from participating in service to the community. The organization sponsors an immensely popular Art and Cultural Month for the public annually, as well as a yearly parade for the children, with floats displaying Walt Disney characters.

INNOVATIVE CONCEPTS

Today, Metacentros is deliberately following two principal strategies:
(1) Expanding their shopping center complexes outside the capital city to the less-developed interior of the country;
(2) Finding ways to serve low-income families.

The majority of the people who live in the interior of Guatemala are farmers who can only find the goods they need in small neighborhood stores with limited stocks on their shelves. These consumers have to travel to the capital city to purchase larger items. The planned expansion of Metacentros will eliminate this hardship and will offer modern goods and services in towns and cities where they have never before been available. Metacentros projects that the majority of the parent company's expansion will occur outside Guatemala City. Recent statistics show that 80% of the Guatemalan population lives in poverty, mostly in the rural areas. For example, Metacentros finished the first enclosed shopping mall in Quetzaltenango, Guatemala's second-largest city, 200 kilometers outside the capital. Now it is possible to find in this smaller city all the modern forms of retailing which formerly existed only in the capital.

In addition to expanding into less-populated rural areas, Metacentros is constructing stores and markets which offer families in the lower-income bracket an opportunity to shop for affordable goods. Presently, the Paiz Organization has expanded to include discount and convenience stores, electrical appliance outlets, and toy shops. While the Paiz supermarkets are generally for the upper and middle-income families, the Despensa Familiar (Family Discount Stores, as described earlier) is a chain for the majority of the people in the lower economic bracket.

A FLEXIBLE ORGANIZATION

In the 1970s the Paiz Organization began formulating five-year plans. Since 1928, their success had been principally as a retail outlet, but at their 50 year mark, they decided to diversify. They chose to push "backwards" into creating their own industries which would manufacture the articles they sold in their stores; they also wanted to push "forwards" into businesses that processed their products. For example, they started a hamburger franchise, called Wimpy, imported from the United Kingdom. They also decided to go international and opened three joint-venture supermarkets in Honduras.

It did not take long to discover that the system they were building was not able to manage such diverse types of businesses, and they had to divest themselves of all the "backwards" and "forwards" companies, as well as their international investments. They saw that the system they had originally built was really a retail type of business and that their systems operated much better growing horizontally. They decided not to continue to push growth into areas of weakness, and learned that removing these sources of limitation made their growth more viable. They are now rapidly continuing to expand in a horizontal direction. Metacentros today only selects, designs, and implements projects that continue along this retail outlet path. As a result, the system is more focused and the 12 teams can more easily see themselves as part of an overall system that has a clearly defined direction.

EMPLOYEES SPEAK OUT

Members of the 12 Metacentros teams all speak out of the same vision. Each is proud and exhilarated at being part of a series of projects that will make a tremendous change in the development of the country. Each of the 12 teams is also aware of its own impact on this development. When the teams have their quarterly meetings, the members listen to the plans of each team. In supporting one another, they have a palpable sense that they are each a part of a grand vision. The company's ambience reflects its involvement in building a dream for Guatemala. As one walks through the offices of Metacentros, one senses this shared vision from viewing a series of models and drawings of present and future projects. Talk to the company architects and their eyes light up as they explain the steps they go through as a team to create the design of a new concept which will involve tens of thousands of people. Walk into any office and immediately everyone will start talking about his/her part in this great dream. It's contagious, this sparkle in their eyes. As Dr. Paiz says:

We have many young people here at Metacentros. For example, we have architects just out of the university. They are designing massive projects that many established, well-known Guatemalan architects would probably not have the chance to do.

Beatriz Ramirez, Dr. Paiz's Executive Assistant, who has worked for him for 13 years, exudes the same enthusiasm. She loves being a part of this great dream and is actually proud to spend so much time at work. At Metacentros, there is a colleagueship and challenge for her that is unlike any other work. Occasionally she will work until 3:00 a.m. to help finish a job. Pride and self-assurance fill her eyes when she talks about her experiences:

> Dr. Paiz never looked over my shoulder when he gave me a job to
> do. He never kept coming around to check on me. As a result, I have
> developed a great deal of self-confidence in my own ability to work.

The General Manager of Metacentros is Maria Olga de Olavarria who, as liaison and communicator on the various projects, must keep in constant contact with the Paiz retail outlets. The daughter of Carlos Paiz, Executive Director of the Paiz stores, she fulfills the Paiz family's rules set for any member of the family who wishes to become part of the managerial staff of the Paiz Organization. First, she has had the required work experience outside the organization. Second, she has a Master's degree, and third, her salary has been decided by a family council. No nepotism is allowed in the organization; working for this group requires competence! While Dr. Paiz does the negotiation for land and coordination with outside investors, it is Maria Olga's role to handle communication and coordination within the Paiz Organization. As she explains:

> When I first started working here, I was working on projects
> already set up. Now it's exciting to work on a new project from
> its birth. It's stimulating to work on the signing, getting the land,
> working through the negotiations with someone with whom we
> had been working for over two years before he finally said yes.
> My father had given up on getting this particular land, but
> Rodolfo and I pursued it, persisted, and won!

She embodies an enthusiasm that can only come from participating in a common dream.

Another participant in this dream is Jorge Cambronero, Director of Design and Store Set-up, who reflects Dr. Paiz's belief that a flexible organization allows its staff to be challenged constantly. As he explains:

During a six-month period, I designed three stores in all, two of them in the interior of the country. It was a very difficult challenge, especially hiring local people where there is a scarcity of trained workers. We did all this with only five people on our team! After his designs are approved, he and his team create a plan and sell out all its implementary steps. This takes from three to six months for each project. He normally is involved in designing four to five large projects a year. For people like Jorge, Metacentros offers the opportunity of a constantly motivating challenge.

Another motivated employee is Cesar Cordon, the coordinator of the Commercial Buildings Architectural team. Cesar describes the work of this team:

> We learned how to relate to investors. There is constant work; we are working on five or six projects at the same time, but I am very satisfied with the work, all of it. I learned a great deal about new projects from my trips to Mexico, to the United States, and to Colombia. Very few people have such opportunities as we have at Metacentros.

This team follows the lead of Dr. Paiz who develops the original idea for each commercial project. They look at the land to be developed and do a topographical survey on the services, water, light, telephone, parking, and all the needed infrastructure. They then do a feasibility study, on all factors involved, including the soil. Next they talk to the sales team so that the salespeople can explain the design to potential investors. It is necessary to design more than one option for the same project, evaluate each one, and do the design again to keep all the alternatives open. Every two weeks all the groups involved in a particular project meet together.

Another example of how a flexible organization stimulates all its personnel to work together comes from Adriana de Dominguez, the Systems Manager who has responsibility for all the accounting to the point of disbursement, control, and income. She finds the work very dynamic and loves working for an organization with a global vision:

> After 19 years in accounting, which for me was a tunnel career, I have been fulfilled. I feel satisfied, more useful, and more developed in my career. I have experienced a radical change. My husband has even said to me, 'You are another person,' as though I had changed physically!

One of the hallmarks of maintaining flexibility in Metacentros is its constant training of all the employees. The organization offers many opportunities for personnel to participate in courses in human relations, communications, and building self-confidence, as well as in sessions on thinking and planning. Dr. Paiz encourages this same attitude in the self-development of teams, too. During interviews with the ICA consultants, many of the managers of the teams involved wanted to include the other team members in the interview. They would spell out each other's role and emphasize how they worked together and trusted each other to get the job done. They also find it crucial to meet with other teams and coordinate their work. One would be hard put to find any jealousy either within or between teams. Everyone not only feels personally involved in satisfying work, but depends on all the other team members to keep the corporation moving. It is as if everyone is pushing a giant rock up a hill and understands that the rock will not move unless each person puts his or her weight behind it.

The Market Research team, headed by Cosmo Alessio, does feasibility studies of each project. Team members check competitive prices on fruits, vegetables, meat, clothes, and other merchandise, and study the interior regions of Guatemala to learn about the buying habits of the people. They carry out a customer profile in each Paiz store every year. Market Research also looks for land for new projects. Cosmo describes his role as head of the team:

> I worked at Metacentros before the new changes Dr. Paiz introduced. I love being part of the Metacentros system even more today, because it is doing very important projects for our country. Our team is making a substantial contribution to the total work.

Sandra Garcia, Manager of Administration, and her team are responsible for coordinating the work of all the shopping centers. Sandra talks about the many changes the organization has had to confront:

> When I started here, there was a crisis because the administrators did not make any decisions. I had to change their own images of their roles. The administrators needed training in self-confidence, words of encouragement, plus more responsibility in making decisions. Now, their self-confidence is high and there has been a great change in their attitudes. They plan all the work of a shopping center condominium and manage the personnel. They are also responsible for publicity, for special sales, and for safety

programs. The key points in accomplishing this new level of initiative were: building self-confidence; a 25% to 30% increase in salary; training courses on how to process evaluation; and working on their self-stories.

It is obvious that people with high levels of personal mastery like Sandra are more committed to working with a team which encourages a broader and deeper sense of responsibility for and involvement in the task. Besides, with this kind of participation, everyone learns faster.

Perhaps the transformation of Metacentros lies in Dr. Paiz's ability to break through the traditional authoritarian approach in which the managers organize and control every decision, to introduce a horizontal system in which everyone shares in the decision making. Dr. Paiz talks excitedly about a new experiment in participation:

> I called together our seven technical teams of architects, designers, and engineers with their support team of draftsmen. I told them that we had a large tract of land near one of Guatemala City's main arteries and wanted to construct the largest shopping center in the city. This time we were not going to have the design team plan it, but, instead, we were going to have a competition among interested people who wanted to present a project. They would have two weeks to come up with a design that would best deal with balancing the costs of the land plus construction with the most feasible use of the property, and the most functional commercial design. Some of those interested immediately started to form interdisciplinary teams of architects, designers, engineers, and draftsmen. All who participated selected the colleagues with whom they wanted to work.
>
> We ended up with four teams who worked day and night, seven days a week for two weeks. Some of them were locked out of their own houses by angry spouses when they arrived home in the early morning. When the day arrived to show their designs, the four teams came up with a total of ten different complete projects. Now we have more designs to compare and choose from than we ever had before. What excites me most is not the project itself, but that everyone worked so energetically as teams. This is a great example of participation.

Dr. Paiz believes in hiring young enthusiastic people who believe in his dream for Guatemala. Young people's assumptions about the way the world works can still be formed, whereas older people may often find themselves resistant to change because the changes do not fit their own mental models framed by long standing habits. When asked about what they would like to see for the future, several of these enthusiastic employees had suggestions:

> We need even more communication with the Paiz Organization so we don't have to wait too long for project approval.

> I would like Metacentros to do more projects for itself (that is, the Paiz Organization) and not for the owners of the land we develop who make questionable changes in what we do. Our good name is involved.

> I want to see all the systems computerized so that no matter what office you are in, the information you need is right there.

> There are seven technical teams and sometimes we lose communication and necessary feedback; we need to involve all the new people in the process.

> When Dr. Paiz is not here, few decisions get made; deadlines are crucial, and we need to be able to make those decisions even when he is not present.

> I want to see Metacentros continue to grow. We want to build a tall, central office in this location for all the offices of the Paiz Organization.

> We need packages of courses for different levels of employees so that there is training for everyone. I want to prepare all employees technically for change.

> I hope Metacentros will have enough money to fulfill all its projects. It is costly to get the amount of money we need. If there were ever a real estate crash, we would be in a great deal of trouble.

When teams get together to create project designs, everyone's models are out on the table. No one is afraid to express inner beliefs; there is nothing hidden. It takes an engaged, flexible group of people with a common vision to be able to express their models in a way that keeps the total organization moving ahead. When they see obstacles to their corporate progress, they talk about them publicly so that they can create strategies for overcoming them.

TECHNICAL AREA

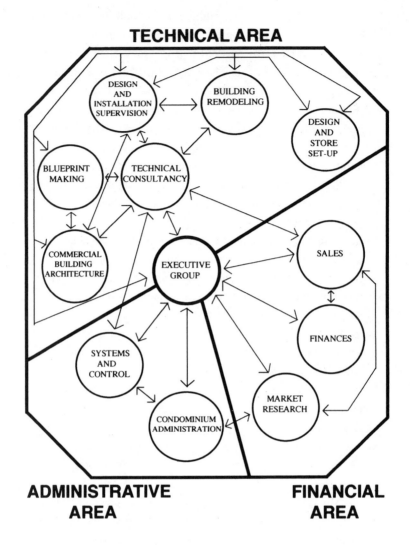

Twelve-Team Metacentros Structure

To ensure participation such as this for everyone on its staff, Metacentros is preparing another innovative strategy called, "Administration of Projects and Not Departments." A different coordinator will be selected for every project and for every new program. The coordinator will be responsible for selecting members from each team: Market Research, Promotion, Sales, Financing, Engineering, Architecture, and Human Resources. Management will also participate in each project. The clients, the new store owners within a shopping complex, and the investors are also considered in this design.

Metacentros anticipates that this new configuration will allow better use of the company's resources and will be:

(1) Done without any top-down hierarchy;
(2) Be more dynamic;
(3) Improve the communication between groups;
(4) Ensure an interdependence between each area of work;
(5) Strengthen the team spirit;
(6) Increase profitability.

They expect this strategy to increase the understanding of the whole project, and improve the communication between people with different skills. It will also create more awareness as well as optimism about a very real project for which they are responsible, and develop more confidence and creativity in each member. The entire staff is very enthusiastic about this new design. They feel empowered with this responsibility and enthused about the impact that their work will have on Guatemala.

OUTLOOK FOR THE FUTURE

It is clear that Metacentros is an important entity in the transformation of a country in need. Guatemalan families at all socioeconomic levels have much better shopping options because of the Metacentros projects. Though the organization is still dependent upon the creative energy of Dr. Paiz to engender new projects within the organization, the seeds are there to grow more and more internal independence in the future. Metacentros is poised for the important transformation to a more creative corporate mind. Here is an organization that is not trying to "hang on" in a competitive way, but one that is making an important contribution to ensure social and economic development throughout Guatemala. In giving all its employees challenging opportunities individually, and as teams, Metacentros is truly a human endeavor.

„ЗОСТРО“ АО

8. RECOVERING A CULTURE OF PARTICIPATION IN RUSSIA

by

DAVID DUNN WITH ALEXEY KUZMIN

The story which follows is about the adventure
of helping Russians remember how to participate.
It is about helping them recover and nurture their
own historic culture of participation, which,
though forced to remain dormant during the Soviet
era, can now be placed at the service of both
profitable business and social development.

Describing Poland in terms also apropos of many nations in the former Soviet Union, Polish businessman Waldemar Borys, told a *Time* magazine reporter (*Time*, March 1, 1993), "It's strange, so much building amidst so much crisis." The forces at work in the nations of the former Soviet Union do indeed form a precarious balance of demolition and reconstruction. Take Russia, for example. Because a legal framework does not yet protect business interests, business leaders must resort to extralegal and seemingly irrational means to guard their own investments and operations.

Diversification for survival reaches the level of absurdity. Small ventures which are springing up intentionally divide their enterprise into several "small boats." A Russian friend describes a firm that makes small electronic parts, buys oil, and repairs autos. "If one operation sinks, the company can still survive in another," he says. Because it is so hard to produce goods, it takes less energy to experiment with private enterprise by simply buying and selling other people's goods. At the same time new business organizations are being created at a frantic pace. Many of the earliest new organizations were founded by former Communist Party or Komsomol leaders and capitalized with Party funds. Other new entrepreneurs announce themselves as "businessmen" without the foggiest idea of what they will do.

In this new business climate, failure is frequent and painful. For Russians it is a period of learning how to fail. Making money is no longer forbidden and money is suddenly a medium of real exchange. Some people do not yet know how to make it, and others who may have a lot of it, don't know what to do with it. For many, the question of how to make money and what to do with it has become a source of serious conflict between partners and long-time friends. And yet people enthusiastically continue to go into business, and attitudes toward private enterprise are changing rapidly. Parents who were embarrassed to speak about a son's work with a cooperative just four years ago now speak with pride about the son's new private company. Many business leaders take great pride in creating new workplaces.

In such a frightening business climate, it seems important to assess the realistic prospects for the future. A closer look at Russia—a complex society that produced autocratic Czars and sublime literature, sociopathic revolutionaries and Sputnik—reveals an unexpected surprise with relevance for business development. A heritage of participation and teamwork lies just beneath the surface of the Russian consciousness. Ask almost any Russian with a love of tradition, and a string of relevant proverbs comes easily to the mind:

- "One head is good, but two heads are better."
- "One person in the field is not a soldier."
- "If everyone gives a small piece of cloth, the beggar can be clothed."

Traditions of participation spread across many areas of Russian life. A delightful symbol of traditional participatory practice is the "tamada," the Russian master of ceremonies of marriages and celebrations. Russians smile as they recall that tamadas are usually pleasantly extroverted persons who know funny anecdotes, tell stories well, and are often good singers. Tamadas are invited to lead celebrations precisely because they know how to keep everyone happily involved; they know the procedures for participation. The tamada thus represents a traditional profession and can also serve as an intriguing metaphor for a Russian way of life—and of doing business— based on creative participation. In a culture steeped in tradition, use of the example of a tamada is a perfect way to introduce participatory process in management. The story which follows is about the adventure of helping Russians remember how to participate. It is about helping them recover and nurture their own historic culture of participation, which, though forced to remain dormant during the Soviet era, can now be placed at the service of both profitable business and social development.

Participation is not easy in a society coming apart at the seams; chaos begs the question of participation. The precarious restructuring of the Russian economy is raising havoc with the lives of ordinary Russians, while at the same time making it possible for an economic elite to become wealthy overnight. The ongoing struggle to redefine the balance of political power seems, at best, to lead to paralysis, and at worst, to a reactionary return to totalitarianism. In the face of such daunting social challenges, Russia's potential in a global marketplace seems decidedly gloomy.

Yet the opportunities for profit seem so great and the contribution to international security so important that corporations around the globe must enter the Russian marketplace, like it or not. Companies willing to brave this uncertainty face complex calculations of risk and return, with their strategies for minimizing the former and maximizing the latter largely untested. The nagging question—Is there any real hope for a return on investment?—confronts every corporation contemplating the Russian marketplace. As these companies survey the Russian business landscape, however, they discover a most promising sign of Russian business acumen. The Moscow-based Process Consulting Company (PCC) is a successful Russian business helping clients creatively participate in the transformation of their own enterprises, government agencies, social institutions, and communities.

PROCESS CONSULTING COMPANY

In September, 1993, PCC—in Russian, Kompanya Protsess Konsalting—celebrated its first anniversary as a small consulting firm whose founding partners work full time in the field of organization development. Like many Russians doing business together, PCC's partners—Alexey Kuzmin, its Director, Nicolae Tatarinov, its Business Manager, as well as Alexander Chesnokov and Vladimir Balakirev, Organization Development Consultants—have been associated as professional colleagues and friends for many years. They represent a vanguard of innovative consultants introducing techniques of participation to those business and social leaders emerging throughout Russia today. When the old laws governing cooperatives were revised in 1990 to permit for-profit corporations, Alexey became the Director of a new firm with interests in language training and business tours, protection of intellectual property, and consulting.

But by the time Alexey and I met at a conference in Moscow before the abortive coup in August, 1991, he and his colleagues were already thinking about developing their own organizational development consulting firm. The struggle these four remarkable men went through during 1992, while deciding to form their own company, would be familiar to many people in business in other parts of the world. Because Russians consider a corporation's mission to be something akin to an organization's vocation or higher calling, the four colleagues talked for months about their new firm's focus and aim. They debated how large their team should be and wondered if they could generate enough business to support themselves. Each agonized over the decision to leave secure employment to join a start-up team.

Their stories illustrate the laborious process by which many Russians disentangle themselves from their Soviet past. Alexey Kuzmin was graduated with a degree in engineering from the Moscow Machine Tool and Small Tool Institute in 1979, where he specialized in computer control of machine tools. As a young engineer working in industry during the early 1980s, he developed several inventions along with an interest in creative solutions to technical and industrial problems, and made, as well, a commitment to educating inventors. He joined a group of young engineers and scientists who founded the Moscow Institute for Technical Creative Work (MOITT) in 1981. Using a do-it-yourself, "bootstraps" approach, this core of innovators created a two-year program to help fellow scientists and engineers understand and develop their creative potential for solving difficult technical and industrial problems. Because MOITT quickly developed a reputation for creative teaching, there was intensive competition for a place in its program. During the 1980s, many successful inventors and several of Moscow's first wave of successful business leaders graduated from the MOITT program. Feedback from these graduates led to a surprising discovery. As Alexey recalls:

> To our surprise we learned that what was so exciting for people was not the methods we taught, but the environment we created. The key for people at this difficult time in our history was the atmosphere of openness and participation. People liked our methods. We helped people acknowledge themselves as creative human beings by facilitating their self-education. It was a dialogue, it involved joint work, it was fun, and they started being creative.

Alexander Chesnokov, the oldest member of the PCC team with 15 years experience as an engineer in construction and medical equipment, worked with Alexey at MOITT. In 1984, Alexander began creative problem-solving work in the Tupalov Design Bureau, famous for some of Russia's best aircraft designs. Alexander, who at one point in his career had been a professional dance instructor and who to this day remains a thoughtful philosopher, recalls a new direction that was emerging in his own and Alexey's thinking:

> Alexey and I noticed in our work with groups of people that creative achievement was closely associated with the psychological atmosphere of the group. This was my motivation for working on a degree in psychology at Moscow State University. I felt closer to the world of people than the world of technology.

A powerful entrepreneurial chemistry was at work among the Russians learning from Western visitors during the late 1980s and early 1990s. American psychologists helped people trained as engineers see the importance of psychological factors in organizational behavior. Others trained as educators saw the need for new organizational forms and management skills. This contact with Western consultants whetted an appetite for creating independent businesses and initiated an interest in a new professional role: organization development consultant.

Many creative young thinkers in Russia in the late 1980s were drawn to Moscow State University's Faculty of Psychology, a center of ferment in its own right. Faculty member Dr. Julia Gippenreiter, a leading Russian psychologist, was a mentor for many students including Alexey and Alexander. She introduced many of her students to the American psychologists and consultants who were among the first Westerners to work with professional colleagues in Russia. Alexey recalls the impact of hearing the prominent American psychologist, Dr. Carl Rogers, speak in Moscow: "It was one of the most important days in my life; the founder of humanistic psychology was speaking about things I believe, that each human being has creative potential that must be nurtured."

Vladimir Balakirev joined Alexey's and Alexander's circle while at Moscow State University. He was interested in group work for self-awareness and management development, and wrestled with leaving a secure public sector job in the social services to join the PCC team. Nicolae Tatarinov had been a trusted friend of Alexey's for over a decade and had been intimately involved in business discussions from the start.

When I entered the picture in August, 1991, Alexey and his colleagues were in the early stages of developing their business identity and strategy. I indicated to Alexey that I was interested in living and working in Russia. By early 1992, he and his team had decided to take me on as a strategic partner because of my experience in group facilitation and similar interests in organizational development. From the start, the aim of our partnership was to introduce new group process tools that would complement techniques developed by the PCC team in Russia. It was my opinion that methods for group reflection and discussion, for social and organizational analysis, and for participatory strategic planning would be immensely useful to Russians.

At the same time, I was interested in learning how these methods and approaches might be modified to meet the unique needs of Russian clients. Alexey and I agreed that the situation in Russia was so urgent, and the need for effective tools for participation so timely, that we developed a way to collaborate in making these tools immediately available. Alexey and I launched a methods transfer process during September, 1992, with a demonstration strategic planning event for the PCC team, a public facilitation methods seminar for Moscow organization development consultants, and two strategic planning workshops for a client in Siberia. These events were so well received that they precipitated a series of meetings in which the PCC team members re-evaluated their business strategy. They believed that facilitation, especially facilitation of participatory strategic planning, was a critically important new service that could be profitably offered to their clients.

Company Profile

Name of company	Zostro Corporation
Headquarters location	Moscow, Russia
Company product focus	Residential construction and commercial interior renovations
Leader and title	Gennady Kurepin, President
Last fiscal year-end sales (1992-93)	U.S. $200,000
Profit percent on sales (3 qtrs)	U.S. $15,000
Number of employees	Approximately 1,000, with 10-150 employees each working in 21 interrelated company units

Over the next year and one-half, opportunities to try out and to share their new tools came in unexpected ways. Alexey led a participatory workshop for an appreciative group of school principals in Siberia. Vladimir caught the attention of both parents and children during a discussion in a school by using a group reflection model we had shared in our September seminar. Alexander taught his college age son, Dema, how to facilitate group discussions and Dema promptly transformed the atmosphere in his psychology class at Moscow Pedagogical State University by simply employing an orderly questioning process. The greatest payoff of our methods transfer, however, was the immediate interest in participatory strategic planning by businesses. Those CEOs, beset with mind-numbing political, economic, technical, and personnel challenges, were looking for ways to engage their managers in effective decision making, honest problem solving, and real action. In an absurdly fluid business environment, they were looking for ways to make serious management decisions without losing two or three months in the process. The stories of two such business leaders who sought PCC's assistance and who have been committed advocates for participation in management of their newly privatized firms make up the rest of this tale.

ZOSTRO CORPORATION, MOSCOW

Zostro Corporation was one of Alexey's first clients. Alexey met Zostro President, Gennady Kurepin, in January, 1991 when Kurepin was the head of the Zodiac Cooperative, a small construction cooperative producing prefabricated wall panels and building blocks. At the time, Zodiac had an annual income of not more than 200,000 rubles (about U.S. $4,000). Gennady Kurepin is a tall, athletic man whose soft-spoken, attentive manner hides an ability to provide tough, aggressive leadership. Kurepin asked Alexey and his colleagues to help assess Zodiac's potential for leadership in building materials, manufacturing, and apartment construction. They began work in early 1991 by helping Zodiac managers envision the future of the cooperative. Privatization was the central goal and evaluating and refining the organizational structure were the essential first steps in the process. The PCC team used a Business Evaluation Workshop to help Zodiac managers evaluate the current state of their business and to provide a baseline profile so they could evaluate their own development over time. In this workshop clients brainstorm—the Russian word means "brain attack"—the elements of the worst organization imaginable.

Typical Russian managers delight in this brainstorming session of negatives, but can still seriously discuss the desirable characteristics revealed when negative features are turned into their positive mirror images. Teams create rating scales for each positive organizational characteristic, and decide the current status of each one by negotiating the position of rating marks along the scale. In this discussion, team members describe and analyze the dynamics related to each of these factors at work in their organization. Six months after an initial workshop, clients reconvene to consider their previous ratings and to re-rate their organization's effectiveness. Reflection reveals a new picture of the dynamics of change in their organization. Team members confidently analyze the causes of change, for better or worse, and plan strategies for improvement and problem solving.

During the months following their evaluation and planning workshops, Zostro Corporation was formed out of the Zodiac Cooperative. Overnight Zostro became a major construction and construction materials conglomerate with companies operating in ten locations nationally and with an annual income exceeding 200,000,000 rubles (U.S. $200,000 at the rate of 1000 rubles to the dollar). Amidst the triple threat of privatization, rapid growth, and hyperinflation, the Zostro managers experienced their daily work as pressurized and chaotic; life was rushed, changing, and uncertain. To help Zostro managers keep ahead of the chaos around them, the PCC team has had to become an ongoing partner working regularly with the Zostro man-

Company Profile	
Name of company	Primoroski Sugar Corporation
Industrial focus	Processed sugars and sugar byproducts
Headquarters location	Ussurisk, Russia (50 miles north of Vladivostok)
Leader and title	Alexander Khomenko, Director-General
1992 sales	U.S. $52,000,000
1992 profit	20%
Number of employees	1,500

agement team. Joint seminars with visiting British or North American managers sparked new images of management. Monthly workshops were held to address current operational challenges: how to recruit qualified professionals, how to clarify and solve management problems, and how to measure and evaluate performance. Alexey reflects:

> When the Zostro management team confronts difficulties and has to make serious decisions, Gennady Kurepin calls us. The managers appreciate our participation because we don't make decisions for them; we help them work them out themselves. Our Zostro partners feel they need our participation as, let us say, guardians of technology. Because we work in such close contact, participatory approaches are becoming a part of Zostro's culture.

In January, 1993, Mr. Kurepin decided to use the strategic planning process I had shared with Alexey and his team in September, 1992. Alexey reports that the Zostro staff liked the participatory approach and comments, "We brought an environment and methods that worked for them. They achieved better results in a shorter time." The Zostro managers created the following six-part company vision:

(1) Create an industrial construction company competitive in a global marketplace;
(2) Develop and implement new technologies;
(3) Achieve and maintain a high level of technical excellence;
(4) Preserve the environment;
(5) Create a flexible organizational structure;
(6) Attract people willing to work with high integrity and competence.

The turmoil and flux of Zostro's business environment have made implementation of their strategic vision plan extremely difficult. The winter of 1993 was a particularly difficult time and the management team had to take radical action so that the Zostro organizational structure could survive. Twenty-one independent but interrelated ventures were created, all related in some way to residential construction or renovation of commercial interiors. Some of the companies will handle construction; others will produce windows, roofs, or other building components. Zostro will handle overall management, but the operating companies will contract with each other. Zostro's challenge is to quickly line up major construction contracts that can use the products and services of several of the operating companies.

Gennady Kurepin and the Zostro management team continue to rely on PCC to lead participatory workshops "in-house." The ongoing partnership with PCC has produced a level of trust in which Zostro's managers are able to confront daunting challenges openly and creatively. As Alexey notes, "We are able to create conditions where people are able to be more creative, cooperative, integrative, and organized." Mr. Kurepin wants to build participatory approaches into the cultures of Zostro's 21 small operating companies, which range in size from 10 to 150 employees each. But for the moment, even with PCC's involvement, external forces continue to raise havoc with even the most gifted efforts of Zostro's management team, and the company's survival, stability, and profitability are yet to be assured.

PRIMORSKI SUGAR, USSURISK

Another company with its own challenges relating to privatization is making a name for itself as one of the most profitable businesses in the Russian Federation. Located in Ussurisk, seven time zones east of Moscow near the Pacific Ocean, Primorski Sugar is one of PCC's newest clients. In September, 1992, Andrew Bisorovni, an employee of Venture Invest, the firm that represents Primorski's interests in Moscow, attended Alexey's and my public seminar on facilitator methods. He was impressed with the experience and with what he learned about PCC. Because he thought that PCC might be able to help Primorski deal with some of its management challenges, Alexey was invited to visit Ussurisk the following month.

The city of Ussurisk, a major industrial center serving much of far eastern Siberia, is located 50 miles north of Vladivostok in a region called

Primorski Krai. The Primorski Sugar plant imports raw sugar from Australia and Southeast Asia, and its 1,500 employees annually produce 170,000 tons of refined white sugar, as well as other sugar products and yeast. Plans are under way to build a distillery as well as a construction materials plant to recycle the by-products of the refining process. When Alexander Khomenko was elected Director-General of the plant by employees in 1988, he inherited a discouraging history of unsolved problems, e.g., an antiquated plant, a history of low employee initiative and achievement, as well as sporadically scheduled management meetings that were unproductive when they were held. Khomenko, a 44-year old manager with experience in construction, but not sugar refining, concluded that the only way to solve the plant's problems was to challenge the old guard management either to change or leave.

Most left and Khomenko has been hand picking the most highly qualified young professionals from all over the former Soviet Union ever since. In his four years as Director-General, Alexander Khomenko put together a new team of six deputy directors for marketing, finance, research and development, construction, production, and personnel. His finance person has a reputation for being the brightest in Ussurisk; his R&D man came to Ussurisk from Moscow; for production, the top sugar technology expert in the former USSR came to Ussurisk from Ukraine. Alexey accepted the invitation to visit Ussurisk in October, 1992, to meet Primorski's Director-General, and to discuss the needs of the plant. Alexander Khomenko is an avid sportsman who uses sports metaphors to describe his hopes for Primorski's future in sugar refining. He had decided he needed help in building "a perfect, effective team." About his future plans he now says very decisively, "I knew we had to move step-by-step—from village to region, to republic, to world champions."

Alexey and the PCC team began work with the Primorski Director-General and its new deputy directors in February, 1993. Members of this management team had just become the actual owners of the company and had advertised their new company for the first time several months earlier. As Alexey recalls:

> They were all very interested in developing their new business. Each manager wanted to be able to participate and to express his point of view. They wanted enough time to be able to hear and understand each other.

The retreat, which Alexey and the PCC team designed for the management group, was held at the comfortable Hotel Ocean on the Pacific Coast. The PCC team proposed that the group get better acquainted, clarify each other's functional roles, analyze the dynamics of their organization, and conclude with a three-day strategic planning workshop. Alexey knew that Khomenko had hired a group of strong-minded, independent professionals, and he reasoned that it would be necessary to help these new deputy directors examine their relationships and affirm their interdependence. They would need to make an intentional decision to be a management team before they could take on the challenge of strategic planning. Alexey commented, "We knew if they chose interdependence, they were a team; if they had not chosen interdependence, they would not have been ready for the strategic planning."

In a Team Roles and Relationships Workshop, Alexey and his colleagues ask their clients to identify the responsibilities or functions of each team member's position. Individuals brainstorm the responsibilities of all positions. The group then discusses each position's responsibilities, and works out a consensus about the key responsibilities of each position and how they can be implemented most effectively. The group first listens to comments from the person in question and then to reactions from the CEO. Managers then write down their views of the responsibilities they share with colleagues. In pairs, managers clarify and negotiate each other's view of joint responsibilities until a consensus is formed about the essential responsibilities of each. A diagram of these working relationships is drafted on a large wall poster and participants discuss insights about this illustration of interdependence. Following this Team Roles and Relationships Workshop, the Primorski deputy directors were ready for an intensive three-day strategic planning workshop. One result of this burst of activity in the strategic planning session—they worked from 10 a.m. to 11 p.m. each day—was a picture of the management teams's vision which they said would stimulate the company to:

- Create a world-class, high-tech sugar refinery;
- Become competitive in a world market;
- Employ highly qualified professionals;
- Lead in the development of Russia's new market economy;
- Pay the best salaries in Ussurisk;
- Address employees' social issues, such as housing, within one year.

In commenting on his experience with the workshop, the Deputy Director for Marketing said:

> It was the first time in my life that I was fully motivated and interested for three days. I didn't want to sleep. It felt like I was watching an interesting movie; I wanted to see the next reel immediately, but had to wait until the next day.

The management team created a set of action plans for the following month and decided to work together for two to three hours each Monday to check progress on each other's action plans. Alexander Khomenko subsequently reported, "People have become motivated. They are developing plans themselves and everyone is fulfilling his own plan. Each week they check with each other and ask, 'Are we moving forward?'" Alexey adds:

> The deputies feel that their meetings are more effective due to what they call 'the approach,' i.e., participation that involves step-by-step listening to each person's point of view, coming to consensus, and fulfilling plans. Mr. Khomenko liked his people's motivation. He is a talented manager in a unique position. He wants to facilitate and not push; his goal is to build a participative culture carefully and exactly. Actually, when he sees that people aren't taking part in decision making, he becomes upset.
> We like him. His beliefs and values fit ours.

As the relationship with Primorski develops, Alexander Khomenko reveals more of his own aspirations for the future: "I want to be a coach; I want my partners to become more and more active and responsible."

Alexey further reflects on how participatory planning and team building are new experiences for a Russian manager:

> In the past, people had no experience working in an organized and structured way where everyone participated. They used to work in hierarchical organizations where people were only told what to do. It is an exciting process to move from silence and fulfilling orders to taking part in decision making and problem solving. Now Russian managers, including the team at Primorski, consider brainstorming, clarification, and negotiation a natural process which they find both useful and enjoyable. They appreciate coming to consensus on questions that had been difficult or impossible to address in the past.

As Primorski's relationship with PCC has developed, it has taken on its own unique character. In some respects the process of refining sugar has helped systematize and organize the dramatic changes that are taking place at Primorski. The company is gaining recognition for being a high-energy enterprise with tremendous future potential. The PCC team helps the strong-minded deputies, hired for their individual expertise, bridge professional gaps to build a joint management structure. Alexey says the management team members are working like fanatics, even on Saturdays and Sundays, because they love their work. Alexander Khomenko is an energetic leader in his own right who commands both respect and fear as a manager. But like a highly disciplined team sportsman, his commitment to participatory approaches in management arises from the fact that systematic participation is what gives his team its power.

BUILDING A WORLD-CLASS BUSINESS CULTURE

It is too early in what will surely be a decades-long process of building a world-class Russian business culture to make sweeping statements, but Alexey and I predict that Russian business managers will be among the most innovative and successful in the world. Russians have had to survive against preposterous odds and are cunning in their ability to invent something from nothing. If one adds the gifts of intuition and openness to the realm of the human spirit, one has the makings of a powerful alchemy for entrepreneurial achievement. The striking feature of the work of PCC's clients, who are struggling simultaneously with survival and invention, is its similarity to work that might be done in a sophisticated business environment almost any-where in the world.

And yet, most of PCC's approaches were conceived entirely within a Russian context. The inescapable conclusion is that whatever the cultural context, there is a natural affinity among managers for participation and for an orderly progression of thought to a productive conclusion. That Russian business leaders with huge organizational challenges so willingly undertake rigorous self-analysis and strategic planning is a hopeful sign. The commitment of PCC's clients to using participatory approaches to shape organizational change is another indicator, perhaps signaling the potential for commitment to participation as a norm in Russian society at large. However, it would be naive and misleading to insinuate that a culture of participation is the main feature of contemporary Russian society, or that participatory approaches will be welcomed by every enterprise and organization.

The contrary is probably closer to the truth. But Russia is basically a group culture, and not a hero culture, a fact which the Communist Party ignored to its own undoing. This participatory feature of Russian society is clearly illustrated by the intimate networks of family and friends which are the basis for getting things done, solving problems, and, indeed, for celebration. This observation brings us again to the image of a tamada facilitating a celebration of marriage. Alexey mimics a tamada, "Now, dear guests, let us ask the young couple, 'What do you feel?' 'What do you think?'" A consummate tamada in his own right, Alexey reflects:

> The tamada keeps his eyes on the guests and can not drink too much himself. He sings songs and organizes the process so everything happens at just the right time, so everybody feels good, and so everyone takes part. In fact, this has become a profession for some people today who are actually making good money facilitating celebrations.

The Russians I know and have worked with are full of ideas, energy, and hopes for dealing with life in a creative way. In fact, they are so full of opinions and plans that they seem to boil over in a group discussion or planning workshop, unless they have the clear guidance and encouragement of a facilitator like a tamada. With such direction, though, they immediately catch on to a way of working that begins with their own best ideas and ends by formulating the best insights of the group. When they have finished this work, they love to celebrate. It is clear from a significant body of experience that many Russian business leaders see the benefits of participatory planning that helps their employees achieve meaningful, tangible results. Such planning assists in ensuring the soundness of at least two elements in the complex calculus of business development: organizational design and effective personnel performance.

One of the most powerful strategies to help Russian managers deal with these two elements is a joint Russian/U.S. team that demonstrates the values and skills of participation and partnership in business. When a Russian and a U.S. facilitator co-lead a planning workshop, an extraordinary kind of cultural bridging takes place. Russians report a startling release of energy and a recovery of internal power, stability, clarity, and creativity. Alexey and I often observe this release of energy when we work with clients, many of whom are experiencing being on a Russian-U.S. team for the first time. A major paradigm shift seems to take place in people's minds: broken, chaotic thoughts and resolves seem to fit together better when these clients experience our bicultural team. It may be that the wounds of Cold War deceit and manipulation heal in the atmosphere of candor and safety established by a Russian-U.S. team. Perhaps the affirmation of the Russians' creative intelligence and cultural wisdom by an international partner supports a sense of internal assurance that inspires Russian people to work together effectively in spite of external chaos.

Whatever the dynamics, cultural bridging is a powerful tool for business development. Cultural bridging also is one of the major benefits of participatory processes, which are inherently open and lend themselves, therefore, to unique constructions and configurations in situations that remain divisive without participation. The PCC staff members are themselves a kind of cultural bridge; they both embody and transcend their own Russian culture in their ability to work with and use the gifts of other cultures. The PCC experience is also an example of entrepreneurial prowess and of a new kind of Russian professional firm entering the global marketplace. The team at PCC works to embody in its own work style the very values it recommends to clients. Alone and with international partners, the PCC team models the benefits of effective participation in management of an enterprise. Their clients' cultures of participation are emerging in the struggle to create order out of chaos—profit out of human enterprise.

V.

MOTIVATING THE WORKFORCE

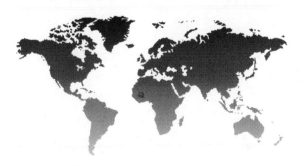

JK Synthetics Ltd.

9. CREATING THE SECOND TAJ MAHAL

by
CYPRIAN D'SOUZA

*The hard technology—the engineering side of resetting
machines or statistical data control—is one aspect of the
manufacturing industry. Soft technology—the process of
leadership and team development—is the other important
dimension. If leaders do not know how to receive
information, how to plan, reflect, and invite
participation, then all the hard technology in the
world will not help them. Working to keep a balance
between the two is the art of leadership.*

The celebration started with ice cream—as much as one wanted. On a warm Tuesday in October, 1992, a large refrigerated truck pulled up in front of the JK Fibre plant in Jhalawar, in the eastern hills of Rajasthan, a border state that separates India and Pakistan. The doors of the truck opened and immediately JK's personnel staff started distributing generous scoops of frosty goodness to everyone in sight. The truck remained there 24 hours, time enough for all three shifts to come and go from work. They never finished all the ice cream the truck brought.

"That was the day we made 60 tons of fiber!" brags M. K. Mathur, General Manager of the four-year-old unit which manufactures acrylic fiber for textile industries. He speaks proudly:

> We'd never done that before. I knew by the end of 'B' shift that we would surpass our best daily production figure. We'd been averaging 50 tons a day throughout September. But to reach 60 was ice cream on the cake. That's when I ordered the truck to come with it.

It was a festive celebration indeed. Spontaneous dancing had broken out on the shop floor. The 350 member team of technicians and managers created a miracle and brought the plant back from what had been the threat of permanent closure barely six months earlier.

"The managers were in the pit of despair," recalls Mathur of that meeting in January, 1992 when management met to discuss the company situation. On their list of woes: dismal production levels, missed targets, late deliveries, inconsistent quality. The biggest quality complaints—excessive moisture in the fiber, the presence of long fiber, and poor dye affinity—meant customers were leaving them right and left. Money was tight; the company coffers were squeezed for cash. Owing to heavy capital investments in the Jhalawar facility, the parent company, J. K. Synthetics, would not offer further financial support. "Things reached the point where it was no longer feasible to keep the plant going," agreed Ramapati Singhania, full-time Director and the visionary force behind the fledgling unit. "The raw material and electricity alone would have cost us more than we could obtain by way of prices." Everything ground to a halt. At that point Singhania called in LENS Services Private Ltd., a consultant firm from New Delhi, and explained that something had to be done or the plant would be permanently closed.

The LENS team, familiar with JK Fibre operations from previous work they had done to analyze quality improvement issues, was well aware of the problems. One consultant remembers:

> I told Mr. Singhania that I thought it was time to look at a whole systems approach, one that would take every part of the operation into consideration. No half-measures were going to serve them for long. It was 'pull out all the stops' or 'no go.'

A big gamble? Perhaps, but there was simply too much to lose by not at least giving it a try.

CREATING A NEW COMPANY MILIEU

In 1989, the new plant in Jhalawar was Ramapati Singhania's dream for initiating a working culture style quite divergent from the traditional operation in Kota, JK's first acrylic plant, located two hours away from Jhalawar by car. The Kota factory pioneered in bringing acrylic technology to India in the late 1970s and paved the way to develop what was an approximately 100,000 tons per year capacity industry. The Indian market consumes about 60,000 tons; the rest is planned for export. For over a decade, Singhania's plant had the acrylic fiber monopoly all to itself, but by 1989 there were two new players. Learning from the experience of the Kota plant, Ramapati Singhania was eager to make the Jhalawar plant a model of innovative management technology. Changes began to be made, starting with a refocusing of management policy from governance to the involvement of people. Everyone recruited into the new plant was a graduate, mostly with engineering and technical diplomas.

Workspace at the new plant is completely open, with cubicles replacing closed offices. Computerized operations hum out the latest information on production figures, raw material consumption, and sales each morning. All financial and operational data are available to anyone. This openness even applies to salary figures, which are posted on the bulletin boards for all employees to read. The decentralized operations established at this plant mean that individuals take responsibility for their own quality inspection, maintenance, and housekeeping. In other words there are no supervisors to give orders or helpers to carry papers around. Managers are required to fill out their own forms, and to keep their own files. If you need a letter typed, you do it yourself. In fact, there are few papers to carry around. There are no memos. As much as possible, all communication is verbal, face-to-face. The idea is to take the opportunity to make personal contact with people and talk things through, rather than generate paper commands. Devoid of secretaries to provide the usual tea services, an open tea area was set up where all employees could serve themselves.

The creation of this open office space dramatized the breaking down of the management hierarchy. No walls divide departments. Managers' desks are placed in the center of the hub of activity, with open access to all staff employees. This arrangement was critical for the improvement of interdepartmental communications. To support the open team approach, work starts every morning with physical exercise in teams. Everyone wears a uniform, identification badge, and eats meals together in the canteen. When the director is in the plant, he eats there also. Like everyone else, he wears a uniform and an identification badge. His office, too, is open, a cubicle on the main floor. Although he is not involved in the day-to-day operations of the plant, Singhania prefers to keep a keen eye on the financial management end of the business. His professional, yet informal, style sets the tone for the whole organization, whose company culture reflects openness, minimum hierarchy, and equitable relationships.

Singhania introduced these modern concepts into a culture deeply rooted in traditional structures of hierarchy. In prevailing Indian business culture, there is power in guarding knowledge and information. Information sharing can be extremely threatening, so, initially, his ideas met with strong resistance. Many in the management team were afraid that good people would quit because the changes were too radical. Or worse, they feared that some people who could not adjust to new ways of working would stay on and simply be ineffective and lost in the new structure.

Most radical of all the changes is a "gain sharing" incentive plan for all employees. Employee incentives are added to a modest base salary; a team calculates these monthly incentives based on as many as nine parameters, such as, raw material usage, reductions in receivables, quality norms, etc. Each year a team draws up a new set of parameters after extensive discussions among employees. For instance, a current parameter measures customer satisfaction. In designing this list of customer priorities, JK Fibre brought customers together to decide what the criteria would be, choosing nine factors which were important to the customer's success, such as quality, delivery according to schedule, or accounts' reconciliation within a month.

At the close of each quarter, an independent agency conducts a survey asking customers to rate how JK Fibre performed on each factor. The data weightage of each factor, as compiled from the surveys, is computed to determine the amount of the gain sharing award each employee will receive. Incentives account for a major share of employees' salaries; so, there is big money at stake. People take this very seriously. When all the parameters are met, employees on the shop floor stand to make some of the highest salaries seen in India. In discussing the methods used in responding to the JK survey, one customer said, "We really think hard what rating we put down, because we know it affects an employee's income." For the person on the shop floor, accurate feedback from customers becomes the vital link in a whole systems approach to work performance. "I'm more aware now," says one JK technician, "of my function in relation to all other areas such as packing, finance, or spare parts, because they also have to succeed if we are to match the customer's requirement."

PULLING OUT ALL THE STOPS

After introducing all of these open and participatory methods and establishing a forward-looking company culture, company managers found it hard to believe that all of these innovative ideas did not yield the desired results. Everything that had been put into place, in terms of the two and one-half year investment in Jhalawar, was on the line in early 1992. Still, production was creeping along between 25-30 tons a day. The will to produce was gone, and frustration and despair were rife. Because Singhania was willing to back up whatever the LENS consultant team thought would turn things around, he decided that JK's senior management team needed to be the ones to invite the consultants to work with them as a measure of their seriousness to find a long-range solution to the company problems. Late in January, M.K. Mathur, General Manager, visited Delhi to talk over a 12 month proposal with the LENS consultant team. Mathur muses:

> What sold me was the consultant team's vision for what the Jhalawar unit could be. They asked me if, in the five years that I have until I retire, I'd like to be known for creating a second Taj Mahal, this time in the desert of Rajasthan. I said, Yes.

It is an overnight train ride from Delhi to Kota and then several hours by car to reach the plant. Mathur left Delhi with a lot to think about and more hope for the situation in Jhalawar.

Several days later as the LENS team met with the management team, they decided to test the team's determination to go for a comprehensive solution. Since the LENS consultants envisioned a five-year 'whole systems transformation' for JK Fibre, the keystone of their plan for the first stage was to build a committed core team and begin to put self-managed teams in place. They planned to build on the open structure that was already present in the factory, opening up further interchange and communication patterns. A concerted focus on leadership skills for everyone would be essential for strengthening the interior 'fiber' of the workforce. They presented to the senior management team the following conditions to be agreed upon before entering into a working arrangement for the project of whole systems transformation. The senior management team must be willing to:

- Change any system, structure, or procedure. Nothing would be sacred.
- Suspend any financial measure of success or failure of the project for one year. They would have to find other criteria to measure success.
- Require the core team to be the change agents. Nothing will happen in the plant unless a group of people decides to make it change.

These three conditions became the bedrock decision point for the project. The LENS team asked the company's management team to think the conditions over and decide before further discussions could begin. It took the top management team two to three weeks to decide to proceed with the three conditions. Owing to a raw materials shortage, the plant shut down totally in February and March. Beginning in April, while the plant was still closed, senior management met for five days to begin to form a coordinated plan of action. "I think it was the first time we ever felt like a team," commented one of the members. "It was a powerful event that really bound us together."

LAUNCHING A NEW STRATEGY

The five-day April Launch session with the senior management team was a mixture of team development, organizational planning, and individual growth through mind/body/spirit exercises. They talked about what was important to each individual, professionally and personally. "You can work next to a person year after year, and never really know him," acknowledged one team member. The session balanced drawing up a thorough three-month implementation plan with a right-brained focus on singing, creating a corporate story, song, and symbol, and even a short course on reflexology. The reflexology session was to prove particularly moving, as managers were called upon to touch and massage the feet of their colleagues. In a country where feet are considered a sacred part of the body, this was a critical exercise in the honoring of each person, as well as a way of laying the foundations of connecting in a very personal way as a team. Following this session, as the group members prepared to initiate their plan, high on the list of priorities was how to start up the factory again. This was no easy task, given that no new capital was available and credit would not be provided to them since they were not producing anything. It was a classic 'Catch-22' situation.

So, what did they do? The team came up with a bold plan to go to their customers. "How difficult it seemed," groaned Mathur, shrugging his shoulders. "Can you imagine what it was like to go back to our customers, the same customers who complained last year about the poor quality of our goods and the late deliveries, and now ask for money?" The team decided they had to convince customers that it was a new day for JK; that they had a plan to deliver on. Organized in groups of twos and threes, they visited every customer. They talked about their commitment to produce top quality acrylic fiber which would more than meet expectations. It worked! The teams collected enough in cash advances to purchase the raw materials needed. Within two weeks of the day when they created the plan, the team started up the plant.

In May, 1992, the plant produced an average of 30 tons a day; in June, July, and August, more than 50 tons daily. Each month surpassed the last, breaking all previous records, reaching a peak production of 60 tons the day in October when they had the ice cream celebration. Total figures for 1992 were 9,700 tons (the lion's share was May to December) compared to 6,000 tons in 1991. The team achieved this increase without any new equipment, with the same people, same machinesbut with a new spirit.

ELIMINATING THE ROOT CAUSE

The overall strategy for the first 13-month phase decided upon during the April team session, called the April Launch, was three-track:
*   Develop the leadership and expertise of the core management team;

- Effect necessary improvements through specialized teams (CATs or Corrective Action Teams);
- Focus on organizational webbing through improved communications between departments and across levels.

The first target of the newly unified management team was to clarify whether they could produce 50 tons per day. To boost morale, it was important at this time for technicians to see managers working alongside them. This move broke down several of the barriers that existed between managers and technicians. The "owner concept" was therefore created, whereby managers "set an example." Thus, wherever a problem surfaced, a person in a managerial position would go personally and focus on it, encouraging technicians to solve the problem, and conveying that no matter how "insignificant" the error, it was important to the whole factory. The entire plant as a team, managers and technicians together, worked upwards of ten hours daily on the shop floor. Problems that arose were treated instantly, the sole objective being to keep operations running. At the end of a month, the unprecedented amount of 35 tons per day had been reached, with a corresponding improvement in quality. (In the making of acrylic, quality is directly dependent on smoothly running operations, thus increasing production levels, and also improving quality.) Flushed with its first victory, the plant surged ahead in its determination to reach the daily 50-ton target.

RECOMMITMENT TO COMMUNICATION

At the same time, techniques encouraging greater participation of all employees were slowly being incorporated into organizational life. The uniforms and a common canteen, which had been adopted from the outset within the Jhalawar complex, now truly reflected the company's open culture and the new changes in working relations among managers and technicians. Additionally, the concept of an "Open House," a forum held monthly for all employees to speak openly with management about factory problems, generated new ideas and cleared the air as well. Daily managerial meetings began in April, 1992. Previously, managers had met only once a month. In resolving the issues together, the management team experienced the gradual disappearance of departmental boundaries. For the first time managers began to form an understanding of the interrelatedness of their functions. The decisions and plans, made collectively, necessarily took into account the needs and requirements of all departments. Whereas previously managers had been preoccupied mainly with the completion of their departmental duties, now emphasis was placed on how to coordinate their activities with those of other departments in order to achieve a shared aim.

The senior management team set aside one day each month to report to each other on accomplishments, issues, and ideas in relation to the overall action plan. No one missed these sessions, called Review Forums. If someone could not make it, the meeting was rescheduled so that everyone could be present. The Review Forum day was an event from start to finish—lively, thought-provoking, and celebrative. Nothing was allowed to disturb the proceedings, even though the meeting was held on the factory premises. Once every quarter the core team took two days off-site to continue to build skills and work on individual development.

With the senior management core team leading the transformation process, many insights about creating good team spirit were learned. Some of the insights include:

- **Having team composition be voluntary and committed.** Once people volunteer, make certain they know the full responsibility for the entire task and require full attendance at all meetings.
- **Using victory lists.** List accomplishments, no matter how small. Make a visible list. This builds team spirit and a sense of momentum.
- **Putting everything in context.** Begin all introductions and reporting with a brief explanation answering the necessary questions of what, why, where, when, and how, especially the, "why." A good rule of thumb for agendas is, "The future before the past" and "the big picture before the details."
- **Making the working decor attractive.** The meeting space is the home of the team spirit. Well-constructed, colorful charts, graphs, and assignment lists impart a keen sense of discipline to the team. Keep them up-to-date and beautiful.
- **Balancing the meeting agenda.** Almost all meetings include the following segments: (1) Setting the tone—a brief conversation on a current event, or a reflection on an article/reading not directly related to the present task, to set the mood; (2) Reporting—brief and to the point, one-page summaries where possible;

(3) Planning—brainstorming or issue clarifications; (4) Assignments—everyone has a role to play. An hour is usually adequate for a well-facilitated meeting.

- **Honoring everyone.** Find ways to let the spotlight fall on everyone. Get people to their feet reporting and leading, and give insightful feedback individually on performance at a later time.
- **Celebrating as a team.** Find opportunities to have regular team celebrations. Build in spontaneous and surprising events. Have fun. Assess the team's spirit by the amount of laughter and the number of smiles present.

Once the April, 1992 Launch initiated the process, the consultant team spent an average of eight to ten days a month at the plant in Jhalawar working with the senior management core team, individually and collectively, through attendance at the Review Forums and Open House, and spending time on the shop floor. Meetings with Ramapati Singhania, once or twice a month, served as forums for the exchange of ideas and concepts, although Singhania encouraged the consultants to try out new approaches. Many of the discussions with Singhania focused on keeping the balance between soft and hard technology. The hard technology—the engineering side of resetting machines or statistical data control—is one aspect of the manufacturing industry. Soft technology—the process of leadership and team development—is the other important dimension. If leaders do not know how to receive information, how to plan, reflect, and invite participation, then all the hard technology in the world will not help them. Working to keep a balance between the two is the art of leadership.

CORRECTIVE ACTION TEAMS (CATS)

Long and short-term planning, unheard of in the past, became a crucial part of managerial discussions. Through the pooling of perspectives, managers had grasped the underlying causes of JK Fibre's predicament. With the high rise in production, the managers worked together to address accompanying changes that would support continued progress. Without a doubt, the introduction of CATs to JK Fibre gave the operation tremendous momentum. The CATs attack and quickly solve quality and system issues within a three-month timebound plan. Anywhere from 8 to 12 people from across functions serve on a CAT. They meet for a day or two to analyze a specific problem such as excessive moisture in the fiber (the cause of frequent customer complaints), or the frequent breakdown of electronic control systems. Using a set of tools for analysis, they examine the problem from every angle, looking for the root cause. Once the CAT members determine at least four of the possible approaches, a plan is then put together, assignments made, and work begun to solve it.

The Raw Material Unloading CAT, looking at the issue of delays in offloading chemicals, found a solution in three days which reduced unloading time from eight hours to two hours. Within another month, the CAT further reduced unloading time to one hour. The Hot Rollers CAT took a little longer. Acrylic fiber moves rapidly in a spiral path along 32 rollers being fed with computer controlled temperature jets of hot steam. The temperature variances, roller by roller, if not carefully maintained, produce the excessive moisture that frustrates textile manufacturers because too much moisture adds weight to the fiber. The manufacturer then ends up paying for water and not fiber. An extremely complex process, uniform temperature maintenance forced the CAT to take a full two to three months to tabulate all the temperature deviations, to discern the necessary corrective steps, and train co-workers to maintain the required temperature on the rollers. As a result the excess moisture content in the fiber was totally eliminated.

Because of the great sense of satisfaction that comes from resolving long-standing problems, employees volunteer and look forward to serving on a CAT. At any time four to five CATs are working on breakthroughs: Super Tenacity CAT (stretch ratio of the fiber), PC CAT (personal computer care), Free Flow Polymer CAT, People-Oriented CAT (dissatisfaction with personnel and administration attitudes and record keeping), Safe Work Environment CAT, and many more. The senior management team forms CATs out of the effective ideas that emerge from the Open House sessions, daily management meetings, or employee suggestions. The CATs are a living example of participation in action.

FACTORS FOR SUCCESS

This transformative process at JK Fibre has provided many lessons which point out the necessary factors for participative success:
- The essentiality of a company champion who has the authority and provides the context for the journey and process.
- A strong ethical and human values base within the leadership and organization.

- An open-minded leader who trusts the wisdom of the people and is detached from the need for immediate results.
- Regular study of and dialogue about edge thinking and its applicability to the corporate task and responsibility, both collectively and individually.
- Alertness to the paradigms, frameworks, patterns, and mental models that are operating in the team and organization.
- Awareness that the process evolves through constant dialogue about the internal and external realities, which calls for flexibility with the master plan. This does not detract from one's commitment to the larger objectives.
- A powerful collective vision of the organization and its potential which enables the organization to transcend the everyday anguish and pain of the change process.

INVESTING IN PEOPLE

In any change process, the necessity of keeping the entire organization informed and 'on board' is essential. At JK Fibre, a unique communication tool was a one-day company interchange meeting or 'Sabha'. Since production at the factory goes on around the clock, it was important to devise a plan which would involve every employee in one of four planned Sabha eventsone for each of the three shifts, and a fourth for general staff. The Sabhas, or company interchange meetings, are semi-annual events which give everyone an opportunity to talk through the company's vision and future plans, as well as a chance to initiate action proposals for each one's particular function. When a Sabha is held, within a period of four days, every single person in the company is part of an information flow system that produces alignment around new directions. Here again, the pace of the event is lively and filled with participation through workshops, reporting sessions, sharing of experiences, and singing. There are snacks and a closing banquet to complete the day's work. Representatives of the four Sabhas meet to compile a summary of results which are then highlighted in the weekly newsletter (in Hindi and English).

The training program, Leadership Skills for Participative Culture, is perhaps the largest training investment to date at JK Fibre. The primary focus of this program is to train persons in the skills of developing, leading, and nurturing teams. Three modules, each lasting three days, impart facilitation skills to 84 coordinators, or team leaders, who represent two to three members of each of the self-managed teams operating at JK Fibre. Training inputs include both personal development methods (pranayama (balanced breathing), journal writing, individual expression through art, and facilitation skills, methods of leading meetings artfully, problem solving, team building, etc.

The key impact of this training from the perspective of the participants is that it developed their self-confidence as team leaders. They now have facilitation skills that enable them to work and solve problems as a team. On the shop floor, as a result of the training, they sensed that they had created a better work environment and developed greater team consciousness. Many reported that their personalities were blossoming and that they sensed a greater commitment to improving themselves. Several participants indicated that as a result of their training, they experienced much more peace and harmony in their families because they had used the methods at home.

R. Singhania, A. P. Bajpai, JK Vice-President, and M. K. Mathur were present for the graduation ceremony held at the conclusion of the training program. At this celebration the graduates received a certificate illustrated with the banyan tree, dubbed the "giving tree," which graces the training center grounds. Singhania's support of the serious effort to retool minds and hearts was evident in his closing statement at the graduation exercise, "We will realize the impact of this work in five years."

PROMISE OF AN OPEN CULTURE

One year of the turnaround project is complete. The senior management team is putting together its assessment of where the Jhalawar plant is, and rebuilding the plan for the next phase. Many new ideas for how to use the information gleaned from customer meetings to increase employee participation or to improve export market strategies are foremost in people's minds. In January, 1993, the market for acrylic fiber totally collapsed owing to political unrest in the country, cheaper import of fiber, and an overcapacity of fiber in the market. Even if one produces and produces well, people are just not buying. So now a whole new market-orientation strategy must be developed. Meeting that challenge will greatly test the 350 member team as it embarks on the next phase in the transformation of JK Fibre.

_____of J.K. Fibre

has successfully completeda course in

Leadership Skills for a Participative Culture

at the Sir Padampat Management Training Centre, Amjhar

conducted by

LENS Services Private Limited

Mary Kurian D'Souza
Director
LENS Services Pvt. Ltd.

Mahendra Kumar Mathur
General Manager
J.K. Fibre

Ramapati Singhania
Whole Time Director
J.K. Synthetics, ATC Group

One would never expect to find a model of innovative thinking and practice in a modern management setting stuck away in a remote part of Rajasthan. The state can not even boast about having a school of management located within its boundaries. Historically known as the "place of kings" (Rajas is the word for kings.), fiercely tribal people, Rajput warriors (men and women) resisted all efforts to be subdued by the British; they maintain, even today in some parts, an unbroken succession of rulers for 44 generations. Could it be that Jhalawar's JK Fibre with all its innovations, its success, and its promise, is the jewel in the raja's crown? Could it be that JK Fibre is the modern day "living management school"?

Mills

10. CRISIS: THE ALLY OF PARTICIPATION

by
NANCY GROW

When the external market collapsed and an internal crisis
exploded at the same moment, directors of the Mills
Group[1] had to decide whether they would continue with
their dream of participation or return to autocratic
decision making. The temptation to return was strong.
Results could determine the survival or death of the company.

C risis is the name of the game in Brazilian industry. Over the past 30 years that country has seen military takeovers, nationalization of industry, movements toward free trade, a return to privatization of industry, inflation in four figures, stringent economic controls, no controls, booms and recessions. Running a company in conditions like these is like driving over very rough terrain. Nelson Piquet, a Brazilian hero of Formula One car racing, says that winning on the race track depends on a talented driver, a better car, the right teamwork, the right time, and a good dose of luck. The same combination could be said for winning in industry in Brazil.

---

[1]The Mills Group is known in Brazil by the name of the holding company, Mills Andaimes Tubulares do Brasil, S.A.

Over its 40 year history, Mills Andaimes Tubulares do Brasil, S.A. has weathered many crises. It has a talented "driver" in Andres Cristian Nacht, company President and owner. It also has a good product, scaffolding, and a good reputation for quality and service. It has a staff that combines youth and energy with wisdom and experience. And its good luck as a company was to hit a moment of internal and external crisis that required the staff to become a competent, participative team.

MILLS ANDAIMES TUBULARES AND THE MILLS GROUP

Mills was founded in Brazil in 1952, a spin-off from Mills Ltd., a company dealing with scaffolding in England and France. It introduced into Brazil steel tubing, and later, aluminum for scaffolding in building construction and civil engineering. Until 1986, it was a small company with a factory in Rio de Janeiro, and sales and rental offices in major cities of Brazil; yet it participated in some of the major construction efforts in the country, such as the 14 kilometer Rio/Niteroi Bridge and the hydroelectric dam at Itaipu.

The year 1986 was a benchmark at Mills, the beginning of a company transformation. Pulling out of an economic crisis in 1985, and recognizing the need for a new vision and new strategies, Mills contracted with the Institute of Cultural Affairs (ICA) for a three-day strategic planning event in April, 1986. This event is a process in which the participants themselves identify their corporate vision and the obstacles they confront in reaching it. They suggest strategies to deal with the obstacles and finally produce a timeline of tactics that will implement the strategies. That Mills strategic planning event is now recognized as a vital turning point in the company's growth and development. In the three-day April, 1986 workshop, managers projected a vision of expansion and growth that the company directors and owners had not articulated beforehand. In addition to expanding the usual markets for the company into materials for civil construction, the group discerned markets for services, such as industrial maintenance and leisure services (grandstands and platforms for sports and cultural events).

Shaping this company forecast later involved a certain amount of upheaval. However, the analysis of the contradictions they faced and their proposals to deal with them revealed professional strength and know-how they had not fully recognized. Mills' good reputation and good customer relationships would provide entrees into new fields of civil construction as well as other areas in which opportunities were clearly present. Moreover, they saw they could quickly acquire subsidiaries in related fields such as construction materials, data processing, and direct marketing. The external vision of diversification and growth was matched with a vision of internal changes: decentralization and division into three companies which would form the nucleus of the Mills Group. With this April, 1986 three-day ICA participative event began the major transformation of Mills and the assumption that it would be big and strong in the near future. However, this double vision, of diversification along with decentralization, was also to be one of the key factors in the later internal crisis that forced total participation.

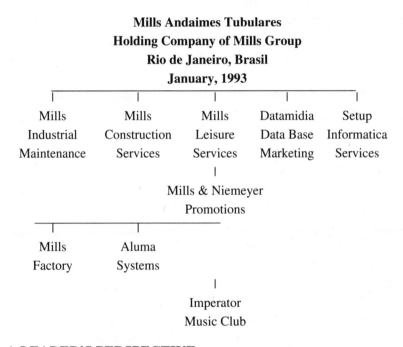

Mills Andaimes Tubulares
Holding Company of Mills Group
Rio de Janeiro, Brasil
January, 1993

| Mills Industrial Maintenance | Mills Construction Services | Mills Leisure Services | Datamidia Data Base Marketing | Setup Informatica Services |

Mills & Niemeyer
Promotions

| Mills Factory | Aluma Systems |

Imperator
Music Club

A LEADER'S PERSPECTIVE

Basic to the success of the company has been the leadership of company President, Andres Cristian Nacht, a man of global perspective and broad interests. An Argentinian educated at Cambridge University in England, he approached his role in Mills with concern for quality and for the well-being of employees. The latter was not a matter of altruism, he will tell you. He believes that employees will not be sensitive and responsive to needs of their clients if as employees they do not themselves receive sensitive respectful treatment from their company. This involves both adequate salaries and a chance to reach his or her potential in the workplace.

Once he entered the business world, Cristian's style raised questions for others. "Cristian," his father would say to him, "you don't have to share everything you know with everyone who works for you." "But why not? It's their company, too!" was Cristian's reply. He demonstrates his recognition of the importance of workers by occasionally doing specific tasks in the factory, at a supply depot, or on a job site. In recent years, Cristian's tendencies towards a particular leadership style have been strengthened by his readings and by observing a new management style introduced into Brazil by the Brahma Breweries, rated the outstanding company of the year in 1989 by the prestigious Brazilian business magazine, *Exame*. Brahma levelled its hierarchy, relaxed its structure, and increased responsibility of employees; at the same time, it pulled ahead of market competition. Cristian was inspired by the fact that this was possible, even in the paternalistic culture of Brazil.

However, Cristian's style and convictions have not always been acceptable to everyone within the company. Some would prefer the "comfort" of closed doors and a careful organizational chart rather than free association and intuitive responses. For some employees, working with him demands too much flexibility. His style is too free and demanding for those who like the security of a chain of command and a clear job description. Some have expressed a feeling that Mills lacks a rudder. Still as President, Cristian believes the company's survival depends on the initiative and creativity of all staff members.

INTERNAL GROWING PAINS

By 1990, Mills had achieved most of the external goals it had set in the strategic planning of 1986; it had grown and become diversified. The three areas of activity had become three divisions, soon to be independent companies: Mills Construction, Mills Industrial Maintenance, and Mills Events. In addition, five subsidiaries had been acquired.

Internally, however, Mills was suffering. Management systems were inadequate and the burden of decision making still rested on too few people. There was no enthusiasm or spirit among their troops; they seemed to have burned out and had no willingness to take risk. The directors assumed all of

Mills Andaimes Tubulares (Mills Group)

Year	1985	1990	1992
Employees	200	736	491
Laborers		899	809
Invoicing	U.S. $12 Million	U.S. $52.4 Million	U.S. $31.6 Million
Structure	One Company: Sales/Rental Offices in four cities	Three Companies: Mills Construction Mills Events Mills Industrial Maintenance Plus a Joint Venture	Three Companies Plus a Joint Venture
Subsidiaries	None	Five	Two

these negatives to be the results of rapid expansion. Day after day managers asked the same questions, "Why don't they have the same zeal we have? They are all just waiting for us to solve the problems. Why aren't they willing to build the company, take risks, work hard like we've done?" Stagnation had taken the place of the burst of energy that exploded after the 1986 strategic planning session. Expansion had given a false sense of well-being. The company was getting fat. Even some of the "old hands" who had brought about the external transformation were resting on their laurels. The directors were frustrated that what they considered to be the original "spirit" of the company was visibly failing at a time when it was badly needed. They feared this was a result of the influx of new personnel who lacked a historic sense of the Mills culture and style.

By 1990, a clear rivalry was developing between new divisions soon to be companies and newly acquired subsidiaries. Both needed the attention and the finances available through the President, Cristian, and the Vice-President, Elio Demier, also a dynamic visionary and doer. The two men recognized that only quick action would surmount these problems. Two directions were chosen: (1) Bring freshness and "healthy chaos" [1] to the directors themselves by shuffling them laterally; (2) Train lower management employees to take greater initiative. These seemed to be compatible ideas, except that they were not coordinated. In accepting both suggestions, the company was hiring two different builders on the same lot. Directors who were asked to take over a totally new area threatened to leave. The suggestions came to them as traumatic and unnecessary additional burdens when they already felt swamped with expansion and decentralization. They had no energy left even to concern themselves with seemingly harmless but time-consuming training courses. It was frustrating to have this training imposed from above. Further, no one could imagine what it might involve.

EXTERNAL SHOCK

While these rumblings were going on within the company, something much more like a financial earthquake was shaking Brazil. In an attempt to pull in its reins on inflation, the Brazilian Government froze all bank accounts in March, 1990. Companies were allowed to draw only enough to meet payrolls; as a result, for a while, markets were paralyzed. But soon, although the market never fully recovered, there was a return to runaway inflation. Many companies collapsed. The firing of masses of people led to general social chaos and violence. Temporary lulls in the market had been experienced before, but this had a powerful impact and lasted much longer. From January, 1991 to December, 1992, investment in industrial expansion dropped to 14.8% of the Gross Domestic Product, the lowest in Brazil's industrial history. During 1992 alone, there would be a 16% decline in retail sales and per capita income would drop by 3.3% [2]. Brazil was on the verge of economic catastrophe.

The first company of the Mills Group to feel the pinch was Mills Construction. Except in Rio, Brazilia, and Sao Paulo, major construction work was discontinued in 1990 as the recession took hold. Not only did the cancellation of jobs produce a drop in activity, but the low bids required to secure the few jobs available made them unprofitable. To secure contracts, budgets were slashed to barely cover costs.

The second company, Mills Events, found that its market virtually disappeared as the recession deepened. From invoicing up to U.S. $1 million a month and employing 220 in 1990, it became a real struggle to invoice U.S. $250,000. The number of employees dwindled to fewer than 80 by September, 1992.

The last company to feel the recession was Mills Industrial Maintenance. It, coincidentally, was also the last to embrace participation. Generally speaking, flow process industries require regular maintenance in the petrochemical

Timeline of Crises

1990	1991	1992
March	**February**	**January**
Incoming President Collor freezes all bank accounts	MILLS 2000 launched	Divisions legally become companies
October	**April**	**February**
Directors complain of stagnation, indifference	LENS II crisis of confidence with internal shifts	Unilateral firings
Decentralization "epidemic"	**August**	Industrial Maintenance hit
Construction industry stops	Internal financial crisis	National crisis of impeachment
ICA contracted/ facilitators brought in for consultation	**October**	**August**
Inflation 1,477%	Crisis of participation	Crisis in Mills Events and consolidation of space, reduction in employees
	Pain of decision making	**October**
	Firings	MILLS 2000 ends
	Inflation 480%	Inflation 1,158%

industry, especially where the safety of refineries and oil wells is concerned. But with a drop of subsidies to these companies and increasing local pressure caused by international competition, maintenance work is being postponed or delayed. Whereas income was U.S. $1.8 million in 1991, the company found itself struggling to reach U.S. $1.1 million in 1993.

PARTICIPATION TRAINING

In this context of crises, in October, 1990, Mills contacted the ICA affiliate, ICA:Brazil about training managers in a leadership style that had become Mills' trademark: a style demanding that managers accept risk and ownership, and embody integrity. A group called Mills 2000 was formed within the company, headed by Nadira Demier, Manager of the Human Resources Department of the holding company. The ICA staff was then contracted as program resources to consult with this group.

The program was formally launched in April, 1991, with a second strategic planning session focusing on how to consolidate and invigorate the talents and services of Mills managers to pave the way for participative management. To allow for greater freedom of expression, no company directors were invited; the managers and supervisors of the three divisions and representatives of subsidiaries attended. The result of the second strategic planning session was a proposal to continue to increase the size and diversity of the Mills group, while at the same time empowering local branch leadership and implanting participation in the management structures.

Elio Demier, Mills Vice-President, appeared at the closing session to assure the group that the directors were supportive and were willing to take drastic steps to confront the crises Mills faced. He also announced widespread changes in assignments of directors, effective immediately. The announcement stunned those present. They took it as a sign that the directors were still trying to pull strings and that the strategic planning session had been only a training event.

Still Mills 2000 (basically made up of the Human Resources Department Manager, Nadira Demier, and the ICA staff) was able to forge ahead. In the next 16 months they put more than 500 employees, including lower management staff members, through training programs, provided assistance in team building, and encouraged the study of articles on participative management, client service, and related subjects. They also helped bring about the fulfillment of the promise of the strategic planning session. Communication channels were then opened and networks formed in the Mills branches throughout Brazil.

One of the first managers to initiate employee involvement was Julio Caesar from the branch of Mills Construction in Belo Horizonte, a city of 3.4 million located north of Rio de Janeiro. From the time of the second strategic planning session, he saw how participation would make the smoother and more effective running of the branch possible. And as he talked with his employees, he realized how little information they had about what was going on in the rest of Mills. To cope with this lack of information and to encourage company pride, he initiated a ten minute news summary that was broadcast over the company loudspeaker system every day. Typical news items might be: "Good news from Recife: today a new contract has been signed...." "The branch in Brasilia continues to lead sales in the ...." "Our supply depot and plant will be moving to a new site in two months time. If you have ideas of how to facilitate the move of your section, please contact...."

At the same time, Julio Caesar invited supervisors to meet with him regularly and to discuss issues and problems they were confronting, such as market decline, increasing competition, and the need to be able to move equipment quickly between job sites. He also encouraged closer links between office and supply depot staff members who had once operated totally separately. In other branches, too, small groups of employees were formed to deal with specific problems and to relate to the Mills Group as a whole. One employee, Beatriz Sequeira Paranhos, then a secretary in the Construction Division in the Mills Rio branch, felt very positive about her own expanding work horizons. She became very well-informed about what was happening in all the other branches and was excited at the possibility of using her knowledge to facilitate the work. When she heard of a job being completed, for instance, she was quick to suggest where equipment would be needed next. Further, she was able to expedite its transfer.

Still, despite many positive changes brought by Mills 2000, confusion and uncertainty ruled the internal and external life of the company. Decentralization that seemed at first to be a positive force, soon was consuming all the resources and energy of the leadership. Externally, the economic situation continued to deteriorate. The process of training the managers and supervisors continued, but the directors were too preoccupied with new roles and many problems to take much interest in what was going on. The lack of funds was becoming a major concern. Finally, in August, 1991, it became clear that the very enterprises they thought were making money not only were not profitable, but were cash-consuming as well.

WATERSHED WEEK AND BLACK OCTOBER

The shock of new financial realities left experienced directors deeply concerned and new directors terrified. The Board reverted to long, secret meetings and avoided workers. Everyone in the Head Office was clear something bad was going on. Participation was not negated at this point; it was simply forgotten in the immediacy of pressure. Still, a process had been started that could not be aborted. By the end of September, 1991, the Board had drawn up a list of strong measures to counter-balance the dilemma. Cristian Nacht tells the story:

> It had been a long day. Late in the evening all the Board's decisions were finally ready. By then, the feeling of accomplishment was great. But the awareness of a major obstacle slowly began to be seen: How were decisions going to be communicated to the

company? Management, supervisors, and senior staff would feel betrayed if after months of training in participation, decisions of this magnitude were thrust upon them without any input. The problem was clear; the solution was not.

A few days later it was decided to follow the suggestion of the ICA consultants:

(1) Change the Board's decisions into proposals and submit them to meetings of employees.

(2) Bring back the employees' comments, doubts, and alternative suggestions.

(3) Reevaluate and decide.

This was done.

A whirlwind week followed during which directors visited each branch and met with company managers. These meetings shook the company. Those invited to the meetings complained that consultations were made too quickly and that not enough information was given for them to evaluate proposals. Directors complained that valuable time was being wasted and that decision making was being taken out of their hands. Many complained that the process generated immense anxiety as everyone became aware that dismissals were inevitable. It was a tense and difficult period, but after two weeks the whole company was clearer on what was meant by participation, and had taken a major step toward achieving it. Although many employees were angry, shocked, and amazed to find out that the financial situation was as bad as it was at a time when they were all busily engaged, some, nevertheless, prepared to participate in the new situation the company confronted.

One example of this employee participation comes from the Mills factory. The Board of Directors had decided that the factory should be closed. But two weeks after the branch meetings, 11 of the key factory employees who had been exposed to participative methods asked to speak to the Board. They pleaded:

Let us keep the factory open, just the 11 of us. We know what to do. We don't need a manager. We can accomplish as much as the 40 that were on the staff before. Mills needs a factory so it is not dependent on other producers with lower standards. Let us be it.

Scaffolding Factory: Mills Construction			
	December 1990	December 1991	December 1992
Number of Employees	75	58	18
Production	U.S. $570,000	U.S. $1,201,000	U.S. $884,000
Production Per Employee	U.S. $7,600	U.S. $20,707	U.S. $49,110

The directors were astonished, but they knew these workers. They trusted them and accepted their proposal. A year later, by October, 1992, the factory had grown to 16 employees and was far more productive and profitable than the 11 factory employees had imagined. To the present it continues to be operated by taskforces with a flat hierarchy. The image one gets from observing it is that of a relay race, each runner a manager/employee responsible for his or her own "lap," as well as for the "race" as a whole. There are no rigid boundaries between jobs; all 16 employees are members of one team.

POSITIVE RESULTS OF THE CRISIS

Cristian Nacht outlines one of the happenings that unfolded in the months after watershed week and "Black October" of 1991; an irreversible trend toward shared decision making:

In the year that followed "Black October," crisis was the major player in almost all aspects of the business. The recession became deeper. In February and March, 1992, a small group of directors decided on further dismissals; as a result, a sense of injustice began to fester among groups within the company. The next September [1992] adjustments, which also involved dismissals, were preceded by a day-long meeting of directors with each company to review the real situation of that unit, to discuss problems, and to suggest solutions. Decisions were then made by the directors with their management teams. Even though these changes constituted the third downsizing in 12 months, and took place in an environment that could not promise relief in the short run, morale and enthusiasm remained high.

Sharing in decision making required an increase in the sharing of information. As Cristian remembers, "Fear of openly discussing major and sensitive problems diminished. It was as though the unthinkable had been done and the barriers were down." This lowering of barriers was to result in a new level of communication. Managers welcomed the opportunity to talk over problems and options. They were clear that they themselves had no "magic answers," and were surprised and pleased to discover that office workers and laborers alike had insights and information to share. Employees surprised themselves also with their seemingly newfound ability to generate and articulate positive suggestions. In the past, information, a prerogative closely guarded by both managers and workers, had been a secret source of power. Until 1991, there were many variations of a story describing a manager who in asking why he had not been informed that a client was unsatisfied with the construction job at hand, received the standard answer, "You never asked me!" Since the crisis, one seldom hears that response. Joint meetings are resulting in the creation of new products and new support systems, as well as in new ways of working, and ultimately, in an increase in productivity.

The crisis also created an understanding of the company's need to invest in the future in various ways. One was to offer perceivable improvements in quality and service. Another was to continue creative teamwork and inventiveness. In September, 1992, when Elio Demier, Mills Group Vice-President, took over direct responsibility for Mills Events, he began to include the entire office staff of 10, plus 20 scaffolders, in planning and decision making. At first the latter were startled and ill-at-ease at these sessions, but later they became adept at making suggestions and offering comments that brought about a more comprehensive understanding of issues, as well as more just and effective ways of dealing with situations as they arose. These office staff members knew exactly how much time a job would take and how modifications could be made without redoing initial plans.

In another attempt to confront the business future head-on, Mills Events pioneered with client-oriented versus task-oriented assignments. As a result, Swanny Macedo Dutra, who was formerly a bilingual secretary, no longer performs office duties exclusively. Now she is part of a team dealing with several clients; she can be found at construction sites or in offices of customers, as often as she is at her own desk. This flexibility applies to all employees at Mills. Each is a member of a team that deals with certain clients or tasks, not simply with isolated marketing or administrative chores. The result is an increase in motivation and a sense of ownership of the successes and tribulations of the company among all levels of employees.

In a recent conversation, Elio Demier talked of the changes in his own stance:

I don't ever want to sit in an office alone making important decisions by myself, he said. I have seen the value of including everyone and in creating an ambience of teamship. Today we all eat lunch together in the lunchroom at the same time. There are no distinctions between managers and laborers. It is fantastic what it is doing to all of us.

What "it" is doing is turning the company into a team, and broadening the perspective of all involved. As a result, fewer errors are made and new decisions are implemented at all levels much more rapidly than before. Mutual respect and understanding are emerging. Because clients are better served, invoicing is increasing.

Team management is another strategy that Mills has successfully taken to more than one company site. When the manager of Mills Construction in the Salvador office was moved to Rio, a team of three took his place; although one of the three was later moved to Sao Paulo, the two remaining continue to work as a team. In Belo Horizonte, when Construction Manager Julio Caesar left for Rio, a team of six was chosen to carry on, three men and three women supervisors, with one acting as the first among equals. To date, this strategy has been effective in maintaining quality, service, and flexibility in the face of a drastically reduced market. A related result that has emerged is a new sense of accountability in the Mills Holding Company. In 1990, the directors identified accountability as one of the problems Mills was facing, particularly in the financial arena. Although work would not be progressing on schedule, managers would be reluctant to lay down demands or to question employee excuses. They would say, "What can you do? That's the way things are in Brazil!" Now in the monthly meetings of supervisors and work groups, people commonly ask others why they have not provided services as promised and when promised. At times these questions have verged on nagging or fault finding, rather than objective accountability. Nevertheless, these requests have revealed a new sense of shared responsibility, and have resulted in quicker responses to the requests of internal and external clients.

In the few places where teamwork has not been stressed within the company, there continues to be dissatisfaction. Beatriz Sequeira Paranhos,

Mills Construction Office Manager, provides an example. She was moved to the head office of Mills Industrial Maintenance and was greatly disappointed. "What were you expecting?" her new workmates asked her. She explains:

> I had become used to working as a team, sharing information, knowing what was going on, and how my part helped the whole. I thought it would be the same in the Head Office only more so, that I would know what was happening in all the branches and really be able to make it work better. But all I do is shuffle paper, and I don't have any vision of what is going on.

Beatriz has since left the company.

One way the crisis affected participation was totally surprising. To save money, each company cut back on space. Mills Events was the first to squeeze into one small office. Boundaries between departments and functions became irrelevant. In the process of "surviving," managers discovered that close common space brings about good teamwork and informal but intense verbal communication that results in a better job. Now, in at least one-half of the branches and in the Holding Company, there is a new space design. Walls have been knocked down and private cubicles have been done away with. At the Holding Company, Mauro Scalabrin, Director of Administration and Finance, instigated the change. The ICA consultants had convinced him during the Black October meetings that one cannot expect employees to be inventive and to risk themselves if they have no voice in the company's decisions. He was impressed with the response to the strategy of "talking to the branches." In his words:

> When I became convinced of the practical value of participation, I decided to do everything possible to encourage it. I saw that people at the holding company were retreating to their own cubicles, and had little sense that we were really working toward the same ends, on the same team. I talked informally with everyone about the advantage of working in one large room. So on the day that we actually knocked the walls down, there were no complaints. And since then, communication and a sense of unity continue to grow.

The Mills President now shares a room with 18 others, including directors, managers, supervisors, and secretaries. Proximity makes secrets impossible, all knowledge accessible.

WHAT WAS LEARNED

Ironically, one casualty of the financial crisis was Mills 2000. In the face of pressing obligations, and with growing concern for the immediate situation, the very program that provided the impetus, training, and driving spirit for creatively dealing with crisis was discontinued. The ICA:Brazil consultants continue to facilitate planning, however, and Nadira Demier, the Manager of the Holding Company's Human Resources Department, injects all training with participation skills and consciousness.

When a group of directors and consultants met to summarize what they had learned from the Mills 2000 program, they created the following list:

(1) **Projecting Results**: The directors felt that it would have helped if they had had a clearer idea of what the results of the Mills 2000 program would be before it started. If they had spent more time discussing the steps, the theory, and the likely results, they would have been able to cooperate better, if indeed they had decided to go along with the program.

(2) **Celebration**: Victories should have been celebrated more frequently. A spirit of doom and gloom took over with the increased financial crunch, even though in the midst of crisis many significant things were being accomplished, such as the installation of computer systems.

(3) **Physical Presence**: In times of crisis, more than at other times, the reassuring presence of the directors and managers is important. Instead, they retreated to their offices and closed the doors. Employees tended to follow their lead. There was a direct connection between the lack of friendly chatter in the departments and the productivity drop, which simply exacerbated the crisis. Ironically, this isolation was going on in 1991 at the very time that networks of communication were being established within the Mills 2000 program, and when, in some branches, local committees were assuming more and more responsibility.

On reflection, ICA:Brazil facilitators would add three further learnings to the previous list provided by the group directors and consultants:

(4) **Training**: Participation depends first on practical skills in planning, in communicating, in human relationships, in client service,

especially in the hierarchical culture of Brazil. Secondly, participation is dependent on a vision of personal and corporate possibility. Innovations, like the factory initiative, were spin-offs from
participative training in Mills 2000. Managers, particularly, need
on-the-job assistance to know how to enlist and use participation
and how to create a common vision with their staff members. It is
a learned skill.

(5) **Interrelatedness**: When one element of a culture is changed,
everything changes. Changing workers changes managers,
changes directors, changes managers, and workers again. One
cannot change one part and leave others untouched. Once participation is introduced, there is no way to return to the old autocratic
way without serious loss. The directors' attempts to handle downsizing at Mills in February and March, 1992, unilaterally created
a climate of distrust. On the other hand, when these leaders
described the crisis and strategies, workers themselves were able
to project solutions they could own, even when one solution
involved their dismissal.

(6) **Resident Knowledge**: Those who work at a task consistently
come to know what they are doing and how they can improve it
in a way that even supervisors cannot match. When workers at
any level were freed to express themselves, they revealed a
knowledge of their work and critical and creative skills which the
board had not imagined.

WHAT'S NEXT?

The first strategic planning session introduced participation to Mills;
the second session broadened the participation. Mills 2000 then provided
theoretical and practical participation know-how for the company as a whole.
Even today, Mills continues to be in the midst of crisis. All things are not
equal or moving at the same pace. But Mills takes courage in that there is a
new unity of vision and commitment quite beyond the profit incentive. Mills
is becoming a learning organization, a company that has largely overcome
the fear of change because the employees have the freedom and the will to
innovate and experiment.

One Mills board member comments, "Those of us who have been through at least two crises are much calmer this time in spite of the radical steps that have to be taken." This sense of calm comes, in part, from the sense of not being alone with all the weight of decisions, but having a strong team working together for a strong company, and for a common future.

References

[1]   Peters, Tom. *Thriving on Chaos*. New York: Harper and Row, Publishers (1987) p. XIV.

[2]   Blocker Assessoria de Investimentos e Participaces S.A., "Monthly Report," February, 1993.

VI.

WHAT MAKES PARTICIPATION WORK?

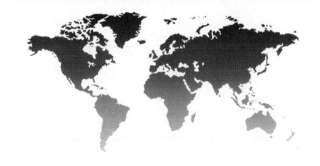

Hudson's Bay Company

INCORPORATED 2ND MAY 1670

PRO PELLE CUTEM

11. PARTICIPATION AT THE GRASSROOTS LEVEL

by
JO NELSON

*"I've been here at Hudson's Bay Company for ten years,
and been a project leader a number of times. Since my
involvement with the 1993 Information Services project,
I've never worked on a project with so much staff motivation,
momentum, and keen interest. And it's been sustained for
more than five months now with none of the usual grumblings!"*
Wendy Smith, Information Services Division,
Hudson's Bay Company

udson's Bay Company (HBC) is Canada's oldest and one of its largest retailers. It was chartered in 1670 as the Governor and Company of Adventurers of England trading into Hudson's Bay. Beginning as a fur trading operation, it established trading routes across much of the territory that was to become Canada. Its trade relationships opened up much of the continent to European exploration. Around the turn of the 20th century, the wool Hudson's Bay blanket with its distinctive red, white, and black stripes, an item developed for fur trading, became known across North America as a symbol of quality and stability. Early in this century, HBC turned its attention to retailing, which became its most important activity.

Today, its three operating divisions cover the Canadian retail market across all price zones and from coast to coast. More than 400 retail stores across Canada bring Hudson's Bay Company to most of the population. At every level, its staff reflects the cultural diversity of modern Canada with employees whose origins represent almost every area of the world. HBC's vision includes a commitment to customer satisfaction through maximum productivity, quality, and teamwork; excellent relationships, products, and service create the greatest value for both customers and employees. The company values feedback on its objectives, and gives honest, respectful, and fair consideration for continuous balanced improvement and growth of both the individual and business.

The HBC Information Services (IS) Division provides information systems and support to the entire company operation. Its mission is to provide high-quality information services and contribute to HBC profitability. Its more than 350 employees provide clients at all levels within the company with data and information to conduct business effectively. For example, millions of credit statements are processed monthly, fast and slow-selling merchandise is tracked and reported, and new technology is introduced to improve customer service. To provide appropriate business solutions to their customers, the IS staff meets with clients in their usual work environment, discerns their needs, and works out a way to meet those needs with computer applications. Often these meetings are intense, as clients have complex problems that need immediate solutions. Clients may have little understanding of computers and what they can or cannot solve, and the IS staff may have little real-life experience with the problems that their clients experience. Communication is not easy. Solving the problems effectively can be a very difficult process, unless both the client and the IS staff have effective methods to collaborate in determining the most effective solutions.

WENDY'S STORY—PARTICIPATION WITH EFFECTIVE METHODS

In February, 1993, Wendy Smith, a technical planner in HBC's IS Division was assigned a project to evaluate HBC's use of a software product installed on the IS mainframe. The software product schedules and restarts computer jobs. This project would also investigate the possibility of acquiring new software products to meet HBC's requirement more effectively. The product in use at the time was old and not as advanced as newer products on the market. Since IS is responsible for processing computer jobs for the whole of the huge HBC operation, a mainframe computer scheduler and restart package is a critical tool that can either enhance or cripple the productivity of many functions in the company. Daily collection and analysis of sales data and regular backup of inventory data, for example, depend on automatic scheduling. Getting data processed rapidly and accurately is critical to the bottom line of the retail business, as its success depends on the effective responses to changing consumer demands.

Wendy describes the complexities involved:

It is often difficult for us as a team to identify requirements up front, including all areas—functional, business, and technical—in the planning for acquisition of a software product. When requirements are not properly identified up front, decisions can be made based on incomplete data. And often this situation leads to feeling at cross-purposes—somebody makes the decision and then others feel like the decision is thrust upon them. There is a problem with ownership of the decision. As a result, we don't always make the best choices that will meet the most needs.

I had taken the Facilitation Skills course taught by ICA Canada, a group of professional facilitation consultants skilled in the use of participation techniques. The course emphasized that solutions are wiser and more effective when all stakeholders are involved in the decision making, and gave me a practical set of methods to really involve people. So for this project, I decided that we should have all those who had a stake in the use of the product set out what their requirements were, then group them together so that we could see where we had similar requirements. Then we would weigh them to create a consensus on the priorities. Only then would we go look for products that would meet those requirements.

As Wendy had a unique and important perspective on the acquisition of the product in her role as the expert on contract terms and conditions with vendors, she wanted to participate in the workshop. So she asked two other people from the Facilitation User Group, a network of graduates of the ICA Canada Facilitation Skills training to lead the sessions. Tom Mavor was to facilitate the meeting, which they estimated would take a half day, and Frank Ramoutar would write down the results as they went. Wendy and Tom carefully prepared the process, and sent out information that would get people thinking about the requirements ahead of time.

The morning of the session, Tom called in with bad news. He was ill and would not be able to facilitate the session. Should they postpone it? Rescheduling all the busy participants would be very difficult. Frank volunteered to facilitate, and the session got underway.

They began using the plan that Tom and Wendy had worked out ahead of time. Wendy explained the context of the workshop, and sat down to assume the role of participant. Frank gave the group the focus question: What are our requirements for a mainframe computer scheduler and restart package? The group of a dozen participants began to brainstorm. As Wendy puts it:

Technical people don't usually say a lot—often they interface better with machines than they do with people. The multicultural nature of our organization sometimes means that there are language problems, which also tend to make people quiet in a group. But in this workshop, there was no problem with getting people to speak! The participatory methods made everybody feel very comfortable from the beginning. Frank encouraged everyone to add **anything** they thought was important. A few of the participants had been in the Facilitation Skills course as well. Everybody was helping everybody in a relaxed way. The meeting was much more productive as a result.

By the end of the morning, the group had brainstormed 142 different

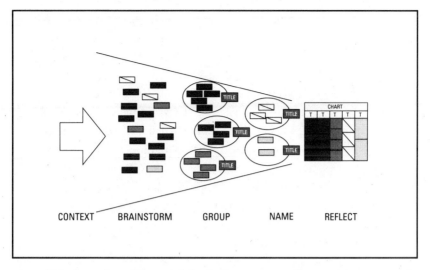

CONTEXT   BRAINSTORM   GROUP   NAME   REFLECT

This flow chart illustrates the basic structure of a participatory workshop as it moves first from considering a focus question to brainstorming common ways to go about solving that question. The next activity identifies or titles the common strategies and groups them. Creating a chart that illustrates all the titles gives the group a chance to view their work, reflect on it, and then move to consensus.

requirements for the software product, put them on cards, and grouped them on the wall into 14 categories. When particular requirements went up that were not clear to everyone, positive discussion went on until everyone understood why those requirements were important. Everyone learned a lot about the requirements of other people in the group. Wendy, for example, learned how much of a difference in productivity particular technical requirements could make, and how much of what was being done manually right now could be automated by the right product. The technical people began to appreciate what impact a business requirement such as a "site license" might make on HBC if it were not included in a contract.

As the group reached the end of the allotted workshop time, they began to realize the immensity of the task still before them. They decided to set aside more time to work together. Wendy recalls:

Usually getting time out of people is really hard. We all have so much to do. But this time, everyone was enthusiastic about how well we were solving the problem and quickly cleared enough time to finish the workshop. Eventually it took us three days to finish weighting the requirements and come to a final agreement on the priorities. Because all the participants were convinced that their input was considered seriously and had an effect on the outcome, they were very motivated to carry out the decisions that we made in the workshop. Five months later, the motivation is still strong. We have taken the list of requirements and have looked seriously at four candidate products. We scored them on how well they matched our requirements, and are bringing in the one receiving the highest score for evaluation. People are doing the work and don't have to be asked for updates on the progress of the project. We have never lost our focus.

As a direct result of the workshop's success, Wendy nominated Frank Ramoutar for the IS Service Quality System Award for the month of March. This award is presented to those employees who have given service to the company above and beyond their regular job. Frank, whose normal job is technical analyst, "had a nice facilitation style in this meeting," says Wendy:

He had an air of quiet authority that kept control of the discussion and kept it moving. The group had a range of personalities from those who generally say very little to those who generally say everything with great authority. Frank never lost his composure for the whole length of time.

The participatory process used in this workshop has had great effects on the productivity of the group. Wendy continues:

Our work is done in a dynamic environment. As things change, often projects get put on hold as other demands take priority. Then we don't reap the benefits of the time we've spent planning because it takes so long to get to the action stage. By that time, people lose momentum. This time, people can see that the new product will help **them**, so they are making the time to see the project through. Management is supportive because they can see the overall good for their departments. There is an achievable goal that will benefit everyone. We plan to use the participatory processes again with similar long-term projects because it has been so effective. I can see lots of applications.

Mary-Jane Jarvis-Haig, Director of Development Support, has been involved in the training of the HBC IS staff and management to facilitate participatory decision making since 1991. As she observes:

I think one of the unique aspects of the way Information Services is implementing participatory processes is that it is a grassroots movement within the company. Management has been supportive, but it is staff members who have decided to make this work. Staff members have been using participatory processes to facilitate team meetings and discussions on how to resolve problems. When they have run into obstacles, they have found ways around them and have not allowed themselves to be stopped. The ICA facilitation methods have permitted diverse groups to work together to a common end much faster, and therefore have increased the productivity of group work considerably. Wendy's group is a good example of this kind of unity.

WHAT PROMPTED THE DECISION TO ENCOURAGE PARTICIPATION

In 1989, IS had a positive experience with involving stakeholders in decisions that affected them. To save money, the development group planned to move out of Toronto's downtown core to a new location. This move meant uprooting over 200 staff members. Other corporations had experienced mass losses when they had made similar moves. Mary-Jane recalls:

Our target was to contain loss to 10%. We designated staff representatives to be involved in move planning and execution. They ensured that communication was open and active from management to staff and vice versa. Staff designed their own new workstations. Despite no new furniture, smaller workstations, and a more remote location, all of which can add stress to the move, our loss was limited to one staff person. The success of this project encouraged us to continue to implement ways of increasing stakeholder participation in decision making.

Shortly afterward, a manager and one of his staff members attended the Facilitation Skills seminar taught by the ICA Canada. This two-day course teaches methods of leading clear discussions, gathering data, and creating consensus. They became excited about its application within HBC and then initiated a process to bring HBC and ICA Canada together. In 1990, they introduced their colleague, Mary-Jane Jarvis-Haig, to ICA. Mary-Jane decided to explore the methods further and attended the course at ICA Canadas office in the summer of 1991.

In the fall of 1991, the global recession was hitting Canada hard. Since the retail business, in particular, was experiencing the crunch, HBC responded with a two-fold strategy to reduce costs and increase productivity. Computer system applications that would allow faster response to customer demand needed to be designed and delivered to clients in a much faster time frame. The IS professionals needed to increase their effectiveness and productivity. As an answer to this need, the Retooling Application Developers in Information Services (READI) strategy was defined and then given high priority. READI was designed to present to application developers specific methodology-oriented skills which would allow these employees to be more productive. Training in facilitation of participatory processes to use when meeting with their business clients or peers was seen to be a significant part of a larger retooling strategy. As Greg Harrison of Development Services pointed out in late 1991:

> There is a hidden frustration in drawing together consensus. Meetings take too much time, and are difficult for everyone. Clients don't like being grilled for requirements, but often do not know how to make their needs understood to the computer experts. We need a way to marry the business client's need for systems support and the Information Services professional's need to deliver that in a more efficient way. We need to reduce the time it takes to deliver the solution.

Mary-Jane used the workshop method she had learned in the Facilitation Skills seminar to define the scope and deliverables of the READI strategy. Management and staff attended workshops together to define what they felt was needed to become more productive. The process worked well. Mary-Jane remembers:

> Groups surprised each other by having very similar requirements. Management was pleasantly surprised to hear of common interest in standards to make the development process more consistent and efficient. The workshops gave the READI team a department-wide mandate.

OBJECTIVE

GETTING
THE FACTS

REFLECTIVE

EMOTIONS,
FEELINGS,
ASSOCIATIONS

INTERPRETIVE

VALUES, MEANING,
PURPOSE,
SIGNIFICANCE

DECISIONAL

FUTURE RESOLVES

The basic structure of the discussion method taught by ICA—a process applicable in many business situations for individual or group decision making.

When the READI campaign began to get underway in late 1991, Mary-Jane called ICA to ask if the participatory processes might be tailored to meet the needs of those designing computer applications to meet business requirements. Mary-Jane and ICA worked together to design a course that would use examples and situations from within the company to help employees learn skills for facilitating participatory design sessions and for other applications within their work. A further session with Greg Harrison of HBC's Development Services in November of 1991 reconfirmed the company's requirements and tailored the design of the course to meet those specific needs.

In January, 1992, the first Facilitation Skills course designed to meet the READI project objectives was offered. The three-day course included demonstrations, explanations, and actual practice of the finely tuned processes for leading effective discussions and workshops. It also focused on ways to apply these methods in a strategic planning program. The first day's schedule centered around a basic discussion method which allows a group to think through an issue together. Three demonstrations of the method got everyone participating. After they learned the underlying structure, each participant prepared a discussion that he or she would use in a real upcoming division meeting, and practiced leading a discussion with a small group of other participants. Supportive individual feedback allowed reflection on the qualities of effective facilitation.

On the second day, the group focused on a basic workshop method that helps elicit ideas from all participants and then synthesizes them to discern the group's consensus. By the end of the second day, each participant had planned an actual workshop that he or she would implement, and had practiced leading a small group. The third day demonstrated the application of the discussion and workshop methods in a participatory strategic planning process. There was great enthusiasm and commitment at the end of the course, when the participants understood the practical applications of the process.

Five of these training courses were held between January, 1992 and January, 1993 under the READI initiative: four in Toronto and one in Montreal. As positive reports of effectiveness of the training spread, increased demand for the course arose. Two courses in the Spring of 1993 were coordinated by the Human Resources Department of IS under their mandate to provide soft (non-technical) skills. Altogether, 85 participants from all divisions within IS were involved between January, 1992 and April, 1993. Most of the sessions included employees from several levels of management and staff and reflected the multicultural make-up of the company. This diversity promoted enhanced communication across the company and demonstrated the effectiveness of the processes in working with widely differing perspectives. Altogether 29 managers, 25 systems programmer/analysts, 16 business/data analysts, and 15 administration personnel attended between January, 1992 and April, 1993.

As more and more of the HBC managers and employees attended the course, the focus began to expand. Not only was participation helpful for designing computer applications with clients, but it could also be used for solving everyday problems and as a tool in participatory management. Participants prepared sessions for determining project requirements with clients, for staff meetings, for one-to-one conversations, and for preparing reports and proposals.

The methods were taught experientially, using discussions and workshops on topics that could involve everyone. One of the side-effects of the course became the products of the demonstration workshops. For example, workshop focus questions such as, What do we **want** to see going on in IS in five years? elicited honest answers. As each group of participants created its own vision of the future of the division, the obstacles blocking it, and strategic directions for tackling those obstacles, a consensus emerged across all divisions and levels of the department. Participants were surprised and pleased that others had similar aspirations. Barriers began to dissolve. Though the emphasis was on methods training, some of the plans that emerged during the sessions were acted upon when the sessions were finished. An objective-sharing session among managers and increased open communication between staff and management are two such examples of these results.

Graduates of the course decided to set up a support network that would allow them to continue developing their facilitation skills. They wanted an easy way to call on each other for facilitation of workshops. Tim Willson created an electronic bulletin board list of all the Facilitation Skills course participants, and people began to use the bulletin board list to find facilitators. Soon a facilitation skills user group began to meet to explore further development of their skills. Recently a proposal to designate a core group of facilitators whose job descriptions would include facilitating participation in problem-solving meetings has been approved by management. As Mary-Jane notes, "Facilitation has become a recognizable soft skill—a skill very valuable to the company's productivity."

WIDER APPLICATIONS

The skill of facilitation has been used effectively by both staff and management in many situations. Bibi Karim, a senior systems analyst, tells of a typical facilitation experience:

I was asked to facilitate the requirements gathering for a project to create a system to allow end users access to real estate and taxation data. There was intensive preparation on IS's part since the participants (mainly managers) were very busy and skeptical about the structured participatory process or approach to the project. Also we did not want them to feel that their time was being wasted. The focus question, How do you see yourself working more effectively today and what are your future requirements for information and business functions? was well thought out and issued in advance to the participants. Initially I was told that everyone could not attend. However, the focus question piqued their curiosity and **all** the participants showed up at the session! The participants were asked to come with a minimum of five responses to the focus question. They did spend the time preparing and used their notes when the workshop started.

The workshop method was the primary process used during the session. The meeting objectives were achieved, and all business requirements were addressed. In fact, the clients were enthusiastic, and requested that we spend a full day rather than the planned one-half day. So we seized the momentum and synergy and continued working until our objectives were completed.

The session delivered a revised data model with clear definitions reflecting the actual information this department used, as well as high level process models, far beyond our original expectations. All clients were excited and helpful to each other, and found that they were all looking towards the same objective. New ideas were raised. At the end of the session, everyone was tired but still positive. This was my first 'work' experience using the workshop method. I felt that the process carried me along to some degree. In fact, it sold itself. In my opinion, preparation was a key factor for the success of this session.

Another group used the participatory planning process to enhance its teamwork. Greg Harrison, Manager of the IS Development Support Department, carved out time from his schedule to attend the course. He reports:

The most interesting facilitation I have been involved in is the staff-driven 'Development Services Visioning' exercise that I was asked to facilitate. The focus question for the process was: How will Development Services become the best possible Information and Business system delivery vehicle for the Hudson's Bay Company? The process that we pursued was the standard ICA strategic planning process based on the workshop method, from visioning exercise to action planning. The group is currently completing the detailed definition of strategic directions and related action items.

Greg Harrison also noted that there are several interesting elements to the process. The group involved is a self-motivated, independent group of functional staff from different teams within the Development Services organization. They were prompted to define what they felt Development Services could do to become 'the best' according to the READI initiative and to their observations of its strengths and weaknesses. They also used as a motivator their desire to deliver a solid, professional effort in their varied tasks. Key individuals decided on a facilitated process because they had observed its relative success in other exercises.

They felt that it was an appropriate method for enabling the development and delivery of objective, reasoned input regarding their perspective on the topic of how to provide high quality business and information systems quickly and efficiently. They were so motivated that much of the work effort was delivered outside of normal working hours. The facilitation framework allowed for a relatively smooth flow from visioning to obstacles, to new directions, to action planning, even though the sessions dealing with the process were widely separated in time (several weeks to a month). This considerable time separation has been identified, however, as a weakness in this particular exercise.

According to Greg Harrison, the general consensus of the key participants in the Development Services Visioning exercise is that the facilitated workshop approach:

- Supported the development of team spirit
- Enabled improvement in the morale of the participants
- Promoted communication across existing boundaries
- Ensured that **all** related variables were at least identified if not addressed
- Provided the cohesive structure for the ongoing process
- Ensured clarity of focus
- Maintained a sense of progress and initiative
- Provided the base outline for a structured action plan.

He sums up all of these achievements:

From the staff perspective, the results of the session have been a clear statement of vision for Development Services; it is a clear expression of challenges and new directions, and a clear, qualified action plan (under development) for pursuing these identified new directions.

My impression is that the facilitated workshop method provided the structure necessary to turn what could have been a 'whining' session into a productive, constructive 'planning' session. The results of this session have significant value for Development Services management as they pursue planning for development excellence.

OVERALL BENEFITS

In the highly competitive retail business, it is critical that information flow rapidly and smoothly within a company, and that people work together effectively to solve complex problems quickly. In HBC, the exchange of information in IS has been accelerated by the use of structured yet flexible facilitation processes. The application of these processes is highly varied. Having the widespread training throughout IS enables employees to understand and support each other as they work together to find appropriate solutions to the problems.

Mary-Jane sums up:

Staff and managers are now using participatory discussions and workshops to facilitate team meetings and discussions on how to resolve problems. A wider group of stakeholders is being involved, and issues are being seen in a broader perspective. Diverse groups are able to articulate obstacles more quickly, and to create effective strategies to deal with them. The usual territorialism is being addressed or minimized. Staff members in the facilitation user-group meetings comment on how surprised they are at what they learn about each other when they use the techniques. They find themselves more sensitive to other points of view. Facilitators go into meetings much better prepared, which makes the meetings go much faster and have much more effective results. Even people who are not usually effective at communication get good results through using effective process. When we use effective processes that create active participation from all stakeholders in solving problems and designing solutions, we produce quality results faster.

12. CHAMPIONS OF PARTICIPATION: ORGANIZATIONS' LEADERS

by
GORDON HARPER

Leadership must invite people to join together in a great adventure to create the future. As the senior partners in the change enterprise, leaders build motivation by making time for people to share their ideas, listen to, and learn from one another.

Throughout the world, businesses face the challenges of managing change. On their feet—running—managers must answer the question of what it really takes to lead an organization through a virtual transformation of its existing concepts, styles, and systems.

The case studies in this collection illustrate the importance and benefits of developing broad participation in change. They also illuminate the critical role an organization's leader plays in managing that change. Only with strong leadership from the management team can significant change happen and be sustained. Anyone who has tried to bring about change in an organization knows how frustrating such an endeavor is without the full support of management. As a result, organizational transformation has become a joint venture between employees who participate and managers who lead *and* participate.

The normal routine is that people in an organization look to their leadership for direction. This is doubly so when an organization seeks to change. Even small changes that disrupt long-standing patterns generate some resistance, but major changes will always produce very strong resistance somewhere in the system. Shifting an organization's mind-set and traditional habits, to say nothing of its established roles and relationships, is no easy task. It requires a sustained leadership effort and calls upon all the skills that good managers can bring to that role. For managers, neutrality in the midst of a change process is not an option; others in the organization will see the leaders as either part of the fresh energy for change or as supporters of the forces resisting change.

When an organization confronts the challenge of change, a leadership team must perform three critical roles:

(1) Personally model the desired changes;
(2) Partner change in cooperation with others;
(3) Orchestrate the total process.

Each of these includes overlapping yet discrete leadership activities. Taken together, they form a coherent style for successfully guiding the transformation of today's organizations.

MODELING THE NEW DESIGNS

When major changes are afoot in any segment of society, people look for role models. In organizations, employees keenly observe all the little signals that communicate their managers' values and priorities. In an environment of change within a company, employees become especially skilled at distinguishing between the articulated corporate values and actual or operational valuesand they learn to trust and go with the latter. The well-known adage, "What you do speaks so loudly, I can't hear a word you are saying," aptly describes an organization's relationship to its leadership. People may listen politely to what their managers say, but they will act according to what they see these leaders do.

We see this every day in our organizations. The Human Resources Director of a U.S. microchip manufacturer describes how irrelevant their corporate value statements used to be:

They were beautifully framed and up on the walls everywhere. People all knew they said that quality was our single most important value, but everyone also knew that finally nothing was to stand in the way of getting our product out the door.

In this case it took the CEO's leadership to change the situation. He led his managers through a process of reviewing and reshaping the old value statements. He then insisted that the discussion of items on the staff meetings' agenda make specific reference to these new value statements and that decisions be made in light of them. In the management meetings, he began asking people to relate their contributions directly to the corporate values. As he demonstrated the expected tough accountability to their stated company values, other managers quickly got the message. Within a relatively short time, what had been lip service to the "quality first" ideal was transformed into an operational priority. The company now provides assertiveness training for its quality supervisors so that, when necessary, they can stand up and say even to a factory manager, "I'm sorry, but this product is not going to ship." This kind of change in behavior in an organization happens only when it is first modeled by the corporate leadership.

The new President of an American oil company's operation in Taiwan discovered upon arriving at his new post that he had stepped into a long-standing corporate culture of secrecy. Over a 20-year period, all policy decisions had customarily been made by two or three company leaders in what the Chinese staff alluded to as a "black box." The new President decided that this clandestine behavior would have to change if other things he hoped to accomplish were to happen. One of his first moves was to institute a weekly meeting with his divisional and departmental managers and to make it clear that this open forum would be the setting for corporate decision making.

Within the corporate culture of the oil company, people perceived this move as a dramatic change. As it became apparent that the new President was actually putting the new decision-making style into practice, it sent shock waves through the ranks. The open discussion of issues by the entire management team created a climate that encouraged the company to begin a long overdue process of change. The President rightly saw that to initiate that process, he had to establish his own credibility and commitment by making the first moves and embodying the changes himself.

Modeling this willingness to make very personal changes for the sake of the organization is of paramount importance in organizational transformation. We have seen too much downsizing and cost-cutting where everyone in the organization is called upon to change and make sacrifices for the good of the operation—except the top managers. When this happens, an understandable cynicism quickly pervades an organization. In a thousand ways, leaders' actions convey to others the degree of personal commitment that lies behind their words. For people to be willing to change themselves, they have to see unmistakable evidence that their managers are willing to change.

By visibly modeling change, leaders become credible witnesses for the new directions. Leading a change process means actively promoting and interpreting it. As it did with Chrysler's Lee Ioccoca, leadership entails a vigorous advocacy, continually explaining the reasons for particular changes and their anticipated benefits to others both inside and outside the organization. In the midst of organizational transformation, people need to have their vision of the future regularly expanded and focused by those they look to for direction. As difficulties arise along the way, they need assurance that their leaders are keeping the faith, that they still trust the process, and believe the objectives to be worthwhile and achievable. Managing a change process means putting oneself consistently on the line as a champion of it.

PARTNERING THE JOURNEY

Modeling the new designs is basic to the leader's role, but organizational change is never simply a virtuoso performance. It requires the active participation of many others. Leadership's second major role has to do with enlisting other people in the challenge of working together to transform their organization. Leaders need colleagues they can count on when the chips are down. Employees who support the changes need to see that they have allies within the organization. It is the role of leadership to develop and continually expand this partnership for change.

In many ways, this activity is similar to building a movement. Leadership must invite people to join together in a great adventure to create the future. As the senior partners in the change enterprise, leaders build motivation by making time for people to share their ideas, listen to, and learn from one another. A common characteristic of the companies described in this book is their monthly, bimonthly, or quarterly team gatherings for reporting and celebrating progress, and for planning their next steps. Without such communication, people are often unaware of what is happening and feel cut off. Even members of the management team are frequently surprised in these sessions to discover how much the other taskforces have accomplished since the last meeting. Scheduling regular opportunities to share stories and reflect together builds the team's sense of accomplishment and pride, and, consequently, a greater readiness to take the next steps.

As people become active partners in designing and implementing change, they develop new capabilities. They become initiators and innovators and assume increased responsibility for the organization as a whole. They even discover that they can try out approaches that their superiors may question. This release of energy occurred when the Operations Director of a supermarket chain in Taiwan decided that the system his area supervisors were using to monitor store quality was no longer doing the job. Instead of simply revising the system himself, he challenged his supervisors to come up with their plan for improving store quality. Although unaccustomed to such direct responsibility, the group developed four new sets of procedures and tracking forms in a two-day workshop and tested them over the coming weeks. The Operations Director had doubts about the new designs, but he gave them the open space to try them out. Within two months, they had scrapped or revised three of these plans, but they were deeply excited about what they had learned and how they were beginning to function as a self-managing team. In one departure from traditional practice, they developed a series of ways to elicit direct customer input as a tactic for improving store quality. These employees were free to learn from their mistakes, as well as from their successes.

Partnering change is similar to helping someone learn to ride a bicycle. Beginners have to master this skill by themselves, but support and encouragement can play a determining role in their actually doing it. Falling down, getting up, and trying again are all part of the process. The spills and the opportunity and encouragement to try again are what finally develops the selfconfidence, along with the balance, judgment, and coordination that people need in order to succeed. Leaders play the role of partners who then help others learn from their own initiatives.

We see another form of partnering in the story of the Metacentros organization in Guatemala City. People in this organization have come to share their President's vision of a commercial enterprise that will make a significant contribution to the needs of residents in the city's low-income suburbs. The result is a large shopping complex that makes available a wide range of needed items at reasonable cost. Employees of Metacentros derive much of their motivation from being partners not only in organizational change, but also in the socioeconomic development of their society. While not every business has this direct a social mission, one of leadership's roles is to help define an organization's distinctive contribution to its community and to the wider society. The change process then becomes empowered by the sense of partnership in a larger purpose that includes but also transcends the organization itself.

Partnering change means working with both individuals and groups as they struggle with new and unfamiliar challenges. As an organization changes, people are called upon to alter their own former patterns of thinking and acting. Key players in the organization do not always welcome this and see that some of the changes will be difficult for them to accept. In the case of Widia (India), the machine tool company, the CEO himself stood up at one point in a planning session and spoke about how painful some of the changes being proposed by the group were to him. Without trying to block the new directions, he let people know the feelings he was experiencing. Not only did this release the group to share at a deeper level, but it also allowed other members of the team to affirm him in his struggle and to bring some healing humor into the situation.

At the same time, the change process often helps individual leaders make needed personal changes and learn new ways of partnering. Sometimes people are surprised to discover that they really prefer the new operating mode. The Head of the Maintenance Department in a U.S. chemical company operating in Taiwan was viewed by his colleagues as a difficult person to work with because of his highly directive style. In one planning session, he was tapped by the ICA facilitators, whom he had engaged, to lead the group in a participatory brainstorming and consensus-building workshop. To the surprise of his colleagues, he did a first-rate job and received strong affirmation from the group. He, in turn, was delighted with the results of his workshop and deeply appreciative of the affirmation of his peers. At the next planning session, he astounded his colleagues by reporting that he had led 15 similar workshops with his own group during the preceding two months.

One of the most challenging aspects of organizational transformation is to facilitate journeys of personal change as well. Enabling people to share their inner feelings and honestly examine old assumptions takes a special combination of sensitivity and skill. In the course of changing a corporation, people who have devoted their lives to building an organization can suddenly feel outdated or abandoned. At times, the leadership may even need to facilitate a kind of grieving process, a necessary step in helping group members leave the past and support the new directions.

This is time when even the best leaders can use some assistance from partners outside the organization. Outside consultants who work closely with the management team bring valuable expertise and objectivity to situations that could otherwise become painful interpersonal conflicts. As outsiders, they can make valuable generalizations derived from experience in other companies. For instance, they frequently recognize places where progress is blocked. Often they can anticipate obstacles better than an organization's leaders, simply because the leadership may be too close to these barriers. Consultants can help an organization analyze its current situation and aid in designing an effective strategy for change. As they facilitate events that require a high degree of participatory skill, they can also train others in the organization to become capable group facilitators.

Consultants also play a valuable mentoring role in the midst of a change process. They often become personal confidants to the leadership team, providing informed feedback and offering their own creative suggestions. They offer individual and small group support for those in the organization who are still wrestling with some of the changes, as well as for those who are moving briskly ahead. Even skilled leaders within the organization find that they benefit from the range of resources which outside consultants bring to the table. In several cases, these "outsiders" become some of the leadership team's most trusted partners.

Not surprisingly, benefits often flow both ways between an organization's leaders and its outside consultants. The ICA staff in India worked with that country's premier hotel chain when it began its major national and international expansion. They worked so closely with the company's Vice-President that they rapidly became a single highly interactive team. As they shaped and reshaped the project's ongoing designs and procedures, both experienced a lively flow of new insights. The Vice-President has since continued his relationship with the ICA, contributing to its other programs, and becoming a valuable resource for *its* staff. Developing and deepening these external as well as internal partnerships for change are important leadership functions.

ORCHESTRATING THE PERFORMANCE

In a change process, the third major role of an organization's leadership is to keep it all together and to keep it moving. One way of looking at the word "orchestration" involves the idea of arranging and combining experience and skill. To achieve effective change, leaders have to be able to see the whole and the parts, the one and the many. It is their job to ensure the integrity and ultimate effectiveness of the total transformation that has been set in motion.

There are always internal and external stakeholders who can and often will have an impact on organizational change. These groups may not all be directly involved in the change, but their understanding of it and support for it can be important. Among these are stockholders, people in the larger organizational matrix, customers, vendors, unions, the media, public interest groups, the immediate community, and the larger society within which the organization operates. In Taiwan, for example, environmental groups recently blocked factory expansions when the corporation's leadership failed to take public concerns seriously enough to make a convincing case for the safety of its operations. As orchestrator of the change process, the leader needs to develop and maintain support even from groups outside the organization.

The early experience of the American oil company in Taiwan points up what can happen when leadership does not assume this role. The first time this organization tried to launch a change process, the three officers who represented its shareholder companies decided that they should not participate when the management team met to develop a vision and strategic plan for the organization. Their concern was that their presence might block other people in the group from openly sharing their own thinking. The rest of the management team gathered and produced a long-term plan that set forth major changes in the organization. When the three officers reviewed the plan, they were startled by and resistant to its scope and far-reaching implications. Their resistance caused many of the proposed actions to be quietly put on hold or assigned to special taskforces for an indefinite period of "further study." As a result, predictable despair set in within the block management team and led to the departure in the coming months of several of its members. Only after several years and the arrival of a new president was the change process to be restarted—this time with the full participation of all the key players.

The case of the Mills Group in Brazil also shows what can happen when people are blindsided by realities that good leaders might have foreseen and prevented. In the midst of the Mills Group's transformational process, the Board of Directors met in closed session to make some decisions about cutbacks required because of an economic downturn. Presenting these plans to their employees afterwards, the leadership encountered widespread anger, anxiety, and misunderstanding, resulting in a work stoppage. In this case, after considerable effort, operations got back on track, and the Board recognized the stakeholder role of its employees. The Board now has a policy of sharing information with employees on a regular basis so that they can participate constructively in decisions that directly affect their future. The orchestrator's role is to anticipate such potential pitfalls and either take steps to prevent them or prepare people in advance to deal with them.

Whether or not timing is "everything," it is a critical component of orchestrating change. Because change requires a sense of momentum, the leader needs to see that this energy is generated and sustained. In its early stages, organizational change can produce a high level of enthusiasm. As the process continues, people's motivation for tackling the hard work depends increasingly on their perception of the progress the organization is making and how energetically its leadership supports the process. Keeping the momentum for change going requires that the company leaders work with others to help set the pace and phasing of the projected changes. Managers' intuitions are important when it comes to deciding the rhythm of the change—where it is most strategic to begin, when it is feasible or imperative to move quickly, and when action is best deferred to a later time. It is generally best to initiate change within projects that can produce rapid and visible results, rather than with ones that may take longer to reform. Orchestrating change means making sure that the process does not bog down; people need to see the productive fruits of their efforts. The team in Brazil's Mills Group has hit upon one creative way to do this by broadcasting daily over the employee public address system ten minutes of news about the changes occurring in the company.

Orchestrating transformation draws on leadership's capacity to think systemically. A systems thinker sees beyond the usual arenas of managerial responsibility to recognize how an organization's overall systems actually work and how they need to work for the sake of the desired changes.

Systemic thinking sees individual operations as components of larger systems which have the often unrecognized capacity to empower or frustrate any particular changes made within them.

The experience with quality circles illustrates the need for such thinking. These quality programs, started in U.S. manufacturing plants, were conceived of as ways for employees in small groups at the factory floor level to propose innovations for improving the quality of their operations. Early adopters of quality circle programs found their employees very receptive. Too often, however, implementing these proposals was frustrated by resistance from the larger system (e.g., slow decision making or a reluctance to grant more than token responsibility to line workers). Many organizations lose faith in planned change when its scope is too limited to affect the whole or when it is "toothless." Orchestrators of change make it their business to understand these larger systems and figure out how to deal with them so that they support rather than impede change.

Perhaps the most critical role of the orchestrator is that of caring for the mood and spirit of the people involved in the drama of organizational transformation. Change disrupts people's lives, raising their hopes and expectations, but also their anxiety levels. Transforming an organization can profoundly alter human relationships. We see this when a top-down chain of command system is replaced by a more participatory style of leadership, with its cross-functional taskforces and greater delegation of authority to front-line employees. While organizational change empowers people in countless ways, it calls into question some people's self-images and how they view the value of their work. Though the change process can give people a powerful sense of owning their future destinies, it can also be perceived as threatening their future livelihoods.

Even when organizational change is welcomed, it can raise the stress level and the FUD (fear, uncertainty and doubt) quotient in the workplace. When leaders fail to recognize and address the FUD reality, tensions and conflicts build and often the organization loses good people unnecessarily. It is, after all, the human beings in the organization who will finally determine what it can and will become. People need recognition for their best efforts, especially when these do not always succeed. These individuals need affirmation for what they are learning from these endeavors and for how they are growing as a result of that learning.

Orchestrating change involves a high degree of sensitivity and responsiveness to a group's mood. A good leader supports that mood when it is up and finds ways to raise it when it is heading for the cellar. When the General Manager of India's JK Fibre plant saw that his rejuvenated team was about to set a new daily production record, he ordered an ice cream truck to the plant site to distribute free scoops for everyone throughout the day. In Guatemala's Metacentros organization, the President has introduced monthly social events, where all the employees can celebrate birthdays, see movies, and demonstrate their performing abilities. This kind of care for the human spirit renews commitment in the midst of the hard work of organizational change. An effective leader provides innovative interventions that refresh and restore that spirit.

LEADERSHIP'S ONGOING COMMITMENT

Even the greatest leader cannot single-handedly transform an organization. As the case studies in this book illustrate, broad participation in the process is essential today. Without vigorous and skillful leadership on the part of management, however, participatory change is hardly imaginable and certainly not sustainable. For centuries, good managers have intuitively performed many of the critical leadership roles described above. In an environment of organizational transformation, these roles must become the very lifestyle of leadership.

Finally, it would be wrong to conclude that these leadership activities are temporary roles, assumed for the sake of effecting certain changes and then laid aside once those changes have been executed. The journey of organizational change has become an ongoing rather than a transitory reality. Managing in a time of stable routine is no longer an option. While a particular set of changes may have a beginning and ending point, the process of change itself does not. A leader who is an effective member of an organization's leadership team assumes responsibility not only for the organization's but also for his/her own journey of perpetual change. Inventing and juggling the new roles of modeling, partnering, and orchestrating the change define what leadership in today's successful organization is all about.

13. CROSS-CULTURAL LEADERSHIP

by
ROY STANSBURY AND CHRIS YATES

*Countries represented in the DuPont region called Asia
Pacific are: India, Pakistan, Malaysia, Philippines,
Singapore, Indonesia, Thailand, Hong Kong, Taiwan, Japan,
Republic of Korea, People's Republic of China, Australia,
and New Zealand. Within DuPont there is an attempt to
unite these nations in the corporate construct of the
region called Asia Pacific. One might say that Asia
Pacific stretches from Karachi to San Francisco!*

Depending on whom you talk to, what you read, and what your life's view is, it is easy to gather many answers to the question, What is a leader? Within the wide range of answers to this question is one clear point of consensus: leadership is critical to our well-being, even survival, in today's bewildering business environment of change. If this is true for any company trying to adjust to doing business in a global economy, it is doubly so for a corporation like DuPont Asia Pacific which operates in a unique cultural context.

The countries represented in the DuPont region called Asia Pacific are India, Pakistan, Malaysia, Philippines, Singapore, Indonesia, Thailand, Hong

Kong, Taiwan, Japan, Republic of Korea, People's Republic of China, Australia, and New Zealand. Their peoples speak a minimum of nine major languages other than English, practice several forms of religion, and variously struggle for and against democratic forms of government. From the Chinese nations to the Aboriginal tribes of Australia to the kaleidoscope of Indian peoples, everyone can draw on millennia of proud history. It is erroneous to think of 'Asia' as a homogeneous grouping, although recent global market imperatives have compelled many countries to link, for instance ASEAN (Association of South East Nations), or CER (Common Economic Region - Australia and New Zealand) and the Pacrim members.

FACING CULTURAL AND CORPORATE COMPLEXITIES

Almost every company today confronts the reality of working in a culturally complex global economy. As a U.S. company, led predominantly by North Americans, DuPont Asia Pacific has had to learn to operate effectively in the non-Western cultures of Asia. In addition to learning the realities of each of the different cultures, competing in the Japanese market with the quality demands of that market was an added challenge. To meet these challenges, in the mid-1980s, DuPont's senior leadership recognized that the company had to change the way it was doing business. In such a large corporation as DuPont, the corporate direction setting is largely centered in the worldwide headquarters. As this direction is filtered down to the operator on the 'shop floor,' it begins to lose its meaning. An example of this kind of conceptual direction is DuPont's corporate vision, "Becoming a Great Global Company through people by using the continuous improvement process to excel in serving four key constituents worldwide: customers, shareholders, employees, and society. Given such a wide-ranging corporate vision, the first question that a person working at the operational level might ask is, 'What does this have to do with me?'"

It is the job of the company's leadership to help all the stakeholders answer that question, despite the size and cultural spread of the corporation. It is a complex task. In certain instances becoming a 'Great Global Company' might mean growth at a rate that far exceeds the current rate. At present DuPont Asia Pacific is achieving double digit growth in many of the countries where it operates, with the expectation that core businesses, in many cases, should be able to grow at an even greater rate than the nations in which they operate. Those who must make such rapid growth happen can see that this pace is nearly impossible. They struggle to keep up as it is. In difficult situations such as these, an effective leader can reconcile this apparent gap. From one perspective, leaders are accountable for delivering the results expected of them by their superiors. From the other, the same leaders have the responsibility to support their subordinates who are struggling just to keep up.

RECONCILING DIFFERENCES

Leadership must, in such situations, reconcile the two seemingly conflicting responsibilities to discover what is really possible. The use of the word 'reconcile' is deliberate. Ronnie Lessem, at London's City University Business Development Program, describes reconciliation, or integration, in the following way:

Integration involves first, the discovery of difference, and, second, the unifying of apparent opposites. After all, we attain unity only through variety. Differences must be integrated rather than annihilated or absorbed [1].

'Reconciling' differences is essential. Leadership cannot hide from the demands of those who set strategic direction and the existing capabilities of those who make it operational. Many times, corporate stakeholders find themselves facing several of the same issues over and over. It is important for leadership to enable the organization to advance beyond repetitive problem solving. Reconciliation focuses on gaining the greatest possible unity among all the stakeholders involved to serve the greater good of the organization and, by extension, the society in which it resides. Ultimately, we depend on people to create this sense of unity and to consider all of the values involved.

In an organization, effective leadership discovers and then removes limitations on human endeavor; leaders do not create obstacles. Good leaders continually enable the organization to envision its own opportunities and possibilities, thereby creating among each stakeholder the sense of leading one's own destiny. DuPont Asia Pacific achieved this sense of self-direction when it decided to follow a strategy of high performance work systems in its manufacturing operations. This approach increases levels of self-management within the organization, and redistributes decision-making responsibilities to levels where they can be most effective. In this arrangement, leaders act as resources, and shed to a great extent the role of manager or controller. With this divesting of hierarchical control, the organization's stakeholders assume a more important role in the corporation. Employees, suppliers, customers, members of society as well as shareholders, all who care for the organization, are then aligned with its larger purpose. It is leadership's task to translate the company's strategic direction into terms understandable to those operating and managing the value-adding process, for example, those who are enabling the "Great Global Company" to acquire 'X' percentage of the China market.

DuPont Asia Pacific has been tackling this assignment for a while. In 1987, the company began to improve its ability to provide leadership and manage overall organizational effectiveness. DuPont traditionally had seen itself as a company that makes things; from its origins of making gun powder, to the invention of nylon, to the widespread application of products such as Kevlar® and Lycra®, it has depended upon its strong R&D and technology base. Several years previous to its 1987 effort, DuPont had already recognized the need to be more focused on the market. An either-or mentality would have said to focus either on R&D or on the market. But, it was time to go beyond that. It was time to reconcile this strong internal technical capability with the needs of the market, and demonstrate that both could coexist peacefully.

By employing an organizational change technology referred to as OE (organizational effectiveness)—jointly developed by Charles Krone, a Carmel, California-based organizational development consultant, and Dupont—the company moved towards continuous improvement (CI) of the company's functional as well as business excellence. A conscious effort was made to improve DuPont's ability to transform things internally, by turning material into a product, or an order into a delivery. At the same time, DuPont recognized the role of CI in understanding and meeting customer needs. Providing a value-adding offering to customers was essential to the company's longer-term success. The demands of manufacturing things and at the same time meeting the needs of the customer had to be reconciled. The company had to understand, for example, that the Japanese were not asking for anything unreasonable when they demanded what seemed to be extremely high quality standards and on-time delivery.

FITTING ACTIONS TO WORDS

It soon became clear that as internal consultants with DuPont Asia Pacific, we needed to work on its corporate culture; otherwise the company would have continued fixing the same things over and over. As facilitators of change in organizations, we have spent a great deal of time and energy enabling various businesses to articulate new visions of the future, only to arrive at a certain point and be disappointed. With action speaking louder than words, we frequently have witnessed the 'hierarchy of leadership' do the opposite of what the organization has been 'led' to expect.

On many occasions in working with appointed leaders to increase employee involvement, we have heard leaders react with, "This sounds good when time allows it, but what happens when a quick decision is required?" Too often leadership's actions reinforce this mindset; stakeholders are told their participation is important. However, when there is a company crisis and quick 'executive' decisions are required, the leadership reverts to old patterns and abandons stakeholder participation in decision making. Leaders often speak about breaking down hierarchical managerial patterns, and their words create specific expectations. The right words are used, yet what is actually being done trumpets business as usual. How then does an organization break this cultural pattern that returns to the same old ways once pressure builds?

To change what the organization and its leadership are doing, it is necessary to understand the existing corporate culture and align it with concrete external needs. To begin this process at DuPont, we needed to clearly comprehend what is communicated to employees as important, when employees are rewarded and recognized, how they spend their time, and what tolerances of behavior the management will permit. Once we understand these elements we can begin to examine how well they support or hinder necessary corporate culture shifts. Elements that are supportive of the new culture remain; ones that hinder are removed or changed.

We saw three areas requiring change before DuPont Asia Pacific could transform its company culture. Our first struggle began with the desire to have people work together in teams. DuPont's culture has traditionally nourished and supported the individual contributor over the team, by way of individual objectives, performance reviews, and rewards. We saw that these systems must change so that the organization places greater value on teams and teamwork.

Our second task was to help the company see that if a major responsibility of leadership is to manage the corporate culture of the organization, then a clear understanding of future needs must be developed. All the shifts in the company's state of being then can move towards this new direction, and help revise its way of doing business; if the corporation fails to execute these shifts, it runs the risk of continuing to do things as they always have.

Unless the culture that exists within the organization promotes and supports its vision, then it is likely that the vision will remain a dream. Our third assignment was to help the company understand how visions function in corporate transformation. Visions of the future are important, but equally so is the need to understand the company's state of being that produces behavior. Without this understanding, the focus of people and their organization becomes cloudy. How well the stakeholders understand and deal with the culture outside of the organization determines how effectively they can create new and better culture within the corporation. Leadership is the primary instrument in achieving this balance, particularly in DuPont Asia Pacific, where the environment in which leadership must operate, with corporate and national cultures colliding, is very complex.

IDENTIFYING CONTRADICTIONS

One way to arrive at some understanding of the prevailing national cultures is by identifying contradictions. In this sense, contradiction affords the opportunity for reconciliation. Such a line of inquiry into a multicultural environment where contradictions are plentiful, therefore, should prove more than useful to us to abstract reconciliation, just as the leadership might put reconciliation into action on the 'shop floor' of any work organization. To carry out this task, there is fertile ground, not only within the culture of DuPont, but also externally, in the sharply differentiated national and racial cultures of Asia Pacific.

There is a very strong work culture in DuPont as seen in the way people from very different business perspectives come together for group experiences, and need little time to feel a sharing of common values. Some of these corporate values are:

(1) Care and protection of the body (safety value);
(2) Paramount importance of the customer (external focus value);
(3) Adherence to corporate and national laws (ethics value);
(4) Respect for individual uniqueness (diversity value).

At an intensive three-week development course for high potential leaders, held at the Australian Management College in Victoria, Australia, in 1992, the host faculty noted that the group of 26 nationally diverse people, many of whom had not previously met each other, took an unusually short time to function as a collective. The faculty also noted that, replicating their 'back home' work environment, some members of this group felt that it was imprudent to challenge corporate core values publicly, except on pain of being in disfavor because of perceived inappropriate eccentricity. Obviously organizational values are powerful and overt in this corporation.

INFLUENCE OF WESTERN THOUGHT

Western organizational change technology, including that developed by Charles Krone and DuPont, cannot escape the influence of Western thought. Rooted in individualism, based on the belief in the potential of individual growth, this type of change process is insinuated into cultures whose sources, generally, are founded on contrary notions. Asian cultures are based upon the relative importance of the group (family, tribe, nation). To stand aside from the group is, in fact, to lose an individuality which can be expressed only within it. When attempting to implement a change process, one ignores the contradiction between the application of technology and the hostility of the environment at the expense of ineffectiveness. An example is the reluctance of the typical Asian leader to subject the technology to the critical debate which it demands, so that new possibilities can be revealed. Contradiction is obviously implicit in the environment.

The paradox is that Asian management culture has no indigenous storehouse of management knowledge from which to draw to help its members compete, so to speak, on a 'world-class' level. Even the much vaunted (in some cases overly so) Japanese business leaders need, as well as exploit, Western management systems without which many of their great corporations would not be successful. Asian leadership, largely drawing on a Confucian and Buddhist heritage which suborns vigorous public debate, needs the very technology against which it uncomfortably struggles. Its need and our struggle as change agents to facilitate an apparently contradictory process demand a great deal of our attention. The essence of our paradox is contained in values hitherto unexpressed in either Western or Eastern form.

At the level of technology delivery, we have had to cope with the expectation that DuPont's global corporate values be manifest in leadership behavior. The typical reaction by Asian leadership to this expectation is that mere compliance will do. Thus, for the Asian leader, organizational values are transmitted. This transmission, however, does not satisfy the premise demanding that the individual undergo and accept a personal awakening that truly changes the individual. For the Asian leader, a mysterious (to Western thinking) trust is placed in the ability of the group, rather than in the individual, to pass through these thresholds of change. If this is so, then we do not have a way of assessing the developmental change which has taken place in groups of Asian leaders. At the moment we have faith that it is so.

A positive sign that the corporation has adopted a so-called learning environment conducive to change is the genuine support provided by several key and influential senior leaders throughout the organization. Although such support comes from expatriate managers, this does not indicate a lack of support from indigenous leaders (who presently have limited representation at 'top' levels). It must be said, however, that for the most part, few Asian leaders sympathetic to our leadership change process have self-awareness of their own relationship to the change process. Their 'support' is limited to their belief in a causal link between a process application and a successful 'result.' When we expose a group of leaders to the change process in workshop form, and they can see a pay-back in rapid and positive behavior change, their support grows. To grasp a straw like this is a significant way for us to maintain our faith in the value of the process.

One should not be beguiled into thinking that the environment is consciously hostile. On the contrary, it is vital, hopeful, and entrepreneurial, if a trifle serious by Western standards of humor. Recognizing the enormous energy potential in the paradoxes of this region, we feel that a humanizing change process like ours will succeed, but only by borrowing traditional Asian qualities such as patience, humility, and pragmatism.

CONTINUOUS IMPROVEMENT INITIATIVE

In 1991, on a global basis, DuPont went like a bull at a gate into a continuous improvement (CI) effort. Like other organizations, DuPont had been bitten by the quality bug, and not for the first time in its two centuries of existence. Unfortunately for DuPont in Asia Pacific, this CI initiative was met with a degree of skepticism and cynicism. Typically, it was asked, "Is this yet another flavor of the month?" A long series of such well-intentioned programs had been inflicted upon the company. In a worldwide organization, such as DuPont, with huge resources, global initiatives for change are often uncoordinated; not every business, country, or stakeholder understands their purpose.

As the CI effort hit Asia Pacific, our first reaction was like that of everyone elsethat it would go away like all the other "stuff" they throw at us! Until reality hit home, that all that we had been working on was about to be perceived as passé, replaced by the 'new' program. Even though new programs are received with skepticism, compliant leaders still tend to substitute them for 'old' programs. As we began to ponder our response to this latest venture, our first thought was one of almost going to war. We began to mount our defenses, for clearly it was our virtue that was being threatened! With some gentle old-fashioned prodding from DuPont's leadership, we began to realize that our chances of winning, defined here as "keeping the game in play," would be higher by cooperating and not by competing. In other words, we should have been paying attention to our own message.

Our work as internal change agents is based on a premise that an organization can evolve to a point where it can maintain or renew itself. However, certain elements must be in place and interact with each other in such a way that evolution or change is a natural part of the organizational process. These elements comprise something we refer to later as a 'developmental learning organization'. Our work related to organizational and leadership effectiveness employing the OE technology was about enabling this organizational evolution. We can see that the CI initiative and our work were not at odds, but complementary.

The first step in marrying CI with our work on organizational and leadership effectiveness took place at a meeting of country managers in Chiba, Japan, where the DuPont Asia Pacific country managers were attending an orientation session with a number of DuPont managers who had been designated as CI resources. At these sessions, they learned a variety of CI tools, e.g., business process mapping, supply chain improvement, and problem-solving techniques, in addition to pertinent OE technology. At this meeting country managers discussed their overall intent regarding an organizational development strategy. Earlier we had reviewed with them the concept of a developmental learning organization.

DEVELOPMENTAL LEARNING ORGANIZATION

Our feeling was that our longer-term business success depended not on new programs, initiatives or interventions. Rather it depended upon developing this capability so that the organization could evolve and transform itself by ridding the company of old patterns. Krone has related the term "entropy" to this work. We found ourselves in an environment where most people would say that the kind of organization that works in most of Asia is a hierarchically oriented organization. At the same time we were attempting to address the question, Where will this region of the world be in five to ten years? That issue caused us to think differently about how we approached our work within DuPont. With change taking place at such a rapid pace and labor being in short supply in several places in Asia, we felt we had to focus leadership's energy on a future organizational form. The country managers, with whom we were working, felt that a developmental learning organization made sense as a goal. But first they had to understand what a developmental learning organization actually involves.

A developmental learning organization depends on highly self-motivated teams, empowered people learning and working interdependently. Involvement and participation are basic to these teams since they have the 'authority to act,' are highly disciplined, and provide their own guidance by creating standards and regulations themselves. As they consider the team approach, many managers express concern about losing control. In such a team environment, control or discipline is no less important; rather what is crucial is the question of the source of control. Effective teams reconcile their value-adding ability through clearly articulated missions derived from well-defined visions. They understand completely what is required of them; all or part of the team is actively involved in developing its 'own' direction.

In many of the plants where work systems, referred to earlier as high performance work systems, are based on the developmental learning organization approach, plant operators do develop their own understanding of their individual mission and their connection to the greater corporate mission. Direct connection with the stakeholders of their particular business motivates the team whose members understand the needs of the stakeholders whether they are suppliers, customers, shareholders, society, or fellow employees. Rather than creating a conventional hierarchy of people and individual responsibilities, the organization structures itself around the work which needs to be performed. People are rewarded and recognized for acquiring additional skills to support this work. These individuals perform a wider range of work than is typical in the more conventional organization which would limit people to particular jobs. For example, in Singapore manufacturing operations, one goal is that everyone will support the manufacturing process. It would not be unusual for the plant manager or a secretary to know how to pack product or perform some other task to support the manufacturing process.

For a developmental learning organization to be able to renew itself, the individual members must be able to have greater control over their own development. After receiving formal classroom instruction, workers themselves perform in a way that continues the process of personal development; they recognize their responsibility to teach themselves and others. Whether the setting is formal or informal, the organization becomes one in which teaching and learning are highly valued. Life-long learning is an integral part of the long-term success of organizations in today's climate of change. One of the cultural difficulties which this implies is that of the Oriental veneration of the teacher, and the relegated position of the taught.

However, two unifying concepts, leadership and principles, may help coalesce the elements of teamwork, vision and mission, needs and values of stakeholders, as well as learning and teaching. On the one hand, the leadership concept should be inherent in the minds of all organizational members (and certainly those in the hierarchy). However, leadership must be seen both to be authentic and capable of creating an environment where trust and empowerment can flourish. This kind of leadership needs to be demonstrated not behind closed doors but, on the 'shop floor,' where leaders are seen as visible, approachable, and most importantly, willing to have the organization connect with its stakeholders. The second concept of principles, on the other hand, then provides the guidance held in common among all the stakeholders within the developmental learning organization. Principles help provide parameters, but do not limit the creative energy of the organization. Principles create a different order; they bring freedom and discipline to thinking.

Such a view of a developmental learning organization was appealing to the country managers in Asia Pacific. They all agreed that these characteristics needed to be in place in their organizations. The task we faced was how to bring into being what seemed to many of these leaders to be a very idealistic end state. In our sessions with these country managers at this meeting in Chiba, we learned once again the importance of getting issues out in the open for discussion. Second, we saw how powerful the participative process can be in helping members of a group confront a common issue and commit themselves to the greater good of the organization. At the beginning of the meeting in Chiba, only a minority of the country managers felt comfortable with the challenge of putting the developmental learning organization concept to work. One in particular was unsure about its practicability in his assigned country. At the end of our half-day session, they all had decided to embark on the journey and to acquire the skills necessary to move towards the ideal.

INCENTIVES FOR CHANGE

As in-house consultants at DuPont Asia Pacific, we continue to support the country managers as the corporate learning organization evolves. Some of those who advocate such journeys of change claim the only imperative driving DuPont and other organizations towards such a concept is the need to remain competitive. The question we are faced with is, Does that mean that if DuPont could remain competitive without adopting such a concept, we would not be doing this? This is not a motivating thought. Futurists, John Naisbitt and Patricia Aburdene, tell us that "the best and brightest will gravitate towards these corporations that foster personal growth" [2]. This is part of the competitive reality. However, transforming an organization should be done not only to remain competitive, but also because it is the right thing to do.

Leadership has a bewildering array of choices for dealing with the need for organizational change. Is it a sound option to employ hierarchically-oriented, 'need-to-know' organizations? Most people spend over one-third of their waking hours at a workplace (indeed for many it is easily more). Surely it is better to be in a work culture in which we experience joy, as well as a feeling of being more productive, rather than one in which we constantly ponder what we would prefer to be doing. For far too many, the workplace is their only humanizing community, the only place that they regularly experience true social interaction. Not only should it be a place where people can freely do a day's work, but also where they can feel as though they are nourished by participating in decisions which affect them.

REFLECTING ON A PARADOX

Our experiences with DuPont Asia Pacific have taught us that an environment riddled with work and national contradictions is a huge challenge for leaders, but also is rich ground in which to develop effective and progressive leadership skills. The conversion of contradiction into paradox may well be an undiscovered skill in the leader's armory, undiscovered because the nature of multicultural work environments has had scant attention from culture change agents. Our behavior as agents working with leadership was derived from a cognitive technology which is very difficult to facilitate. We do not believe, that, as an organization, we are the worse for the attempt. The passion that carries us forward is our belief that human beings are more important than people-made entropic systems, of which DuPont is one. We asked for reflective comments from several leaders who had worked with us in reshaping DuPont's leadership culture. This sampling of leaders is all male because a combination of conservative transnational and male-dominated Asian cultures has limited the promotion of women into leadership positions.

To the question, What do you consider to be the dominant outside force on our businesses?, most leaders nominated 'economics.' For example, a senior U.S. executive working in the region replied that the dominant outside force is "primarily economic, which has made it more difficult for consistent direction and to see the payback of the developmental organization." Because it drives social and political change, economics preoccupies leaders in this region. We should point out that while economics as an imperative might be universal, the use to which national wealth in Asia Pacific is put varies considerably. In Japan, for instance, welfare payments are low compared with New Zealand, long established as a 'welfare state.'

We also asked DuPont's leaders to articulate their images of leadership. Most saw the ability to 'see,' 'listen for' or 'feel' the onset of change as important characteristics of a good leader. It is as if a leader senses the need to be developed, rather like a gamekeeper whose stewardship over an estate depends upon sensory intake, as much as intellectual understanding of what needs to be done. A Japanese leader commented:

> They [leaders] do not invent or develop new products, but help
> their subordinates in taking risks to do so. Empowerment of peo-
> ple had been and is the key to success.

What kind of base have we actually established at DuPont Asia Pacific? This question brought wildly swinging responses, reflecting the varying progress of participative work cultures in countries and businesses in Asia Pacific. It seems though that something has begun to embed itself, even if it is only vigorous debate. For instance, to quote a Japanese leader:

> We have not yet clearly defined who the leaders in DuPont in
> Asia Pacific are. Locals, whose traits and styles are different
> from typical American leaders, need to be understood and
> accepted globally.

Lastly we asked, What role does a developmental learning organization carry out in meeting these challenges of leadership in changing environments? A Korean personnel specialist responds, "We should maintain what we have learned and then improve that. We have introduced too many new concepts, and must avoid destroying past achievements and learnings."

Leaders in large corporations such as DuPont resent the plethora of new ideas and sometimes competing (but not ultimately conflicting) change programs such as OE and CI. Though some accept change as the dominant outside force, they nevertheless attempt to stabilize the internal organization, in many ways protect it from change. On the whole, however, we find the corporate CI effort to actually energize the building of developmental learning organizations. The view of one CEO in DuPont Asia Pacific outlines the route to change:

Developmental learning organizations need to be viewed as a real route to advance people and business. They need to be put in place in harmony with local culture. That's the issue today. They must be driven by nationals in each country.

Hidden here is a contradiction. How does the situation in which organizations are driven by local nationals (with which we heartily agree) sit with the objective of global business organizations based upon simple value chains from maker to user? Work and leadership cultures differ widely along the chain, making it not a simple but a complex task to reconcile these differences. The paradox of complexity serving simplicity is a major job for leaders, and shows perhaps that change is not only the dominant force without, but also within, organizations. Flushing out this contradiction and converting it into useful paradox seems to be a way of bringing some sense to the difficult task of knowing, understanding, and acting on the states of being within organizations. In this way we may be able to do more of what leaders envision as the appropriate response to change. It has been difficult to operate in often adverse environments, in corporate and national cultures frequently unresponsive to the need to radically change outmoded thinking and practices of leadership. In our experiences with DuPont Asia Pacific over the past five years we have witnessed both the wonder and the divisiveness of participation. Wherever we have achieved advances, it has been worth the effort. Not least has been the pleasure in working in this new world with delightful people.

References

[1]   Lessem Ronnie. *Global Management Principles*. New York: Prentice Hall, 1989.

[2]   Naisbitt, John and Patricia Aburdene. *Megatrends 2000*. New York: William Morrow, 1990.

14. FACILITATION SKILLS IN ACTION

by

ROBERT R. VANCE

*"I can state unequivocally that successful facilitation techniques
can span the globe. Effective facilitators can involve people
from very different national and organizational cultures as active
participants in and agents of change. They can build on
cultural diversity and use it as a means of expanding beyond
what could be an organization's limited concerns and outlook."*
Robert R. Vance

Facilitation has multiple roots in a diverse set of circumstances. Seen as a form of specialized group guidance, it is used in teaching, counseling, training, and therapy. Several companies experimented with it some decades ago believing that more employee participation in decision making could result in improved productivity. The term "facilitator" became interchangeable with a variety of roles including consultant, teacher, leader, trainer, and instructor. What once was simply a style preference for directing a group has become a highly effective professional service that is in growing demand. Increasingly, organizations from all sectors of society are hiring trained process facilitators to guide their major planning events in the confidence that guided strategic planning will save the organization valuable time, improve the quality of work produced, and be well worth the cost.

Some companies have both internal and external process facilitators. An internal facilitator is hired in-house and works for that organization only. External facilitators, like those discussed in this chapter, have their own professional practices and may be contracted by many clients. External facilitators provide the objectivity of an outsider and bring to the individual company the experience of working with a variety of organizations. Although this chapter discusses the work of external facilitation, the process and skills are the same whether they are carried out by internal or external facilitators.

The definition of "facilitator" is shifting from the passive role of helper to a new emphasis on a more active guiding role. The facilitator is becoming a disciplined catalyst who stimulates and maintains the overall planning process. Process facilitation takes that a step further. Those who practice the art of process facilitation use both a highly honed set of participatory skills and also a keen intuitive sense of what the group needs. Facilitation in action in strategic planning sessions involves deceptively simple techniques such as conducting self-introductions, printing an agenda on a flip chart, leading brainstorming sessions and periodic attempts at refocusing a wandering discussion back to an agreed upon agenda. These techniques have become second nature for a well-trained person who leads a group meeting. It is rightly assumed that most people can learn these facilitation skills with a minimal amount of training and preparation. Experience is the key to how well they apply what they learn.

KEYS TO FACILITATION SUCCESS

As an experienced process facilitator who has consulted in several countries, I know that process facilitation will work anywhere on the globe. In this chapter, I discuss my work with an international bank in Lagos, Nigeria. **The first key** that links this bank to other groups where process facilitation works is that there are within these organizations highly competent and caring executives who want to win. These leaders are not afraid to allow their colleagues to participate in the decision making and acceptance of new responsibility that leads to genuine success and accomplishment.

The second key to facilitation success is a long-term commitment to stay the course for several years and ensure that a quality organization is established. **The third key** is to use a team approach in which many people share in both the burden of deciding what needs to happen in the develop-

Company Profile	
Name of company	Niegeria International Bank Ltd.
Name of holding company	Owned 40% by Citicorp Overseas Investment Company and 60% by private Nigerian investors
Commercial focus	Corporate, commercial, and investment banking service
Head office	Lagos, Nigeria
Number of branches	8: 6 in Nigeria, and 2 in the neighboring Republic of Niger
Leader and title	Amirapu Somasekhar, Managing Director (1988-1992)

ment and growth of the company, as well as in the satisfaction of seeing those new corporate goals achieved.

PROCESS FACILITATION IN ACTION: IN LAGOS, NIGERIA

Though my wife Cynthia and I often work as the Vance team from our company, Strategics International, Inc., located in Miami, Florida, I joined a facilitator colleague, Sherwood Shankland in putting our experience into action with the Nigeria International Bank (NIB) in Lagos, Nigeria. Between 1989 and 1991, Sherwood and I conducted a series of ten-day management retreats for senior bank management at NIB. Although the bank is a majority locally owned bank, it is fully a part of the worldwide Citicorp operation. The main offices of NIB are in Lagos, the largest city in Nigeria, where all the major corporations and government offices are located.

Unquestionably, NIB is one of the leading international banks in Nigeria. In a banking climate that tolerated a wide variety of quality, NIB consistently offered superior products and service that resulted in the bank's gaining many of the most respected companies and institutions as their clients. Although NIB is not large in terms of numbers of customers, it is a highly influential bank in the overall banking picture in Nigeria. The greatest strength of NIB is its Citicorp connection which allows it to draw on all the banking products created worldwide, and participate in the Citicorp corporate culture that stresses quality service and a determination to serve the client needs.

One of the other great strengths of Citicorp around the world is the large number of international staff members assigned to each country. Out of a group of 30 managers at NIB, ten were from a country other than Nigeria, and these ten were from six different countries. In one way these diverse operating styles and sometimes conflicting cultures can be frustrating. But this diversity eventually became a great benefit in helping the NIB team invent innovative ways to succeed in Nigeria.

During 1989, the first year we were in Nigeria, it was already obvious that NIB was facing dramatic changes in its external environment. The government had just changed the rules for the exchange rates for banks, which up to that time admittedly had been very favorable. This government action was carried out with little advance warning. It wiped out a large portion of NIB's expected revenues that year and consequently their profits. Over the next two years, several dramatic factors affected revenues. These events included a coup attempt, an extensive fire in the bank offices, and the enactment of additional government regulations. All of these forced NIB to expend an enormous effort just to maintain revenues, much less increase them beyond the levels of previous years.

When the government changed the exchange rate rules the second time, it encouraged the creation and expansion of locally owned banks (which were attracted by a subsidy) over international banks (which tend to favor more open markets). Overnight, the local banks started to amass huge profits. As a result, the local banks offered their managers salaries many times those of local NIB managers (and the local managers of other international banks), and promised a quick advancement in rank of one or two levels. This competition, of course, had a great impact on the self-esteem of the Nigerian managers at NIB. Consequently, NIB quickly lost some of its more talented and well-trained local staff members. Since Citibank has an excellent management training program, NIB managers became the most sought after professionals in the country. Interestingly, because of the great depth of managerial skill, even after NIB lost several of them to small upcoming banks, it still had the strongest management team in the country.

CRITICAL ROLE OF THE MANAGING DIRECTOR

The critical factor allowing NIB to maintain its balance amidst this upheaval was the effective leadership of NIB's Managing Director, Amirapu Somasekhar, or Soma as he is known to most people. I had met and worked with him when he was with the Caribbean Division of Citibank International in Miami. Soma is a very capable yet demanding leader who demonstrates a personal concern for his staff. His bold leadership and cooperative spirit create a working atmosphere where policies can be discussed and changed. His willingness to allow such broad-based participation reflects a self-confidence rare in senior management. Sherwood and I saw that he genuinely listened to ideas or issues the bank employees raised. When he thought these suggestions were in the best interests of the company, he was quite willing to move on them. His approach to Sherwood and me, as facilitators, was both collegial and collaborative. He insisted on knowing exactly how we intended to conduct the discussions and then he allowed us to proceed. We greatly appreciated his style and stance which enabled us to work for him in the best possible working environment.

NIB FACILITATION CHALLENGE: INCREASING REVENUES AND TEAMWORK

Our work in Nigeria began in the waiting room of my doctor in Miami. While Soma and his kids waited for their overseas shots, he told me that he had been transferred from Citicorp in Miami to head up the bank in Nigeria. With energy radiating out of his eyes, he said his task at NIB would be to build a team and to increase profits, and that he wanted Sherwood and me to help him with these tasks after he was settled in his new job.

A few months later, we were called to Nigeria by Soma to engage in the following four process facilitation activities:

(1) **Meet with the client to identify the issues and opportunities** the organization faces and to create a participative process for discussing these issues and for building action plans;

(2) **Lead a series of strategic or operational planning sessions that result in specific implementation plans** and directly serve the vital interest of the client;

(3) **Use a range of group methods (team discussions and activities), as well as individual techniques, that will develop strong teams** and improve the *esprit de corps* of the entire organization;

(4) **Act as objective moderators who oversee all aspects of the planning process**. This neutrality encourages all ideas to be heard and assists the group in choosing appropriate strategies.

Though these four objectives were the framework for our facilitation work at NIB, each year we were there, we custom designed the process for the particular emphasis and tasks that Soma required. Our consultations spanned three years, from 1989 through 1991. In general, our sessions began with a review of where we were, i.e., a time-lined perspective in which the attendees told their stories of the accomplishments and key events of the past year, interpreted what they had learned, and determined their directions for the future. Next we created a palette of future possibilities and mapped them on large expanses of paper spread across the front wall of the meeting room where we gathered.

The first year we diagramed revenue opportunities and matrixed them to discover which ones had the potential to provide the highest revenue in the shortest time. The third year Soma asked us to lead the managers' team in creating a five-year shared vision chart with strategic intents, benefits, components, and projected results for each column on that chart. Over one-half of the agenda for each management retreat was devoted to serious work on implementation plans, including product implementation briefs that detailed action steps, assigned responsibilities, and set due dates.

FOCUS ON REVENUE GENERATION

Our first task with NIB was to lead planning sessions that would result in concrete plans for increased revenues; this became the major undertaking of the first retreat in 1989. Several bold and far-sighted plans were created in these sessions and actually executed by the managers in the next four weeks. Although this type of planning facilitation process will work with any size company in either the private or public sector, implementation moves more quickly in the private sector because a company like NIB can mobilize its forces and financial resources quickly to institute change overnight. In the public sector, on the other hand, there often is a weaker pattern of accountability, so there is less pressure for change. Frequently, public institutions' regulations and procedures make any shift very difficult.

Since one of the main intents of the bank's vision was to increase NIB's revenue and profits, the managers' team members decided to insist that revenue generation and cost containment be priorities for every department in the bank. Sherwood and I focused on this challenge in all of the retreats and were pleased with the responses of the participants to our efforts.

Because so many senior and mid-managers had been involved in both planning retreats, they understood exactly why revenue generation and cost containment were so important and why their departments needed to accept this challenge. Consequently, they moved on it immediately and effectively. In the third year, the financial situation had stabilized enough that we were able to go beyond the topics involved in NIB's first objective and conduct a conference on long-range planning. In the third retreat in 1991, the team built a five-year vision of new strategic directions for the bank. Again, this plan for the 1990s was the result of broad-based input throughout the bank; it was a consensus of the best thinking of the entire management of NIB.

During the three years of these facilitated company retreats (1989–1991), revenues increased steadily, and over the five years since the retreats began, the bank has achieved a dramatic increase in revenue. Of course, many factors contributed to this success, but the retreats were certainly a key factor. In retrospect, it is likely that the very difficult internal and external forces also helped to create the success NIB experienced. The dramatic regulatory changes within Nigeria forced people to expend effort beyond anything they would have thought possible. NIB won with it. Even the fire within NIB's own walls had a positive effect as it reminded the team again that they were working in a situation with forces that were sometimes beyond their control. Despite its physical damage to NIB, the fire actually brought people together and strengthened their resolve to win.

CREATING A STRONG TEAM

After increased revenues, our second major priority over the three years was to help NIB establish and maintain a high quality management team throughout the bank. The first year we focused on establishing a strong senior management team to assist Soma who had been in his position for a little less than one year when the first retreat was held. He quickly showed his wisdom and courage in allowing a large group of senior managers to attend these sessions and to openly discuss and struggle with the bank's real situation and important issues. In the second and third years, Soma invited all the other middle managers to participate in these sessions, to ensure total support for the future of the bank.

By the second retreat we realized we would need to spend a significant percentage of our time addressing the "people issues" that had emerged as the result of the second round of changes in Nigerian government regulations. In a marathon ten-hour retreat session, the group examined the underlying issues of the NIB staffing. The NIB international staff members shared their frustrations with some of the local staff members who did not grasp that it was crucial to maintain a strong Citibank culture within the larger Nigerian culture. We encouraged the local staff members to express their long held frustrations with Citibank, with NIB, and with the situation resulting from the government regulations.

NIB had consistently increased salaries to be comparable with those offered by the largest and most influential banks. Nevertheless, local managers explained that their deepest frustration was their inability to build up non-cash personal equity. Nigerian stock opportunities were very restricted and uncertain, and the local owners of NIB had no interest in selling any of their shares. Because private homes are so scarce and expensive in Nigeria, NIB owns and provides housing for its top managers. For similar reasons, the bank purchases autos and furniture and makes these items available to senior managers while they work for NIB. It was common, then, that top local managers did not own outright anything more than their clothing and personal furnishings.

Soma said he understood the local managers' frustration and asked them to brainstorm changes that could be made. He indicated he was quite willing to go to the NIB Board with changes—if they made business sense, and if he could get some certainty that the managers would stay with NIB for the long run. After extensive discussions, we drafted a recommendation that managers, who stayed with the bank for five years or more, could purchase from the bank several of these items, including houses, autos, and appliances.

It is one thing to recommend a list of changes that will benefit some members of an organization. However, unless there are changes in the culture and structure of an organization—and not just in some changed individuals—the transformation will usually not really take hold. To ensure that transforming the organization really did take root, the company did make additional changes in actual policies and procedures. For example, NIB arranged to have several minibuses deliver local staff back and forth to work—a service which was already being provided by other large companies in Nigeria. Soma even agreed to open a clubhouse nearby for recreation and refreshments during the employees' free time.

In the third year, to further solidify the team building that had gone on during the first two years, we added what we called the "NIB Mini-Theatre." In arranging this celebrative event, we reset the meeting space into a theater-in-the-round, ordered some special snacks and drinks, and had the teams prepare skits to present to each other. Right after dinner on one Saturday night, we gave each team its skit assignment and then allowed them 45 minutes to prepare. Working with Soma, we carefully chose five different themes which would allow the managers to kid each other and, at the same time, build cohesiveness among the entire group. Most of the skit themes were general, i.e., "A Day in the Life of the Bank in Niger" (a neighboring country) which would allow room for creativity and humor regarding the real issues the participants were facing. The company fire had happened just a few months before so one skit was named "Fire Recovery Maneuvers—NIB Style" which encouraged some silliness in relation to an event that had been very destructive and serious for several staff members. One of the key managers in finance was always having to say no to extra expenses, so a skit was entitled "The Day Ramiro Said Yes!" The skits provoked frequent and genuine humor. Even Soma was kidded in a very affectionate way. On the whole the skits were very healing and created an even more powerful team.

In looking back at our experience in Nigeria, as well as at this collection of case studies, I can state unequivocally that successful facilitation techniques can span the globe. Effective facilitators can involve people from very different national and organizational cultures as active participants in and agents of change. They can build on cultural diversity and use it as a means of expanding beyond what could be an organization's limited concerns and outlook. In the following section, we outline our facilitation process.

THE CLIENT/FACILITATOR RELATIONSHIP

An example of how the process facilitator and client relationship develops and progresses might follow a scenario like this:

(1) An appointment is set with the client. To prepare for this meeting, the two professional process facilitators talk through with each other what they know about the client, and what the client might need in the way of planning. At the appointment the facilitators urge the client to talk about the organization's vision for the future as well as the issues the organization is facing.

(2) A second meeting, a three-hour design conference, is held with the organization's CEO and some other key players. At this time, these leaders develop the three to four focus questions that a planning session scheduled off-site will address. They finally agree to hold a three-day, all employee planning retreat to build a three to five-year vision, discuss the underlying issues, create strategic directions, and devise a detailed implementation plan for the various action steps.

(3) As the day of the off-site retreat approaches, the facilitators prepare by thinking through a custom designed planning process that will provide an effective and yet eventful and enjoyable three days. By the end of the retreat, the facilitators will have either entered all the discussion data into the computer, or have gathered the necessary materials to complete the planning document. At the end of 90 days and again after 180 days, one of the facilitators returns to lead a two-hour follow-up session to ensure that the implementation is being done and to build consensus on suggested changes that have become evident as the organization carries out its plan.

This is the minimum relationship for a single two-three day contract. In some cases, this schedule will expand out into many spinoffs, as it did with NIB. In those cases, ongoing consulting between the facilitator and client will occur.

PROCESS FACILITATION AND ICA TECHNOLOGIES

The type of facilitation described here is planning process facilitation. It is the intentional use of specific planning processes and skills to effect a carefully thought-out plan, even though particular results will vary greatly from organization to organization. It creates excellent plans and leaves a workforce energized and excited about its future.

Truly great managers have always done this. At one time, we assumed this was done only by managers with charisma and innate skill. Today, every senior manager must have this capacity. It is also obvious that every manager, if not every employee, could greatly benefit from process facilitation training. In fact, just as every organization has its financial and legal consultant, now every organization needs its process facilitator—a master facilitator who can work with senior management to train people throughout the organization in group facilitation skills.

36 SKILLS FOR SUCCESS

BEFORE THE EVENT

- Conducting 1-1 client interviews
- Developing the key focus questions of each planning session
- Leading a management input design conference
- Designing the planning format and participative process
- Developing appropriate overviews for each session
- Overseeing the room set-up to encourage group participation

DURING THE EVENT

- Beginning the planning process from a "high"
- Managing large groups containing different company departments at the same time
- Verbalizing the group consensus; rearticulating it as it changes
- Leading a focused discussion reflecting deeply on issues
- Giving effective overviews of the different planning stages
- Setting the tone and importance of planning activities
- Leading creative brainstorming sessions
- Grouping data into meaningful arenas or strategies
- Giving clear directions for self-directed small teams
- Consulting with the manager to make shifts during the planning
- Assisting the group to clarify their ideas, implications, and plans
- Helping the group to focus on outcomes, not personalities
- Guiding the group to discover their most strategic priorities
- Leading positive group feedback to refine first draft reports
- Changing the process midstream to handle special issues
- Designing templates to focus on the group data
- Designing action plan forms to ensure detailing of tasks
- Intervening in small teams to refocus product outcomes
- Ensuring that follow-up coordination structures are decided
- Scheduling follow-up accountability meetings
- Inventing "spiritizing" activities to build cohesiveness (dramas, role play, roasts, theme celebration, etc.)
- Ending the planning process on a "high"

AFTER THE EVENT

- Producing a camera-ready document of the consultation results
- Reflecting with the manager: results, implications, and next steps
- Learning from participant feedback and evaluations
- Designing and leading follow-up "booster" sessions
- Advising team leaders during the follow-up process

Although many people act as process facilitators, there are specific skills and planning processes that must be perfected by process facilitators who use the ICA methods and the many derivatives of these techniques. For instance, I believe that every consultant session should start from a "high"—so I often ask the participants in a planning session to call out their accomplishments, strengths, and learnings as they evaluate their past working year. We then wallpaper the room with lists of these triumphs. It's rewarding to see the excitement of the participants as they stare at their "Achievement Wall." Once that has happened I know the participants are ready to tackle the hard issues. The first art of a process facilitator is to help people to believe in themselves; creating the Achievement Wall always does the trick.

Our complex society and institutions often overwhelm people, so as facilitators we are driven to provide focus and to make things seem simple. I have always felt that if people could agree to several little things, the big items would follow. The art of a skilled process facilitator is to take diverse ideas and forge them into six to seven strategies. This focused approach empowers people to feel that they are able to cope with their challenges. Allowing honest self-evaluation is another art of process facilitation because it leads to positive suggestions and proposals. Making sure the discussion does not deteriorate into whining and name calling is crucial. The key to success is that the facilitator asks the questions in an objective and positive tone. The art of facilitation involves making sure the participants leave the workshop with clear action plans rather than unresolved issues. For the facilitator this can be quite a juggling act of trying to listen to concerns, stating consensus, and pushing the group to move into an action mode all at the same time.

As may be obvious, any planning event will incorporate, in some fashion, all or most of the following elements:

- **Organization Situation** What are we doing well? Why? What are our key challenges?
- **Shared Vision** What needs to be in place in 1, 3, or 5 years?
- **Obstacle Analysis** What underlying issues prevent the success of the organization?
- **Strategic Directions** What new strategies will ensure success?
- **Action Implementation** Who will do what, and when?
- **Follow-Up Consensus** Who will coordinate? When do we check back?

Process facilitation frequently can catalyze organizational transformation. For extensive and genuine transformation to occur, however, something like a major planning conference or a series of planning events involving several levels of the organization needs to happen. Process facilitation then can function like a midwife who delivers needed changes throughout the organization. Some organizations in the 1980s and 1990s reengineered or restructured from a hierarchical organization to a matrix organization. Process facilitators can assist these organizations in learning new patterns and techniques of decision making that foster increased interaction between managers and their employees. (See the Ten Intentional Skills List at the end of this chapter for process facilitation suggestions.)

The art of process facilitation will continue to change. Technologies of participation will evolve and be refined as more process facilitators experiment and share their successes in different countries and on various continents. Process facilitation is a growing profession that is beginning to be seen as an utter necessity to the different and complex types of organizations in our society. The cry for some form of significant participation in the decision making of an organization is a trend that is increasing. The ToP techniques that this book has described allow for manager and employee involvement that both honors individual members and guards the integrity and the future of the organization.

Process Facilitation: Ten Intentional Skills

The key to effective process facilitation is learning a set of intentional and disciplined skills. You cannot simply fly by the seat of your pants and you cannot simply do whatever occurs to you. Process facilitation has a definite direction and involves skills which must be learned and refined until you can use them effectively. As in any profession, once a person learns basic skills of the discipline, one is able to orchestrate a symphony of processes that can become at times a truly artistic expression.

We have outlined the ten basic skills that are needed. We will not attempt to teach the skills or describe the various ways they might be combined. If you have further interest in the performance of these techniques, see the book *Winning Through Participation*, as described in the Bibliography.

1. **How to conduct a one-on-one interview with a client or a design conference with several people from an organization.** This is done in order to discern the major issues that the organization faces, and to forge an agreement of how the consultant's process will deal with it.

2. **How to build your own planning format and process for approaching the issues and actually lead a planning retreat or conference.** Some people are capable of advising clients, but cannot invent a planning process to lead managers or employees in developing a plan. Process facilitators also need the flexibility to make small adaptations during the planning retreat, yet never lose sight of the focus and direction of the consult.

3. **How to lead a small team or group meeting that results in a clear and tangible result.** It is important to know what a group is experiencing because of its tremendous effect on building appropriate strategies and owning the implementation of the plan. Process facilitators need to understand group dynamics and how to handle diverse and difficult groups. This skill also includes the capacity to verbalize the group's consensus along the way and to be able to rearticulate it as it changes.

4. **How to lead a focused discussion that allows a group to reflect deeply on a particular subject.** This includes an approach that guides a group through four levels of reflective questions which probe the depth of their knowledge and insights, and thereby reveal implications for decision making and action. This method can be used to initiate problem solving, but is particularly effective when you want a group to think through an issue before they begin their action planning.

5. **How to prepare and deliver an effective and powerful presentation and teach others to do the same.** Most people can learn to give an effective speech or report if they are willing to prepare, yet some people shrink from this responsibility. Process facilitators need to learn to give an overview which sets the stage for effective planning. This includes explaining the background work in preparing for the consult with the management team, as well as outlining the key focus questions that will be addressed, the planning process and time-frames that will be used, and the importance of the group's work. During the planning retreat, each workshop or discussion will require a short overview to set the tone and explain the importance of that particular part of the process.

6. **How to lead a workshop that will gather data and insights from a group and help them to forge a consensus.** This method is at the heart of effective facilitation and without skill in this arena, facilitation that makes a real difference is very difficult. Increasingly, process facilitators are using visual templates in which all ideas, proposals, and plans are written on pre-designed overheads or flipcharts or frameworks for index cards. This ensures that everyone understands and follows what is being talked about. Index cards allow you to move ideas around and group them in a way not possible with other methods. All of these procedures help the group to focus on outcomes rather than on personalities or on differences.

7. **How to help a group determine and agree on strategic or operating priorities.** The facilitator must be capable of using techniques of 'reflective group listening' and verbalizing the group consensus.' This technique invites participants to clarify, refine, and agree upon the ideas and strategies. It requires a high level of skill to orchestrate a diverse group so that it reaches an effective consensus where all views are authentically heard and agreement is achieved on a position that everyone can live with. This is particularly important when the group is deciding upon the actual operating priorities or strategies.

8. **How to guide a group to build action plans and detailed implementaries that accomplish the actions.** Any group that does not lay out its action or implementation plans is probably not serious about achieving its goals. Even more important is making sure participants invent tactics that actually can be done and are assigned to individual persons or taskforces with due dates. A skilled facilitator will make sure that the client desires an implementation plan beforehand in order to make the desired organizational change.

9. **How to assist a group to implement its action plan by developing a coordination plan and accountability structure.** Plans frequently are ``new work'' that have to fit in somehow with ``existing work,'' and the facilitator and manager have to develop some organizational changes and coordination structures to assist the group to make the necessary adjustments. It is helpful if the facilitator can return for a follow-up or booster session to assist the implementation.

10. **How to assist an organization to develop high morale by inventing activities that will 'spiritize' the group.** During the retreat, many facilitators and managers use items such as T-shirts, buttons, hats, and session themes to enliven the group. After the retreat and during the implementation period, activities such as department show cases and displays, taskforce celebrations, and weekly and monthly meetings are useful.

AFTERWORD

Around the world, desks are cluttered with all sorts of management analyses for creating corporate value in the next decade—for motivating company personnel, using human resources, delegating to staff—take your pick. Every day, executives struggle to stay on top of their responsibilities, to move beyond their job descriptions to exemplary performance. This book spells out, case by case, in common sense terms, how employees do actually come to the rescue of their company leaders, and in so doing, save their own jobs.

Just because common sense comes into play here does not mean that the people involved in these cases think that every corporate decision, every business meeting, has involved setting easy directions; in fact, quite the opposite is the case. Making these corporate changes has not been easy. Managers in these case companies have been confronted over and over again in various cultural, geographical, and economic settings with the sense of *un*ease to which opening up information and levels of response to other employees inevitably leads.

In these situations the manager has been forced to a deeper level of understanding of his or her own job and how it relates to the whole, and is confronted with expressing to all the other staff members in the corporation how they too must look more deeply at their own functions in the workplace. Teams of people within the company are being asked to support themselves in this assignment. Once started, and proven in small ways to succeed, a corporate culture of participation grows and slowly becomes habitual. But that happens only as the whole organization turns the page on how it is going to operate. First, leadership dares to decide. Then staff dares to follow, and to participate in the process, haltingly at first, and then with much more confidence. People actually begin to *feel* about their jobs, their work, their careers, their companies. It has to do with people's perceptions about coming to work everyday. The reason that this kind of participation works though is not that people feel "good;" it is not only that they feel much more effective. They *are* more effective. (The ideas that characterize this particular business culture are generally spelled out in Chapter 2.)

What causes these people to behave differently? Theoretical explanations aside, differences can be observed. Absenteeism goes down. Numbers of training program participants go up. General cooperation and communication improves. Attention to detail rises. Desire for excellence is born and the idea that it is reachable takes over.

Experienced consultants and facilitators have for some years tried to design ways of talking about this kind of corporate culture with business people who are most used to bottom-line thinking. For many company leaders, there is more comfort in confronting figures on paper than in dealing with the human factor out on the company floor. But the bottom line alone is not working today as a simple motivator for excellence. Establishing a new corporate culture is seen more and more not as an option, but as a necessity.

THE 21ST CENTURY ORGANIZATION

A culture of participation in an organization is like a hologram. The hologram—a three-dimensional picture made on a photographic plate containing all the information necessary to produce a complete picture of its parts—is a useful metaphor for the organization of the 21st century. Strange as it may seem, upon close examination of any part of a hologram, one can see the entire picture. From an organizational point of view, no matter where one gains access to the "holographic organization," the entire culture's values, beliefs, and philosophy are communicated instantly. Participatory processes pioneered by ICA and described in this book are giving way to a new dynamic that might be called "whole-system transformation." Instead of only a department or team experiencing renewal, the whole organization does.

The underlying force that drives a holographic organization is its integrated systems. With participation throughout, every part of the organization is completely integrated into the whole system. This means vertically, hori-

The Five A's

Pamela Johnson and David Cooperider at Case Western Reserve University, Cleveland, wrote in 1991 about five global social change organizations, including ICA. In an article, "Finding a Path with Heart," (*Research in Organizational Change and Development*, Vol. 5, JAI Press, Inc., Greenwich, CT pp. 223-284), these researchers identified in work cultures organizing principles that enhanced competence and created vitality.

The five elements the authors identified that point to this new corporate culture can be applied both to individuals and to the corporation as a whole. They are: (1) **Affirmation**; (2) **Attunement**; (3) **Alignment**; (4) **Authenticity**; and (5) **Action**. These observations recognize that for individuals:

- **Affirmation** engenders a sense of hope and faith in the future.

- **Attunement** fosters individual trust.

- **Alignment** fosters individual commitment.

- **Authenticity** catalyzes self-actualization.

- **Action** supports personal empowerment.

For corporations, these researchers have characterized the ways that teams "feel" about their work. They observe that:

- **Affirmation** inspires individuals on a team to envision tangible results and possibilities for future action; and to celebrate as a group significant events in the organization's life, as well as individual contributions and special achievements.

- **Attunement** enables a group to make a collective commitment with appreciation and respect for the group of people with whom one is engaged in a common cause. I believe that this is living in the gaze of my neighbor without judgment.

- **Alignment** creates an organizational congruence with those individuals who comprise it, so that the organization acts as a vehicle for individuals to express their own goals. In such an aligned situation, organization members ask of one another, "What's worth my life?"

- **Authenticity** allows people to discover and act out their heartfelt values; to the extent that people are real and straightforward with each other, the organization is able to respond authentically to the needs of each member.

- **Action** makes it possible to translate one's commitments into stronger and more confident direct actions on behalf of a larger moral imperative. I believe this degree of influenced optimism is a rare quality.

zontally, functionally, and geographically. It is easy to recognize a holographic organization by following its every day activities:

(1) Every person in the organization can easily and quickly explain the organization's vision, purpose, and mission and their part in achieving them.

(2) Every person will have been trained in multiple functions so that breakdowns occur only for a moment.

(3) Multifunctional teams, taskforces, problem-solving units, strike forces, can be seen everywhere, dealing with cultural, corporate, and customer challenges.

(4) New learning opportunities are an intrinsic part of all systems so that skills can be constantly improved with an emphasis on computer-based and non-technology information systems.

(5) A kind of self-renewing principle is built into the whole system, so that people learn from each other. The holographic system is reflected in each of its parts. This allows the system to learn and function even when it breaks down in a crisis. A quick restart occurs because of the underlying learning capabilities in a fully integrated, participative system.

One hope for the 21st century comes from seeing holographic organizations with cultures of participation beginning to emerge today across the globe in many settings. It has taken a quarter of a century of research and experimentation to create models. But the path is here if a manager has the courage to venture forth as the "chief educational officer"—a new way of being a CEO. This kind of CEO will lead a new paradigm organization that uses its resources in the way the companies in our cases have.

We invite others to join us not only in setting goals to plan their own holographic organization, but in helping to give it form. Perhaps by modeling a new style of organization, corporations will lead the way into a new culture of participation for all of society.

James P. Troxel

ANNOTATED BIBLIOGRAPHY

BOOKS

Ackoff, Russell L. 1981. *Creating the Corporate Future: Plan or Be Planned For.* New York: John Wiley and Sons. Participative planning is introduced as a way of being responsive to the hopes and dreams of the stakeholders of the organization.

Adams, John, editor. 1984. *Transforming Work.* Alexandria, VA: Miles River Press. This is considered by many as the "text book" for organizational transformation.

Adams, John, editor. 1986. *Transforming Leadership.* Alexandria, VA: Miles River Press. This compendium includes articles by organizational practitioners who were ahead of their time.

Anthony, William P. 1978. *Participative Management.* Reading, MA: Addison-Wesley. This book serves as the introductory primer on the topic of participation.

Belasco, James A. 1990. *Teaching the Elephant to Dance: The Manager's Guide to Empowering Change.* New York: Crown Penguin Plume. Belasco writes about the balance between transforming individuals and transforming organizations.

Bennis, Warren and Burt Nanus. 1985. *Leaders: The Strategies for Taking Charge.* New York: Harper and Row. Ninety executives in the private and public sectors were interviewed for this book.

Bergdall, Terry D. 1993. *Methods for Active Participation: Experiences in Rural Development from East and Central Africa.* Nairobi: Oxford University Press. Bergdall describes how the Technologies of Participation are being applied in village development.

Bridges, William. 1980. *Transitions.* Reading, MA: Addison-Wesley. This author uses "endings, neutral zone, beginnings" as the paradigm of the change process and applies it to individuals.

Bridges, William. 1992. *The Character of Organizations.* Palo Alto, CA: Consulting Psychologists Press. The paradigm for change from *Transitions* is applied here to groups.

Burbidge, John, editor, for the Institute of Cultural Affairs International. 1988. Munich: K. G. Saur Verlag. *Approaches that Work in Rural Development.* This is Vol. III of the IERD Series that pulls together the lessons learned from the three-year International Exposition of Rural Development (IERD) in the context of key issues in current development theory and practice. A section of the book is devoted to methods of participatory development.

Cox, Alan. *Straight Talk for Monday Morning: Creating Values, Vision and Vitality at Work.* New York: John Wiley and Sons. Cox calls for a new kind of teamwork that employs "values technology" and advocates for a decision-making process other than consensus which, he says, can be the "lowest common denominator thinking."

Deal, Terrence and Allan Kennedy. 1982. *Cultures Corporate.* Reading, MA: Addison Wesley. Chapter #9, "Change: Reshaping Cultures" has a short case study in it as a model.

Denison, Daniel. 1990. *Corporate Culture and Organizational Effectiveness.* New York: John Wiley & Sons. Organizations that meet the contradictory demands of involvement, consistency, adaptability, and mission are likely to be the most effective.

DePree, Max. 1989. *Leadership is an Art.* New York: Doubleday Dell. "Participative management arises out of the heart," writes DePree, head of Herman Miller Office Furniture Company.

Dolman, Lee and Terrence Deal. 1991. *Reframing Organizations.* San Francisco: Jossey-Bass Inc. This book deals with the frames of structure: human resource, political, and symbolic.

Drucker, Peter. 1992. *Managing for the Future: the 1990s and Beyond.* New York: Truman Valley Books/Dutton. In this book, one in a long line of books from the "grandfather of American management," Drucker advocates that private sector companies need to learn from many of the highly successful "third sector" organizations.

Greenleaf, Robert K. 1977. *Servant Leadership: A Journey into the Nature of Legitimate Power and Greatness.* New York: Paulist Press. Peter Senge recommends this book because it talks about the leader as the "first among equals."

Harman, Willis and John Horman. 1990. *Creative Work: The Constructive Role of Business in a Transforming Society.* Indianapolis, IN: Knowledge Systems. The authors encourage businesses to be the catalytic agents in whole-system change.

Joiner, Charles W. Jr. 1987. *Leadership for Change.* Cambridge, MA: Ballinger Publishing Co. His sections on "A Participative Strategy-Development Process" and "Developing a Participative Structure" are useful aids that parallel the methods in *Participation Works: Business Cases from Around the World.*

Kanter, Rosabeth Moss. 1989. *When Giants Learn to Dance: Mastering the Challenges of Strategy, Management, and Careers in the 1990s.* New York: Simon and Schuster. Kanter is one of the best at capturing the edge state of affairs in corporate America.

Land, George and Beth Jarman. 1992. *Breakpoint and Beyond: Mastering the FutureToday.* New York: HarperCollins. Understanding of the invisible forces of natural change uncovers the hidden patterns that can unlock our potential as individuals and organizations.

Lessem, Ronnie. 1989. *Global Management Principles.* New York: Prentice Hall Press. *Global Management Principles* addresses management values and organizational behavior through exploring theory and practice from around the world.

Lessem, Ronnie. 1991. *Total Quality Learning: Building a Learning Organisation.* Cambridge: Basil Blackwell. If you are ready to go beyond Total Quality Management to institutionalize an ongoing learning environment, take a look at this.

Mahesh, V.S. 1993. *Thresholds of Motivation: The Corporation as a Nursery for Human Growth*. Mahesh's work in India and his message in this book greatly influenced ICA facilitators' work in Asia.

Mills, D. Quinn. 1991. *Rebirth of the Corporation.* New York: John Wiley and Sons. Mills recommends using an organization chart that employs clusters of circles rather than hierarchical boxes to depict the style of organization needed for the future.

Mink, Oscar, James Schultz and Barbara Mink. 1979. *Developing & Managing Open Organizations.* Austin, TX: Learning Concepts. This is one of those "ahead of its times" books that describes the transformed organization.

Morgan, Gareth, editor. 1989. *Creative Organization Theory.* Newburg Park, CA: Sage. This resource book contains articles and short cases that serve as background. Morgan also wrote *Riding the Waves*, 1988, Jossey-Bass.

Owen, Harrison. 1987. *Spirit: Transformation and Development in Organizations.* Potomac, MD: Abbott Publishing. Storytelling is an important tool in the transformation process.

Pascale, Richard Tanner. 1990. *Managing on the Edge.* New York: Touchstone/Simon & Schuster. The McKenzie "Seven S" model is used to analyze the organizational changes at Ford, General Electric, and Hewlett-Packard.

Peters, Thomas J. 1987. *Thriving on Chaos.* New York: Harper and Row, Publishers. The book's section on "Empowering People" serves as an excellent backdrop for the case studies in *Participation Works: Business Cases from Around the World.*

Peters, Thomas J. and Robert H. Waterman, Jr. 1982. *In Search of Excellence.* New York: Harper and Row, Publishers. A decade after its publication, Peters and Waterman's message is still appropriate for the 1990s.

Ray, Michael and Alan Rinzler, Editors for the World Business Academy of Stanford University. 1993. *The New Paradigm in Business.* New York: Jeremy P. Tarcher/Perigee Books. Over 30 articles describe many of the new values emerging in business today including quality service, personal development, community service, and sustainable development.

Renesch, John, editor. 1992. *New Traditions in Business: Spirit and Leadership in the 21st Century.* San Francisco: Berrett-Koehler.

Fifteen contributors offer new paradigms for business operations by addressing human values.

Rowan, Roy. 1986. *The Intuitive Manager.* New York: Little Brown. The farther into the unpredictable future a manager's decision reaches, the more she or he must rely on intuition. With things changing so frequently, planning may do more damage than good.

Schechter, Howard. 1990. *Rekindling the Spirit in Work.* Available from the author, P.O. Box 454, Stinson Beach, CA 94970. Personal and organizational transformation are related. It is necessary for an organization to foster the spirit in work.

Schein, Edgar H. 1985. *Organizational Culture and Leadership.* San Francisco: Jossey-Bass. A leader is one who manages the organizational culture. This book describes how to be an effective cultural manager.

Scully, John, with John A. Byrne. 1987. *Odyssey: Pepsi to Apple...The Journey of a Marketing Impresario.* New York: Harper and Row. Especially note the vignettes between his biographical chapters, particularly "The New Loyalty" and "Spinouts."

Senge, Peter. 1990. *The Fifth Discipline: The Art and Practice of The Learning Organization.* New York: Doubleday. "Forget your old, tired ideas about leadership. The most successful corporation of the 1990s will be something called a learning organization." *Fortune Magazine.*

Spencer, Laura J. for the Institute of Cultural Affairs. 1989. *Winning Through Participation: Meeting the Challenge of Corporate Change with the "Technology of Participation."* Dubuque, IA: Kendall/Hunt Publishing Company. This practical book pulls together 30 years of wisdom and experience from the Institute of Cultural Affairs' work in community and organization development. Focused on the private sector, its teachings can be readily applied to any organization or community. Available through Miles River Press.

Steele, Fritz. 1973. *Consulting for Organizational Change.* Amherst: University of Massachusetts Press. Companies need to design learning events that deepen the organizational change process. Different kinds of events are needed, depending upon where the organization is on the change journey.

Tichy, Noel M. and Stratford Sherman. 1993. *Control Your Destiny or Someone Else Will.* New York: Bantam Doubleday Dell Publishing

Group, Inc. The passionate commitment of Jack Welch, General Electric's CEO, to open as well as inclusive management has made "the GE revolution" one of the most impressive company turnarounds of our time.

Torbert, William R. 1987. *Managing the Corporate Dream.* Cambridge: Oxford University Press. Four phases of development of an enterprise are examined to aid an executive in taking an idea to reality.

Weisbord, Marvin. 1991. *Productive Workplaces: Organizing and Managing for Dignity, Meaning, and Community.* San Francisco: Jossey-Bass. The first part of the book reviews the development of "the search for productive workplaces," from Taylor, Lewin, McGregor, Emory, and Trist. For those not "academically trained" in organizational development, this is an easily read, enjoyable way to get the background history.

Wheatley, Margaret J. 1992. *Leadership and the New Science: Learning about Organization from an Orderly Universe.* San Francisco: Berrett-Koehler Publishers. A professor at Brigham Young University and a private consultant, Wheatley spells out the implications of current scientific thinking for contemporary business practices. She makes a persuasive argument for a participatory approach to management based on the nature of the universe itself.

ARTICLES

Ackerman, Linda. 1986. "Development, Transition or Transformation: The Question of Change in Organizations." *OD Practitioner* (December): 1-8. This is a clear definition of organizational development as "death and re-emergence." The author states that "Transformation is not possible without a leap of faith, individually or organizationally."

Adler, Paul S. 1993. "Time-and-Motion Regained." *Harvard Business Review* (January-February): 97-108. This discussion responds to the question of whether a bureaucracy can be designed to encourage innovation, commitment, and participation.

Argyris, Chris. 1991. "Teaching Smart People How to Learn." *Harvard Business Review* (May-June): 99-109. Sometimes the smartest people find it hard to learn. This analysis provides clues on how to overcome a professional's avoidance of learning.

Beer, Michael. 1988. "The Critical Path for Change: Keys to Success and Failure in Six Companies." Chapter 2 in *Corporate Transformation* by R. H. Kilmann and T. J. Covin. San Francisco: Jossey-Bass. Beer writes about the fallacy of programmatic change, why failures happen, and how to achieve corporate transformation.

Beer, Michael, Russell A. Eisenstat and Bert Spector. 1990. "Why Change Programs Don't Produce Change." *Harvard Business Review* (November-December): 158-166. The article raises the question: Do you begin by training people in new roles, hoping the change will happen, or do you create new structures and require the people to learn new roles?

Bronson, Lou. 1991. "Strategic Change Management." *OD Journal* (Fall): 61-67. Bronson describes a seven-step process of organizational change.

Brown, L. David and Jane Gibson Covey. 1987. "Development Organizations and Organization Development: Toward an Expanded Paradigm for Organization Development." *Research in Organizational Change and Development* 1: 59-87. A study of organizations committed to social change reveals some salient insights replicable for all organizations and for the organizational development practitioner.

Cooperrider, David L. 1989. "Positive Image, Positive Action: The Affirmative Basis of Organizing." Chapter 4 in *Appreciative Management and Leadership: The Power of Positive Thought and Action in Organizations* by Suresh Srivastva and Associates. San Francisco: Jossey-Bass. Cooperrider describes the heliotropic nature of organizations and its implications for management.

Davis, Stanley M. 1982. "Transforming Organizations: The Key to Strategy is Context." *Organizational Dynamics,* (Winter): 64-80. Managers who manage context can make an organization more effective. Those who manage the content rather than the context can improve only the efficiency of the organization.

Drucker, Peter F. 1988. "The Coming of the New Organization." *Harvard Business Review* (January-February): 45-53. Drucker's new image for large businesses is that of a symphony orchestra with fewer than half of the current number of managers participating.

Drucker, Peter F. 1992. "The New Society of Organizations." *Harvard Business Review* (September-October): 95-104. Drucker states that we are moving into the knowledge society and asks what are the implications of that reality for the business as a knowledge organization.

Dumaine, Brian. 1989. "What the Leaders of Tomorrow See." *Fortune Magazine* (July 3) 48-62. The "leaders of tomorrow" interviewed said that they see radically decentralized organizations that go beyond participative management to become learning organizations.

Dumaine, Brian. 1990. "Who Needs A Boss?" *Fortune Magazine,* (May 7): 52-60. Dumaine introduces self-managed work teams and suggests that participation without authority to act is shallow.

Dumaine, Brian. 1991. "The Bureaucracy Busters." *Fortune Magazine* (June 17): 36-50. Employee creativity can be unleashed through constellations of teams, projects, and alliances.

Dumaine, Brian. 1993. "The New Non-Manager Managers." *Fortune Magazine* (February 22): 80-84. Six roles played by managers, such as facilitator, coach, and sponsor, empower their co-workers in self-managed workteams.

Freedman, David H. 1992. "Is Management Still a Science?" *Harvard Business Review* (November-December): 26-38. The old scientific management was about ensuring control. The new one is about making sense out of chaos.

Hamel, Gary and C. K. Prahalad. 1989. "Strategic Intent." *Harvard Business Review* (May-June): 63-76. A whole new model of strategy is needed to revitalize corporate performance. See Prahalad and Hamel referenced below for a companion to this article.

Handy, Charles. "Balancing Corporate Power: A New Federalist Paper." *Harvard Business Review* (November-December): 59-72. Balancing centralization with local autonomy in corporate life when structuring an organization provides the best of both.

Holder, Robert. 1990. "Leadership from Depth." *Journal of Quality and Participation* (September): 70-78. Holder describes four interdependent processes involved in organizational transformation: leadership, vision, organization paradigm, organizational "death and rebirth."

Howard, Robert. 1992. "The CEO as Organizational Architect: An Interview with Xerox's Paul Allaire." *Harvard Business Review* (September-

October): 107-121. Xerox has completely remade its corporate culture and the article suggests that attention to a company's culture is a primary concern of its leaders.

Jelinek, Mariann and Joseph A. Litterer. 1989. "Why OD Must Become Strategic." *Research in Organizational Change and Development* 2: 135-162. New roles and tasks for the organizational development practitioner are required as the profession changes in response to new types of business organizations.

Kanter, Rosabeth Moss. 1989. "The New Managerial Work." *Harvard Business Review* (November-December): 85-92. The post-entrepreneurial company alters the basis of management power and requires new sources of motivation.

Kizlios, Peter. 1990. "Crazy About Empowerment?" *Training* (December): 47-57. Among the pros, cons, and pitfalls of empowerment is the question of whether companies are really willing to hand over power to the workers.

Kotter, John P. 1990. "What Leaders Really Do." *Harvard Business Review* (May-June): 103-110. One distinction between management and leadership is that good management controls complexity but effective leadership produces useful change.

Lammers, Cornelis J. 1991. "Organizational and Interorganizational Democracy," paper presented at the 10th Colloquium of the European Group for Organizational Studies, July 15-17, Vienna, Austria. This study of variant forms of democracy in a variety of organizations provides helpful learnings.

Lee, Chris. 1990. "Beyond Teamwork." *Training* (June): 25-32. A new image of how work gets done through teams is presented. This new approach is linked with training to support it.

Maffei, Benoit. 1991. "Organizational Culture as a Paradoxical Concept," paper presented at the 10th Colloquium of the European Group for Organizational Studies, July 15-17, Vienna, Austria. Can the concept of "organizational culture" be usefully applied as an object of research and investigation?

Miller, Susan. 1991. "Making Decisions Happen: The Cultural Dimension of Implementation," paper presented at the 10th Colloquium of the European Group for Organizational Studies, July 15-17, Vienna,

Austria. In a study of successful implementation in business, Miller isolates two factors of "enablers" and "realizers" and states the practical necessity for developing these two different sets of skills.

Mintzberg, Henry. 1991. "The Effective Organization: Forces and Forms." *Sloan Management Review* (Winter): 54 - 67. The author addresses how to manage contradiction through cooperation and reconciliation of ideology and politics within organizations.

Oyler, Marilyn R. 1992. *Transferring the Skills to Develop and Sustain a Participative Culture.* Master's thesis, Ottawa University. Ms. Oyler laid the groundwork for the present book, *Participation Works: Business Cases from Around the World*, by shaping the image of "participative culture." (For further information: ICA West, 4220 North 25th Street, Phoenix AZ 85016.)

Prahalad, C. K. and Gary Hamel. 1990. "The Core Competence of the Corporation." *Harvard Business Review* (May-June): 79-91. Underneath products, services, and technologies, what is it that is at the heart of your business that needs to be nurtured because it is your most important competitive advantage?

Rose, Frank. 1990. "A New Age for Business?" *Fortune Magazine,* (October 8): 157. This good primer explains some of the new management philosophies and their origins.

Rotchschild-Whitt, Joyce. 1979. "The Collectivist Organization: An Alternative to Rational-Bureaucratic Models." *American Sociological Review* 44 (August): 509-527. The introduction of a new theoretical model to support the rise of worker-based organizations.

Schaffer, Robert H. and Harvey A. Thomson. 1992. "Successful Change Programs Begin with Results." *Harvard Business Review* (January-February): 80-89. Results-driven transformation is similar to and different from activity-centered change programs, such as quality circles, total quality management, training, and so on. They suggest that companies focus on a critical task rather than on quality, participation, or teamwork.

Scott, Cynthia and Dennis Jaffe. 1988. "Survive and Thrive in Times of Change." *Training & Development Journal* (April): 25-27. Scott and Jaffe explore a basic model of death and new life for organizational transformation.

Semler, Ricardo. 1989. "Managing Without Managers." *Harvard Business Review* (September-October): 76-84. A description of the Brazilian Semco company can be compared to the Mills Group story in *Participation Works: Business Cases from Around the World.*

Sherman, Stratford. 1993. "A Brave New Darwinian Workplace." *Fortune Magazine* (January 25): 50-56. This article lists some of the significant implications of the workplace revolution which is complementary to the participative culture.

Stata, Ray. 1989. "Organizational Learning - The Key to Management Innovation." *Sloan Management Review* (Spring): 63-74. Organizational learning serves as an umbrella for systems thinking, planning, quality improvement, organizational behavior, and information systems.

Stewart, Thomas A. 1991. "Brainpower." *Fortune Magazine* (June 3): 44-60. Participative cultures can unlock the intellectual capital that is corporate America's most valuable asset.

Volberda, Henk W. 1991. "Organizational Flexibility: The Paradox between Change and Preservation," paper presented at the 10th Colloquium of the European Group for Organizational Studies, July 15-17, Vienna, Austria. In order to survive, an organization has to balance being both a planned and a flexible organization. Knowing when to do which is the key to leadership.

Weber, Alan M. 1993. "What's So New About the New Economy?" *Harvard Business Review* (January-February): 24-42. In the knowledge economy, the most important work is conversation. Creating trust is the manager's most important job.

**MILES RIVER PRESS 1009 DUKE STREET
ALEXANDRIA, VA 22314**

Additional   1. Phone 1-800-767-1501 for Visa or MasterCard charges
Orders: 2. FAX to 703/683-0827 with charge information
             3. Mail check or money order payable to Miles River Press

___ copies of *Participation Works: Business Cases From Around the
    World* @ $24.95 $_____

    Postage/handling (add $4/1st book ordered, $1 each additional book)
    Airmail overseas shipment (add $6/book) VA residents add 4.5% sales tax

Ship to: _____

Address _____

City _____ State_____ Zip_____

Daytime phone number_____

Charge card (V or MC) Number _____ Exp.Date _____

I would also like to order the following MRP titles:

☐   *Transforming Leadership: From Vision to Results* (John Adams, gen-
    eral editor) @ $25.95
☐   *Transforming Work* (John Adams, general editor) @ $21.95
☐   *Winning Through Participation* (Laura Spencer, editor) @ 21.95